BRING ON THE GIRLS!

The Improbable Story of Our Life in Musical Comedy . . .

BRING ON THE GIRLS!

The Improbable Story of Our Life in

Musical Comedy, with Pictures to Prove It

by

P. G. WODEHOUSE

and

GUY BOLTON

LIMELIGHT EDITIONS NEW YORK

ISBN 0-87910-011-7

MANUFACTURED IN THE UNITED STATES OF AMERICA

LIBRARY OF CONGRESS CATALOGING IN PUBLICATION DATA

WODEHOUSE, P. G. (PELHAM GRENVILLE), 1881–1975.
BRING ON THE GIRLS!

1. MUSICAL REVUE, COMEDY, ETC.—UNITED STATES.
2. MUSICIANS—UNITED STATES. I. BOLTON, GUY, 1884–
II. TITLE.
ML1711.W6   1984   782.81'0973   83-24436

The authors wish to extend their sincere thanks to Chappell & Company
for permission granted them to reprint lyrics from a number of musical
comedies. Those lyrics are copyright as follows:

From VERY GOOD EDDIE, Copyright, 1916, by T. B. Harms Company
From HAVE A HEART, Copyright, 1916, by T. B. Harms Company
From MISS SPRINGTIME, Copyright, 1916, by T. B. Harms Company
From OH, BOY! Copyright, 1917, by T. B. Harms Company
From THE RIVIERA GIRL, Copyright, 1917, by T. B. Harms Company
From OH, LADY, LADY, Copyright, 1918, by T. B. Harms Company
From THE ROSE OF CHINA, Copyright, 1919, by T. B. Harms
    Company
From SALLY, Copyright, 1920, by T. B. Harms Company
From SITTING PRETTY, Copyright, 1924, by T. B. Harms Company
From SHOW BOAT (the song "Bill"), Copyright, 1927, by T. B. Harms
    Company

BRING ON THE GIRLS!

The Improbable Story of Our Life in Musical Comedy . . .

. . . and the Pictures to Prove It

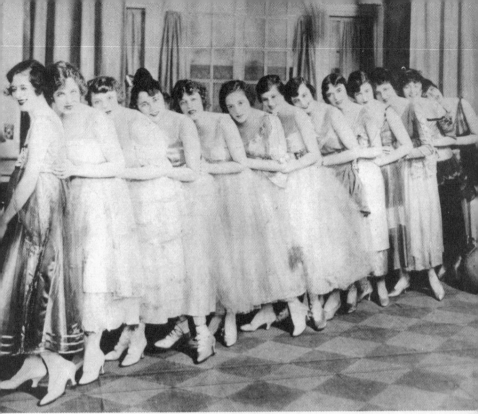

WHEN THEY BROUGHT ON THE GIRLS IN "OH BOY"

Bert Williams used to explain that bringing on the girls was the panacea that never failed to enliven the dull spots in a musical comedy. He claimed that it dated back to the days of ancient Egypt. "When one of those Pharaohs died, they'd lay that ole Pharaoh out, and then, just to make sure, they'd bring in wine—finest wine in the country—and they'd put it beside him. Then they'd bring in rich food that smelled just beautiful an' put that on the other side of him. Then they'd bring on the girls, an' those girls would do the veil dance. An' if that ole Pharaoh didn't sit right up and take notice then ... brother, he was dead." (See Page 1)

GUY, WRITING IN HIS DIARY

With men of the Guy Bolton type memories are like mulligatawny soup in a cheap restaurant. It is wiser not to stir them. (See Page 42)

PLUM

Critics have often commented on the somber gloom which permeates all Wodehouse novels, like the smell of muddy shoes in a locker room. (See Page 83)

EWART MILLAR

COL. HENRY W. SAVAGE

He walked with a slight limp, having probably in the course of his career been shot in the foot by some indignant author. (See Page 33)

VANDAMM

PLUM WODEHOUSE, GUY BOLTON, RAY COMSTOCK AND JERRY KERN

The Princess Theater Triumvirate—words by Plum, book by Guy, music by Jerry—with their producer.

ABE ERLANGER

"He sounds a bit of a Tartar."
"The Tartars, meeting a particularly tough specimen, would say he was a bit of an Erlanger."
(See Page 15)

FLO ZIEGFELD

"He's got an air. You feel that hundred-dollar bills mean no more to him than paper matches to a cigar store. And half the time he hasn't enough to buy a knitted waistcoat for a smallish gnat." (See Page 132)

"OH BOY"

Sheriff Sims (Stephen Maley) catches up with Hal Forde and Anna Wheaton. (See Page 63)

EDDIE, THE RED-HEADED STEWARD

Eddie himself interpolated into "Oh Boy" the best laugh of the show, but it's possible that the line he's delivering here to Edna May Oliver and Justine Johnstone was actually part of Bolton's book. (See Page 64)

BILLY B. VAN (WITH EILEEN VAN BIENE) IN "HAVE A HEART"

"Napoleon was a little guy:
  They used to call him Shorty.
  He only stood about so high.
  His chest was under forty . . ."

(See Page 19)

MARION DAVIES

A reception room, a large sitting room, a small sitting room, a dining room, two bedrooms, two baths, a clothes-pressing room, maid's room, and maid's bath in the old Hollenden Hotel in Cleveland. (See Page 65)

JUSTINE JOHNSTONE

Invited to share Marion's suite, she looked dubious. "Where do I put my maid?" she queried. (See Page 65)

KNOLE

365 rooms, 52 staircases, and 12 courtyards. (The haunted bathroom is the small window on the extreme left.) (See Page 198)

ADELE ASTAIRE

You could dance with her, at Knole, if you could buck the line. There is a rumor that her brother, who tried to struggle on without her after her marriage, turned up in Hollywood, and this may be so. (See Page 208)

CHARLIE CHAPLIN, GUY, AND EDDIE KNOBLOCK

During the Boltons' honeymoon voyage on the S.S. *Olympic*, they planned and helped put on the ship's concert. (See Page 155)

THE ROULOTTE

It could sleep four and had a bath, a kitchenette, and a bar, but it had no ballroom, so the King of the Belgians, for whom it was built, passed it up. (See Page 193)

CARROLL McCOMAS AND HARRY BROWN IN "OH LADY, LADY"

"There was I and there were you three thousand miles apart..." (See Page 2)

CULVER SERVICE

GUY, PLUM, AND JERRY

"This is the trio of musical fame, Bolton and Wodehouse and Kern ..." (See Page 101)

ETHEL WODEHOUSE

Once she made up her mind to give a party, no man nor elemental power could stay her course.

(See Page 67)

MARGUERITE NAMARA

"On Christmas Day she will be appearing in the Bull Ring in Mexico City with Titta Ruffo."

"Become a lady bullfighter, has she?"

"She's singing Carmen, ass."

"I trust she won't wear that red dress of hers."

(See Page 125)

VIVIENNE SEGAL AND CARL RANDALL IN "OH LADY, LADY"

Casting is to a large extent a matter of luck, but she was ideal for "Molly" and he looked exactly like "Bill." They were perfect. (See Page 98)

LEON ERROL AND MARILYN MILLER IN "SALLY"

Ziegfeld hated the idea of Marilyn being introduced as one of six orphan girls all dressed alike in cotton frocks and laced-up ankle boots, but Guy found an ally in Marilyn herself. (See Page 153)

"THERE'S A CHURCH ROUND THE CORNER"

Dolores, Leon Errol, Marilyn Miller, Irving Fisher, Walter Catlett, and Mary Hay in the triple-wedding finale of "Sally."

(See Page 153)

BERTIE, THE PERFORMING SEAL

A hardened comic who always hammed it up—his motto was Anything for a Laugh. (See Page 84)

JEROME KERN

He and Plum wrote "Bill" for "Oh Lady, Lady," but saved the song for years until they found Helen Morgan to sing it in "Show Boat."

IRA AND GEORGE GERSHWIN, AND GUY

They collaborated on "Lady Be Good." George always stipulated that Ira should do the lyrics, and Plum did not blame him. (See Page 206)

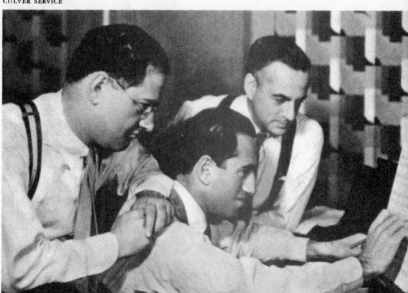

NOEL COWARD

When he was ten years old he stole Gertrude Lawrence's first speaking role. (See Page 220)

SYLVIA HAWKES (WITH DOUGLAS FAIRBANKS)

She had looks, brains, and humor. Even Nell Gwynne didn't cut a much wider swathe. (See Page 196)

GERTRUDE LAWRENCE

Guy wrote her a note asking her to star in "Oh Kay." She replied with a six-page telegram which could have been condensed into the words "Right ho."

The dog is Betty Compton's "Buggsie." (See Page 191)

BETTY COMPTON

Mayor Jimmy Walker, an old song writer himself, turned agent to land her a part in "Oh Kay." (See Page 233)

W. C. FIELDS

"Are you in possession of aspirin?"
Palmer produced a small tin box.
"Thank you, thank you. Don't slam
the lid." (See Page 265)

ETHEL MERMAN AND THE GIRLS IN "ANYTHING GOES"

Cole Porter took the bread out of Plum's mouth by writing his own
lyrics, but Guy and Plum wrote the book for the London production.
(See Page 270)

Chapter One

THE SCENE IS a smoke-filled room in a hotel in Boston or Philadelphia or New Haven or wherever else musical comedies are tried out in preparation for their New York openings. Tonight's performance of the new venture has revealed a dull spot in the second act, and a conference has been called to debate methods for ironing it out.

Various proposals are made. The comedian thinks that if he were given another song there, all would be well. The baritone feels that it is more the place for a baritone solo. The author of the book . . .

In an arm chair in the corner there is sitting a man in shirt sleeves, chewing an enormous (unlighted) cigar. He is fifty-five years old and for twenty-five of those years he has been an impresario of musical comedy. Lending to the discussion the authority of long experience and uttering the slogan which he probably learned at his mother's knee, he says:

"Bring on the girls!"

It is the panacea that never fails. It dates back, according to the great Bert Williams, to the days of ancient Egypt.

"When one of those Pharaohs died," he used to explain to his partner Walker, "they'd lay that ole Pharaoh out, and then, just to make sure, they'd bring in wine—finest wine in the country—and they'd put it beside him. Then they'd bring in rich food that smelled just beautiful an' put that on the other side of him. Then they'd bring on the girls, an' those girls would do the veil dance. An' if that ole Pharaoh didn't sit right up and take notice then . . . brother, he was dead."

The impresario has his way. The girls are brought on.

And how wonderful those girls always were. They did not spare themselves. You might get the impression that they were afflicted by some form of chorea, but the dullest eye could see that they were giving of their best. Actors might walk through their parts, singers save their voices, but the personnel of the ensemble never failed to go all out, full of pep, energy and the will to win. A hundred shows have been pushed by them over the thin line that divides the floperoo from the socko.

It is for this reason that Bolton (Guy) and Wodehouse (P.G.), looking back over their years of toil in the musical comedy salt mines, raise their glasses and without hesitation or heel taps drink this toast:

"To the Girls!"

And they feel that the least they can do in gratitude for all their hard work is to honor them in the title of this book.

· 2 ·

There was I and there were you three thousand miles apart:
Who'd have thought that we would ever have met at the start?
But it's plain to see 'twas meant to be in spite of every bar,
For I met you and you met me, you see, and here we are.

The above is the refrain (or "burthen," as Jerry Kern always insisted on calling it) of a duet Carroll McComas and Harry Brown used to sing in the fourth of the series of Princess Theater intimate musical comedies, *Oh, Lady, Lady*. The idea being that Carroll and Harry, having discovered that they were kindred souls, were feeling how tragic it would have been if they had never met. The thought might apply with equal force to the authors of the play.

At the outset it would have seemed that conditions for an early meeting were just right. Wodehouse was born in Guildford, a small town in England, and almost simultaneously Bolton was added to the strength of Broxbourne, a village in the next county. As the crow flies, Guildford and Broxbourne are not much more than twenty miles apart, and it is quite possible that the two infants, destined to collaborate for forty years, may often have seen the same crow engaged in checking the distance. One would have said that it would have been a mere matter of weeks before they got together and started working on a show.

But it was not to be. Just as Wodehouse, who even then wanted to write musical comedy lyrics, heard that there was a baby over at Broxbourne who wanted to write musical comedy books and resolved to save his pocket money and look him up directly he had amassed enough for the fare, he was stunned by the news that the Bolton parents, who were American, were taking their issue back to New York. And at about the same time he had to return with his own parents to Hong Kong, where the elder, bread-winning Wodehouse won bread as a judge. Collaboration for the moment became, if not void, certainly null.

It remained null for a considerable number of years, during which Bolton ripened into an architect in New York and Wodehouse into a writer in London, and the odds against the two ever meeting were raised astronomically by the fact that the latter's principal means of support was the composition of a daily column, supposedly humorous, on the London *Globe*. It was a steady job—three pounds a week, just like finding it—and in those days no Englishman ever dreamed of giving up a steady job. It seemed as though Fate had definitely arranged that the words "Book and Lyrics by Guy Bolton and P. G. Wodehouse" should never appear on a theater program.

But what Fate had not allowed for was the latter's secret passion for America. From his earliest years America had been to this pie-faced young dreamer the land of romance, and came a day when he decided that he had got to see it, if only briefly. The *Globe* job carried with it a five weeks' vacation per annum, and in 1909 it suddenly struck Wodehouse, an able mathematician, that, allowing eight days for the voyage out and another eight for the voyage back, he could manage nearly three weeks in sunny Manhattan. Packing a toothbrush and a couple of short stories, he set out.

A week after his arrival he had sold one of the stories to the *Cosmopolitan* and the other to *Collier's Weekly*, both on the same day and each for three hundred dollars, and feeling that a good thing like this must certainly be pushed along—the London price at that time for a Wodehouse story was seven pounds ten shillings—he sent in his resignation to the *Globe* and settled down in Greenwich Village with a secondhand Monarch typewriter and plenty of paper.

It was not too difficult, he found, to make a living of a sort as a free-lance writer in New York. He had hit the city at a time when magazines multiplied like rabbits there, and even if you failed to join the swells in George Horace Lorimer's *Saturday Evening Post,* there were plenty of other markets where you could pick up your hundred and fifty or two hundred dollars for a short story, and you could live an incredible time on two hundred dollars in those days. And if everything else failed, there was the Munsey group of more or less half-witted pulps, with Bob Davis, their editor, always ready to bury his head in his hands for a couple of minutes and come up with a plot which he presented to you gratis and bought, when worked into a story, for fifty of the best or sometimes even seventy-five.

The gap between the future collaborators having thus shrunk to a few city blocks, their meeting could not be postponed much longer. For there was now a new link between

4

them—that rising young composer, Jerome D. Kern. A few years before, Wodehouse had written some numbers with Jerry—then aged about eighteen—for a London production, while Bolton had just done a piece called *Ninety in the Shade* with Kern music—the first time Jerry had been entrusted with an entire score.

Wodehouse, moreover, had recently become dramatic critic for Frank Crowninshield's *Vanity Fair*, and in this capacity he attended on Christmas Eve, 1915, the opening performance of *Very Good Eddie*—book by Bolton, music by Kern—the second of the "intimate" musical comedies at the little Princess Theater on Thirty-ninth Street between Broadway and Sixth Avenue.

· 3 ·

It was Elizabeth Marbury, dear, kindly, voluminous Bessie Marbury, who first thought of musical comedy on a miniature scale—musical comedy with not more than two sets, eight to twelve girls and an orchestra of eleven, a celeste to take the place of wood wind. It was one of those inspired ideas that used to come to her every hour on the hour.

For Bessie was a brilliant woman, a dramatic agent who held the entire European market in her plump and capable hands. Her clients relied on her not only to sell their work but to help them write it. If their second act seemed to have blown a fuse, she would tell them what to do about it. She would even suggest plots and characters. She was a sort of female Bob Davis.

She and Ray Comstock were running the Princess Theater at that time and not making much of a go of it. It was difficult to get the right sort of show for a house with only two hundred and ninety-nine seats. The last thing tried there had been an evening of one-act plays, and it had been a painful failure.

It was then that Bessie got her inspiration. Midget musical comedy!

5

There would be a risk, of course. The expenses of production would amount to fully seventy-five hundred dollars. But Bessie thought it could be made to pay.

The venture would have to be economically planned. The tiny Princess could not afford as author and composer any of the men with big names—the Henry Blossoms, the Otto Harbachs, the Victor Herberts and the Ivan Carylls, who, being established, had large views on the sort of money for which they were prepared to work. What was needed was young fellows who were on their way up the ladder but still climbing the lower rungs.

Jerry Kern was the obvious choice for composer. A much less knowledgeable woman than Bessie Marbury could have spotted him as a coming champ. In those days managers were importing large, heavy Viennese operettas with large, heavy scores, and it was always the gay, tuneful, interpolated Kern numbers that put them over. She signed up Jerry at once. The question then arose: who was to do the book? and Jerry suggested Guy.

Bessie not only looked like a very charming and benign elephant, she had an elephant's memory. She remembered *Ninety in the Shade*, she remembered a divorce comedy by Bolton, *The Rule of Three*, and she remembered having heard his name mentioned by Charles Hanson Towne, the editor of the *Smart Set*, who had published some Bolton short stories.

"Yes, I know Bolton's work. He shows promise."

"And now," said Jerry, "you're going to promise him shows."

Nobody Home was the first of the series. It was enough of a success to encourage the management to feel that they were on the right lines, and Bolton and Kern were commissioned to write another. With this one, *Very Good Eddie*, intimate musical comedy—later to be known as the Princess Shows— became definitely a New York institution.

· 4 ·

Very Good Eddie took its title from a catch phrase which Fred Stone had made popular in his ventriloquist act in the latest Montgomery and Stone extravaganza at Charles Dillingham's Globe. It was a farce-comedy which would have been strong enough to stand on its own feet without the help of music, the first of its kind to rely on situation and character laughs instead of the clowning and Weberfieldian cross talk with which the large-scale musicals filled in between the romantic scenes. It was, in fact, intimate. It had no star part, the interest being distributed among a number of characters played by Ernest Truex, Jack Hazzard, John Willard (who later wrote The Cat and the Canary), Alice Dovey, who had made a success in that classic musical comedy, The Pink Lady, and a promising young beginner named Oscar Shaw.

On the opening night Jerry Kern came over to where Bolton stood leaning on the back rail, his face pale, his lips moving as if in prayer.

"How do you think it's going?" he asked.

Guy came out of his trance.

"I'm too numb to tell. There's a large man in large spectacles over there in the tenth row who seems to be enjoying it."

Jerry glanced in the direction indicated.

"Wodehouse," he said.

"I suppose it is," said Guy, "but that's only to be expected on an opening night. The question is, what's it going to be like tomorrow?"

"What on earth are you talking about?"

"You said it's a good house."

"I didn't. I said Woodhouse."

(For the benefit of the uninitiated, that is the way it is pronounced.)

"Yes, of course it is," said Guy petulantly, looking at the set.

"It's supposed to be a small hotel in the wilds of the upper Hudson. Brick would be all wrong."

Jerry continued to be patient.

"Look," he said. "Let's keep quite calm and thresh this thing out. You concede that there's a man over there in the tenth row."

"Yes."

"With large spectacles?"

"Very large spectacles."

"Well, the point I am trying to establish is that his name is Woodhouse."

(We will continue to misspell it until you get the thing firmly in mind.)

"Oh, you mean his *name* is Woodhouse?"

"That's right. Plum Wodehouse."

A gentleman in the last row, down whose neck Jerry was breathing, turned.

"I've no doubt what you two are saying is a lot funnier than what's going on on the stage," he said, "but I can't follow two plots at once."

"Sorry," said Guy, cringing. "Actually what's going on on the stage is very funny indeed."

"Sez you," said the man in the last row morosely.

The teammates withdrew to the balcony stairs and sat down on them. A decent five or six feet now separated them from the audience.

> *Any old night is a wonderful night*
> *If you're there with a wonderful girl . . .*

sang Oscar Shaw.

"Lousy lyric," said Kern.

A standee turned.

"Look," he said, "if you don't like this show why don't you get out?"

8

The pair withdrew to the lobby. If you applied an eye to the crack of the folding doors, the stage could still be seen. The doorman, who had been using this vantage point to watch the proceedings, obligingly made way for them. Guy squinted through the crack.

"What has Ada Lewis done to her face?" he muttered anxiously. "She looks most peculiar."

"That isn't her face," said the doorman. "She's walking on her hands. Saving her face for the last act."

Guy eyed the honest fellow with displeasure.

"We should have come to you for some gags," he said coldly.

"Why didn't you?" said the doorman. "I'd have been glad to help you out if I'd known the show was supposed to be funny."

"How's it going?" asked Jerry.

"It seems to be going all right."

"Ever hear the one about the English author feller that had a show on over here with Charlie Dillingham?" broke in the doorman in his charming, friendly way. Neither Kern nor Bolton had ever seen a man so patently resolved to be the life of the party. "He was in London, see, on account he couldn't get over for the opening, and he cabled Charlie 'How's it going?' And C.B. cabled back 'It's gone.' See what I mean? This feller asked 'How's it going?' and Charlie cabled back 'It's gone!' Get it?"

Guy drew a deep breath.

"I get it," he said. "Very droll."

"Most amusing," said Jerry. "I'm convulsed. What's happening in there? Have the customers rushed the stage yet?"

"Not yet. And that chap with the spectacles is laughing again."

"Probably overheard that story of mine," said the doorman.

The lights on the stage dimmed for the "Babes in the Wood" number.

9

Give me your hand:
You'll understand
We're off to slumberland . . .

sang Ernie Truex in a cracked voice.

"God!" said Jerry. "You never know what words are going to sound like till you hear them with a first night audience. Why don't you get Wodehouse to do your lyrics?"

"Does he write lyrics?"

"He certainly does. I did half a dozen numbers with him for a thing in London called *The Beauty of Bath*. One of them—'Mister Chamberlain'—used to get ten encores every night. As a lyric writer he's the cat's pajamas."

"Rather a dated expression," said Guy coldly.

The audience began to stream into the tiny lobby. The man with the spectacles came up to them.

"Oh, hullo, Jerry," he said.

"Hello," said Kern. "This is Bolton. You two fellows ought to know each other."

Guy and Plum shook hands.

"I hope you liked the show," said Guy.

"Best thing I ever saw in my life."

"I wonder," said Guy, "if you would mind stepping over beside that man with the crumpled shirt front and the rumpled hair? He is the *Tribune* critic."

They moved to where Heywood Broun was chatting with Alexander Woollcott.

"What did you think of our little entertainment, Mr. Wodehouse?" asked Guy in a clear, carrying voice.

"Not bad," said Plum.

After the final curtain Jerry took them to his apartment on West Sixty-eighth Street. There they were joined by a group of English friends who were appearing at Dillingham's Globe Theater in *Tonight's the Night*. There was Lawrie Grossmith, who had played in *Nobody Home*, and his brother George, the *Tonight's the Night* light comedian. There was Lawrie's brother-in-law, Vernon Castle, with his wife and dancing partner, Irene. There was Fay Compton, now and for long a leading London star. They were all eager for news of *Very Good Eddie*.

The two interested parties had decided they would wait up for the notices. They were glad to have company for part of the night. Jerry took his place at the piano, Fay stood beside it and sang. Two or three of the girls were working away in the kitchen making sandwiches.

Wodehouse and Bolton gravitated to a corner. "Do you think *Eddie* got over?" said Guy.

"Of course it did. Didn't you hear the audience as they were coming out? The woman ahead of me said it was the cat's pajamas."

"Really?" said Guy, beaming. "The cat's pajamas—one of my favorite expressions. Very clever and original. By the way, Kern used it about you."

"Me?"

"Yes, as a writer. He says you write good lyrics."

" 'Good' is a conservative word. 'Superb' is more the *mot juste*."

"Have you done any over here?"

"Not yet. But only the other day I missed landing a big job by a hairsbreadth. Somebody gave me an introduction to Lee Shubert, and I raced round to his office. 'Good morning, Mr. Shubert,' I said. 'I write lyrics. Can I do some for you?' 'No,' said Lee Shubert. Just imagine if he had said 'Yes.' It was as near as that."

"Would you like to join Jerry and me?"

"I'd love it."

"Then let's get together."

The Bolton diary of this date has the following entry:

Eddie opened. Excellent reception. All say hit. To Kerns for supper. Talked with P. G. Woodhouse, apparently known as Plum. Never heard of him, but Jerry says he writes lyrics, so, being slightly tight, suggested we team up. W. so overcome couldn't answer for a minute, then grabbed my hand and stammered out his thanks.

Turning to the Wodehouse diary, we find:

Went to opening of *Very Good Eddie*. Enjoyed it in spite of lamentable lyrics. Bolton, evidently conscious of this weakness, offered partnership. Tried to hold back and weigh the suggestion, but his eagerness so pathetic that consented. Mem: Am I too impulsive? Fight against this tendency.

Chapter Two

Eddie was an immediate success and not one of the Princess' two hundred and ninety-nine seats was ever empty, but neither Bolton nor Kern, drawing their infinitesimal royalties, was able as yet to feel that he had made any very noticeable impact on Broadway.

What they needed, to put them up among the Blossoms, the Harbachs, the Herberts and the Carylls, was an equally successful venture at one of those vast houses that could play, when full, to as much as sixteen thousand dollars on the week —say, for instance, Erlanger's New Amsterdam.

Abraham Lincoln Erlanger was at that time the czar of the New York theater, though beginning to be a little worried by the competition of the up-and-coming Shuberts. All the big managers—Ziegfeld, Dillingham, Savage, Belasco, Cohan and Harris and the rest of them—were Erlanger men, booking their plays in his theaters.

One morning Wodehouse had a telephone call from Bolton.

"I've got a job for us," said Guy. "Come on down and I'll tell you about it."

Plum found his partner looking awed, as if he had recently passed through some great spiritual experience.

"It's a Viennese operetta."

"Oh, my God!"

"And what Mr. Erlanger wants is a new story and new lyrics fitted into the score."

Plum tottered.

"Did you say *Erlanger*?"

"Yes, it's a Klaw and Erlanger production."

"And I was just going to advise you not to touch the thing! Why, they might put it on at the New Amsterdam."

"That's where they're going to put it on."

"But how did you manage to land a terrific job like that?"

"Apparently all the men up top had a go at it and couldn't satisfy the old boy, so he scraped the bottom of the barrel and found me. I did a scenario which he liked, thank goodness, and it's all settled. You are to do the lyrics and Jerry some interpolated numbers. You'll have a lot of work, I'm afraid. It's one of those shows where the finale starts halfway through each act."

"That's all right. I'd die for dear old Erlanger. Tell me about Erlanger. He really exists, does he? You've actually seen him? What's he like? To look at, I mean."

Guy considered.

"He's rather like a toad," he said at length. "It is as though Nature had said to itself 'I'll make a toad,' and then halfway through had changed its mind and said 'No, by golly, I won't, I'll make a czar of the American theater.' Not that I have anything against toads. I've met some very decent toads."

"Me, too. Many of my best friends are toads. I look forward to meeting him."

"You'll be doing that in half an hour from now. He wants us at his office at eleven. Be careful not to say anything disrespectful about Napoleon."

"I'll watch myself. But why?"

"Because he has a Napoleon complex. He not only admires Napoleon, he thinks he *is* Napoleon."

"Reincarnated?"

"I suppose so."

"What would happen if I kidded him about Moscow?"

"He would probably shoot you. He keeps a loaded revolver in his desk. They say he did shoot a man once."

14

"Mistook him for the Duke of Wellington, no doubt. He sounds a bit of a Tartar."

"That's our expression. The Tartars, meeting a particularly tough specimen, would say that he was a bit of an Erlanger. Still, he's said to be kind to authors and dumb animals, so let's go."

· 2 ·

The Erlanger office was large and picturesque. In one corner was a punching bag, beside it a barber's chair. The barber who came each morning to shave the imperial face had been specially chosen for that high office because he could speak French. When called on to do so, he would take down one of the volumes of Napoleon's letters that filled a wall bookcase over Erlanger's head and translate. One can picture the stream of small-fry managers and rural "Opry House" owners who drifted in and out of the office being considerably impressed by this display of culture. A man must be quite something when even his barbar can sight-read from French into English.

It being now eleven o'clock, the barber had done his work and departed (no doubt with a respectful *"Vive l'Empereur!"*) and A. L. Erlanger was seated behind the huge desk in one of the drawers of which, probably the open one so as to be handy, lay the celebrated loaded revolver. Lounging in a chair beside him was a small boy in knickerbockers, who gave the two collaborators a cold look as they entered, as if he did not think highly of book writers and lyrists.

"Who's the kid?" asked Plum out of the side of his mouth.

"I don't know," said Guy.

"*L'Aiglon*, perhaps?"

"I shouldn't wonder."

It turned out later that the stripling was some sort of relation, a nephew or the son of a cousin or something, and he was a very valued and esteemed cog in the Erlanger organization. Aged twelve years, he had been selected by Erlanger as possessing exactly the intelligence of the average New York theater audience. If he liked something, Erlanger reasoned, the public would like it, too. If he didn't, they wouldn't. And there may, of course, have been something in this.

It was not immediately that A.L.E. was at liberty to attend to his book writer and lyrist, for he was engaged at the moment of their entry in what—on his side—appeared to be a heated argument with Jack Hazzard. It seemed that Jack had been offered the comedian's part in the Viennese show and was hesitating whether or not to accept it.

This was so perilously near to lese majeste that Napoleon was not unnaturally incensed.

"I don't know what you're wibble-wobbling about," he was saying. "You ought to be down on your knees thanking me for giving you such a chance. Eh, Plymouth?"

"You betcha," said the knickerbocked child. "I'm astounded."

"I'm more than astounded, I'm surprised. It's not only incredible, it's unbelievable. You're nobody. No one ever heard of you. And here I am, offering you—"

Jack stirred uneasily. He was sitting on the edge of a hard chair immediately opposite the desk. Guy and Plum were side by side on a leather settee. The arrangement was faintly suggestive of a courtroom with judge, jury and criminal.

"Well, sir, Mr. Erlanger," said Jack, nervously revolving the hat that dangled between his knees, "I'm in a hit, you see—"

"A hit? What hit? Where?"

"*Very Good Eddie*, Mr. Erlanger. At the Princess."

Erlanger exploded.

"The Princess? That broken-down little cheesebox under the Sixth Avenue El?" (The Princess was a Shubert house.) "Do you realize I'm offering you a chance to appear on the stage of the *New Amsterdam*? And there you sit, humming and hawing—"

"He's crazy," said Plymouth.

16

"It sure is a great opportunity," Jack agreed. "What's the character like that you want me to play, Guy?"

"He's very loquacious."

"Yes," said Erlanger, "and another thing, he talks a lot." He looked at his watch. "Well, think it over," he said. "I've got to go down to the theater to see a run-through of Georgie Cohan's new show. Come along, Plymouth."

He bustled out, followed by *l'Aiglon*, followed by Bolton, followed by Wodehouse. No actual invitation had been extended to the two last-named to join the party, but it seemed to them the prudent thing to do. The first rule a young author learns in the theater is never to let the manager get out of his sight.

The George M. Cohan show was in full swing when they arrived. They had come just in time for the entrance of the policemen, six chorus boys in uniform who marched on to a special tune. It was one of those neat tricks in which Cohan specialized, and it should have been very effective. But unfortunately one of the six, a big, awkward young man with red hair, seemed incapable of moving in time to the music. He made the wrong turn, got out of line and generally ruined the thing.

This did not escape Plymouth's observant eye. His voice rang out like that of the daughter of the Village Blacksmith.

"Hey!"

"Yes, Plymouth?"

"That one's no good."

"Which one?"

"The one third from the end."

Cohan nodded gloomily.

"I've been trying for five weeks to get that boy to march in time, but nothing I say makes any difference."

Erlanger snorted Napoleonically.

"You're too soft with him. You're too easy. You don't know how to handle these guys. Let *me* talk to him!"

His remarks, filtered for family reading, ran about as follows. "You filtered fool, what do you think you're doing? Can't you hear the beat of that filtered music? Can't you pick up your feet, you filtered lummox? Don't stand there gaping at me like a filtered half-wit. Go back and make the entrance again."

Instead of going back, the lummox came forward, right down to the footlights. His manner, if a little reserved, was extremely courteous. At least, it began by being extremely courteous.

"I regret exceedingly," he said, "that I have fallen short of the requirements of the part entrusted to me, Mr. Erlanger. I am not a professional actor. I gave up a good job in a garage to join this production because I'm married to one of the ladies in the chorus, Miss Pansy LeBoeuf, and I didn't want us to be separated. I informed Mr. Harris that I had a very poor ear for music, and he assured me that it did not greatly matter. If it does, you can of course dismiss me. BUT WHAT YOU CAN'T DO, YOU FILTERED SON OF A FILTER IS TALK TO ME THAT WAY IN FRONT OF MY WIFE, AND IF YOU DO IT AGAIN I'LL COME DOWN THERE AND KNOCK YOUR FILTERED BLOCK OFF, AND THAT GOES FOR COHAN TOO."

Erlanger had his coat half off, starting for the stage, but Cohan was ahead of him. He stuck his hand up to the boy.

"Put it there, kid!" he said. "And let me tell you you're going to be one of our policemen as long as you want the job. Practice that walk and see if you can't get it, but if you can't, to hell with it."

The performance continued. Erlanger had slumped back into his seat, baffled. His favorite marshal had let him down. Guy was thinking how typical that generous gesture had been of George Cohan. Plum's mind was occupied with the name he had heard.

"Pansy LeBoeuf, did he say?"

"That's how I got it."

"Quite a name."

"Yes, almost as good as Pickles St. Clair, who's with Dillingham. But we've got a girl in the *Eddie* chorus who tops them
both—Dawn O'Day."

A few minutes later Erlanger rose.

"It's okay, George," he said. "I've seen enough to satisfy
me. You open at the Chestnut Street in Philly, and I'll route
you west to the Grand in Chicago."

Without waiting for a reply, he strode off up the aisle. He
called over his shoulder to Guy and Plum as he passed them.

"Come upstairs, you two. I'll get Klaw to give you your
contracts."

Next morning Plum called at Guy's apartment.

"Yesterday inspired me," he said. "It gave me an idea for a
lyric. I've only done a bit of it, but here's how it goes so far."

> *Napoleon was a little guy:*
> *They used to call him Shorty.*
> *He only stood about so high.*
> *His chest was under forty.*
> *But when folks started talking mean,*
> *His pride it didn't injure:*
> *"My queen," he'd say to Josephine,*
> *"The thing that counts is ginger."*

"And the refrain?"

"I haven't done the refrain yet. But here's another verse."

> *He got too fat. We all know that*
> *From portraits in the galleries.*
> *He never seemed to learn the knack*
> *Of laying off the calories.*
> *But though his waist was large, he faced*
> *And overcame all foemen.*

He knew quite well it's brains that tell
And not a guy's abdomen.

"Erlanger's going to love it," said Plum.

The song was destined for success, but not in an Erlanger production. Jerry Kern wrote a delightful tune and orchestrated it with toy trumpets, and it was sung by Billy B. Van in *Have a Heart*.

· 3 ·

The new piece was to be called *Miss Springtime*. Guy's title had been *Little Miss Springtime*, but that was changed very promptly by Abraham Lincoln Erlanger.

"We don't have nothing little at the New Amsterdam," said Abe.

By a great stroke of good fortune Plymouth had picked up a germ and gone down with mumps, so was not on hand with his sympathy, encouragement, and advice, and rehearsals proceeded smoothly. Everything connected with an Erlanger show always moved with the precision of a Napoleonic campaign. The boss kept an eye on things himself and stood no nonsense.

There was once an expensive foreign tenor who was engaged for a leading role in an Erlanger production, and on the night of the dress rehearsal Erlanger, seated in the stage box, was puzzled and annoyed to note that all that was proceeding from the gifted artist was a faint sound like gas escaping out of a gaspipe. Stopping the performance and enquiring into this, he was informed by the tenor in a hushed whisper that he, the tenor, was saving his voice for tomorrow night.

Erlanger's eyes bulged slowly from his head. He swallowed once or twice.

"Sing," he said.

The tenor went into a whispered explanation. When he said he was "saving his voice," the voice was in fact saving itself.

"She is gone," he said, alluding to his voice, as serious singers will, as if it were an independent entity. "Tonight she is gone, but tomorrow she will be back."

"Sing!"

"But I am telling you, Mr. Erlanger"—the whisper was even fainter—"the vo-chay, she is not there. She does this." He pinched his throat between thumb and forefinger by way of illustration.

"Sing!" said Erlanger.

"Please," the whisper was now scarcely audible. "They are delicate, these great voices. They—"

Erlanger rose from his seat, removed his coat and sprang from box to stage. He placed one large hand on the tenor's left shoulder, another large hand on his right shoulder, got a good grip, and shook him backwards and forwards for some moments, then from side to side. He raised him in the air and brought him down with a bump that shook the New Amsterdam stage.

"SING!!!" he said.

The tenor let out a note that could be heard as far downtown as the Battery.

The Emperor had handed over the preparation of *Miss Springtime* to two of his most trusted Generals—Herbert Gresham for the book and Julian Mitchell for the dances. Martial law had been proclaimed on the first day of rehearsals, and Gresham readily adjusted himself to the military atmosphere. Whenever the Little Corporal of Forty-second Street strode on to the stage, he would come smartly to attention, and it was clearly with an effort that he refrained from saluting.

Julian Mitchell was much less docile. He was a sort of Marshal Ney, an independent spirit who truckled to no one. He would fight manfully against any suggestion, even from the All Highest, that was in his opinion bad for the show. He knew his job, he did his job, and he was not going to have anyone telling him how to do it. He was fired oftener than a machine gun, but whoever fired him always had to take him back again, for Julian stood alone. He was the real creator of the *Ziegfeld Follies,* for two editions of which Flo Ziegfeld was merely the brilliant pressman.

It was amazing that he should have reached such a position, for he was very nearly stone deaf. His method of hearing a melody was to press his ear closely to the back of the piano. If the piano was in the pit, he would seat himself on top of it like a sort of Buddha. For some reason which aurists may be able to explain he could hear a little better in this position.

Thus enthroned, he shook his head at one of Jerry Kern's interpolated numbers.

Kern, never one to accept adverse criticism meekly, shouted up at him.

"I didn't write it to be heard at that end."

This perplexed Julian.

"Who did write it, if you didn't?"

Jerry raised his voice.

"I said I didn't write it to be heard—"

This, Julian felt, was childish.

"You didn't write it to be heard? What did you write for, then?"

"—heard at that end," yelled Jerry, pointing at Julian's posterior.

"It isn't the end I object to," said Julian. "It's the beginning and the middle."

Kern gave it up, and played something else.

Miss Springtime—with Sari Petrass, George Macfarlane, Jack Hazzard, Georgie O'Ramey and Jed Prouty as its principals—opened at the old Forrest Theater in Philadelphia. It moved like clockwork, the beautiful Joseph Urban settings appearing and disappearing without a single hitch. Even the audience did what was asked of them.

As the orchestra struck up the "play-out," the two authors

pressed back through the outgoing crowd to the pass door. Erlanger was already on the stage, the department heads, directors, scene painters, stage carpenters, electricians, head props and costume designer assembled about him. The company stood in lines facing him. Napoleon, with his Marshals about him, preparing to address his troops.

His speech was a eulogy. He scattered medals like bird seed. It was plain that what had occurred tonight had been an Austerlitz. He was particularly enthusiastic about the chorus dancing, the precision and verve of which, he said, had been exceptional.

"The finest line of dancers I've watched in years," he said, and motioned to Julian to say a few graceful words.

Julian, who had not heard a syllable of the speech, stepped forward, a bundle of scribbled notes in his hand.

"I'm ashamed," he said. "I'm ashamed and mortified at the way you girls let me down tonight. The whole lot of you danced as if you were wearing snowshoes. No precision, no verve, the worst line of dancers I've ever watched."

He would have spoken further, but at this point a justly incensed czar of the New York theater, speaking carefully into his left ear, fired him. It was not till late in the following day that he was taken back again.

Guy summoned up courage to ask a timid question.

"Do you think it's a hit, Mr. Erlanger?"

Plum, on his other side, made a similar query.

"It's a hit, don't you think, Mr. Erlanger?"

The Emperor swelled portentously.

"A hit? Of course it's a hit! Do I ever put on anything that isn't a hit?"

"No, no, Mr. Erlanger."

"Certainly not, Mr. Erlanger. Of course not, Mr. Erlanger."

"It will run at the New Amsterdam for a year, and as soon as I have the New York opening off my hands, I shall organize a Western company."

The two collaborators beamed at him. People said unkind things about old Abe, did they? He had ruined people, had he? Well, what of it? They probably thoroughly deserved to be ruined, and as for him shooting that man everybody said he had shot, why shouldn't a fellow shoot a chap from time to time if the situation seemed to call for it? What's the sense of having a loaded revolver if you never use it?

Those were the days. None of this modern nonsense about "Hoping they'll like us in New York" and "We'll have to wait and see what the critics think of us." "As soon as I have the New York opening off my hands, I shall organize a Western company." Just like that. And the West was the West then. A full season in Chicago, fifty-two one-week stands, a third season of three-nighters.

And, as a matter of record, Erlanger was right. *Miss Springtime* ran at the New Amsterdam for two hundred and thirty performances, and was an even bigger success in Chicago. It went on touring for several years.

Chapter Three

BOLTON and Wodehouse were lunching at Armenonville, the charming grillroom of the Knickerbocker Hotel at the corner of Forty-second Street and Broadway. This was a step up from their customary Childs, but they were doing well now and could afford to cut a modest dash. Guy had two hits running on Broadway, and Plum had just sold his novel, *Piccadilly Jim*, as a serial to the *Saturday Evening Post*.

"Tell me about last night," said Plum, when they had finished the important business of ordering. "How did you make out with Belasco?"

The question concerned a play called *Polly-with-a-Past*, a comedy which Guy had written with George Middleton.

"I don't quite know," Guy replied. "It was hard to tell whether the old boy liked it or not. He was hanging pictures."

"What do you mean, he was hanging pictures?"

"While George was reading the play to him. I must say my heart bled for poor old George."

"Where did this take place? The famous studio?"

"Yes, as sinister a joint as I've ever been in. It looks like the scene of nameless orgies."

"But this picture hanging . . . ?"

"Apparently the Master is always tinkering, trying new effects with priest robes, painted cassones, all that sort of junk. Now he was hanging pictures. Well, he told George Middleton to go ahead and read the play. George would read a couple of lines and then there'd be bang, bang, bang. He'd stop, and Belasco would call out, 'Go on, I'm listening.'"

"Pretty ghastly for George."

"Yes, he seemed to be suffering. And that wasn't all. Belasco's secretary was there, the one they call Ginty, and the poor thing was suffering from neuralgia. It was in the left eye that it seemed to be troubling her most. She kept applying hot compresses to it and groaning, 'Oh, my God! This is terrible!' It made her sound like a dramatic critic. George would read a line, and there would be a yell of 'Awful! Awful!' It jolted him quite a bit.

"But George is not a man to be lightly stayed in his appointed course. Pausing for but a moment, he would plough manfully on. Another couple of comedy lines, and there would come a bang, bang, BANG. ('Don't stop. I can hear you.') And Ginty would shriek, 'Ow! Ow! This is frightful!' "

Plum drew his breath in sharply, as if he had had a sudden twinge of neuralgia in the left eye.

"So that's reading a play to Belasco! How did this custom of reading plays to managers ever start, I wonder."

"I believe it's a hangover from the days when most managers couldn't read."

"Now that a fair proportion of them can, why not let them wrestle with the thing themselves?"

"Yes, if they would do it, that would be fine. The trouble is, the last thing managers want to do is read a play. They seem to think it makes them look important having a great pile of unread scripts on their desks. The higher the pile, the bigger the manager."

"Then what's the answer?"

"I know the answer, if you could always work it. I managed it once with Harry Frazee."

"I never knew Frazee had done a play of yours."

"He didn't, but he bought it. It was one evening after office hours. His staff had gone home, and it seemed that there was nothing to interrupt us. I didn't know then that during the reading of a play a manager has to have something to do

26

that will keep him usefully employed. I believe Arch Selwyn does fretwork, while Crosby Gaige catches up on his burnt leather bookmarks. Harry Frazee, sticking more closely to business, uses such time for cleaning out the drawers of his desk, getting rid of empty whiskey bottles, appeals for charity, cancelled summonses and so on.

"After I had read a couple of pages during which he was entirely invisible, dealing with the contents of his lower right-hand drawer, he suddenly bobbed up and told me to stop reading and leave the play with him. I pointed to the vast pile on his desk.

" 'As fairness would demand my play going to the end of the queue, it wouldn't reach you for another two years.'

" 'All right,' he conceded grudgingly. 'Read a couple more pages. But those dialects! I can't make head or tail of them.' He disappeared again on the left side of his desk.

"I must admit the play was rather rich in dialects, though I was surprised he'd noticed it. It was about a bunch of soldiers, an Italian, a German-American, a colored boy, et cetera. I read two more pages as soon as Harry had got back with a pair of old rubbers, a catcher's mitt and a girl's brassière. He again told me to stop reading. He said he couldn't understand a word I was saying, he hated plays with a lot of foreign accents in them and I was wasting his time.

" 'But you've still got several drawers to sort,' I said. 'You might as well let me read a bit more.'

" 'I've just told you,' he said. 'I can't follow you when you do those dialects.'

" 'Look,' I said—I'd had a sudden inspiration—'How about you reading the play to me? If you'd just read to the end of the first act, I bet you won't want to stop. I bet you five bucks!' A bet is something Harry can't resist. He grabbed the script and started to read.

" 'Gosh,' I said. 'It's better than I thought it was. You're good, Mr. Frazee. You were an actor once, of course?'

27

" 'No, I was never an actor.'

" 'You should have been—that's all I've got to say.' That encouraged him. He started to work harder.

"It went like a breeze. I may not be much of a reader, but I was right there as an audience. A first act by a budding playwright was never better received.

" 'I can't wait,' I said, 'to hear what you're going to do with that second act twist. Gosh, I've a treat coming to me there.'

"From then on he was selling the play to me. He took off his coat and stood up so that he could really act. I went round and sat in his desk chair. I could rock better on the laughs.

"By the time he got to the end of the play he was all in. I had to pour him a stiff drink. I took one myself. We were buddies. He asked me to call him Harry."

"He bought it?"

"I left the office with a thousand dollars in my pocket. The little masterpiece was never produced, because he subsequently came out of the ether, but it got me a thousand at a time when I most needed it. And if you can get a thousand bucks out of Harry Frazee, you're good."

"Yes, I've always heard he's a pretty hard-boiled egg."

"Most managers are."

"But not all. There are shining exceptions. One points with pride, for instance, to Savage."

"Colonel Henry W. Savage? Have you met him?"

"I was in his office yesterday, and he's very different from . . . well, somebody like Abe Erlanger. Mind you, I'm quite fond of Abe. He eats broken bottles and conducts human sacrifices at the time of the full moon, but he's a thoroughly good chap, heart of gold beneath a rugged exterior and all that sort of thing. All the same, you couldn't describe him as a *preux chevalier*. He lacks a certain something."

"You don't often get a manager who's a Chesterfield."

"Exactly. That is why I say that, when you do, you should grapple him to your soul with hoops of steel. This Savage, now, of whom I speak, is the answer to an author's prayer, a charming, refined, cultured gentleman of the old school with delightful, courtly manners, frank blue eyes and a heart as far from fraud as heaven from earth. He radiates benevolence. He is without guile."

"His heart is as the heart of a little child?"

"You put it in a nutshell. That gentle soul would not harm a fly."

"How do you know?"

"I've seen him."

"Seen him what?"

"Not harming flies. He is a sort of modern St. Francis of Assisi, dripping with good will to all men and running his business in a spirit of pure altruism. By the way, he wants to see us after lunch."

A man who had been sitting with his back to them turned in his chair.

"Excuse me, gentlemen," he said. "I could not help overhearing your conversation. You were speaking, if my ears did not deceive me, of that hornswoggling old pirate and premier louse of the world, Colonel Henry W. Savage."

"That . . . *what* did you call him?"

" 'Hornswoggling old pirate and premier louse of the world' was the expression I used. I could think of nothing stronger on the spur of the moment."

Guy had recognized the man now. His was a face which since *The Merry Widow* had become a well-known one.

"You're Donald Brian, aren't you?"

"That's right. You're Guy Bolton, I think, and . . ."

"This is P. G. Wodehouse."

"How do you do, Mr. Wodehouse," said Donald Brian, "I will address myself to you, for it was you who were describing Colonel Henry W. Savage as a gentle soul devoid of guile. I assure you, Mr. Wodehouse," said Donald Brian earnestly, "that that man, that seemingly saintly Hank Savage, is so crooked that he could hide at will behind a spiral staircase. Let me tell you a little story. Some years ago this child of unmarried parents sent for me. He was casting a piece called *The Merry Widow*, of which you may have heard. He wished me to play the hero, a certain Prince Danilo."

"You were terrific as Prince Danilo," said Guy.

Donald Brian bowed.

"Thank you. I am a conscientious artist, and I spared no effort to earn my seventy-five dollars a week."

"Your *what?*"

"That was my salary throughout the run. I asked a somewhat higher figure. The Colonel refused and we started arguing about it. 'Look, Donny,' he said at last. 'I'll tell you what let's do. Let's toss for it. If you win, I'll give you what you're asking. If I win, you'll work for seventy-five.' Then he pulled a half dollar from his pocket and said, 'Head or tails?' "

Donald Brian paused a moment. He seemed to be struggling with his feelings.

"Now, psychologists have established," he resumed, "that in seventy-seven cases out of a hundred the answer to that question is 'Heads.' I saw no reason to be different, so I said 'Heads' like all the rest of the boys."

"And it came tails?"

"It had to come tails, because, as I learned later, it was tails on both sides—one of those freak coins that the mint has turned out occasionally. You see, the old boy knew all about that quirk of human nature that gives 'heads' a big preference. And so through the whole run of the *Widow* I worked for seventy-five dollars a week. And when the show had been running for a year to capacity business and he had made a fortune out of it, I asked for a raise. 'Why, Donny, I'm surprised,' the Colonel said. 'I thought you were a good sport. That was your end of a bet—seventy-five a week. You're not going to welch, are you?' "

Brian sighed, and turned back to his table.

· 2 ·

It was a tale that provided food for thought, but Plum, as they walked over to the Savage office, was inclined to make light of it.

"These actors!" he said. "Extraordinary how they love to invent yarns. Anything for a good story."

"You think it was an invention?" said Guy, who seemed pensive.

"Of course. You aren't going to tell me that a man like Colonel Savage . . ."

Plum broke off. They had paused in front of the George M. Cohan Theater to look at the photographs in the entrance. Colonel Savage's star, Mitzi Hajos, was playing there in a piece called *Sari*.

"Someone over on the horizon seems to be trying to pass the time of day with you," Plum said. "He's waving, and I think I caught the word 'Guy.' "

Guy turned.

"Oh, that's Tom Cushing. He wrote the book and lyrics of *Sari*. Hullo, Tom," he said, as the other came up. "Do you know P. G. Wodehouse?"

"We've never met. How are you, P.G.?"

"How do you do? Guy tells me you're the author of this outstanding success."

"Well, I adapted it from the Hungarian original, and it was a hell of a job, let me tell you. You know what stinkers these Hungarian books are. I had to invent practically a new story. I also fitted new lyrics to all that endless music Kalman writes. It took me months."

"Still, you must be making a packet out of it."

A spasm of pain contorted Cushing's face, the same sort of spasm which had twisted the features of Donald Brian when he had been speaking of double-tailed half-dollars.

"Do you know Savage?" he asked.

"Slightly. Guy hasn't met him yet. We're on our way to his office now."

"God help you," said Tom Cushing. "Forgive me if I seem to speak bitterly, but I have passed through the furnace. Do you know what the Colonel paid me for all the work I did on *Sari?* Five hundred dollars."

"Five hundred *flat?*"

"That's what."

"Good Lord!"

"I was to be paid in five monthly installments, which were to cease if the play should close. That was to keep me up to the mark. Unless I did my damnedest, it might close in three months, and then I would only get three hundred dollars."

"It's been running a good twenty weeks, hasn't it?"

"Twenty-four, to capacity. Well, I got my five checks, and then the generous old fellow sent me another. A darned graceful gesture, I thought, and so I told Madison Corey, the Colonel's manager, when I happened to run into him on the street. I said, 'That was nice of Colonel Savage to keep on with those hundred dollar payments because the show is such a success. I appreciated it greatly. What a dear old chap he is!' And next morning there came a letter from the dear old chap saying that his bookkeeping department had made a mistake and unless the hundred was returned immediately, legal proceedings would be instituted."

Guy had paled a little beneath his tan.

"I can't believe it."

"It's true."

"What did you do?"

"I sent him ninety-eight, fifty. I told him I was using the other dollar and a half to buy a frame for his letter. Oh, well," said Cushing philosophically, "it'll be something to tell my grandchildren about when they cluster around my knee."

He passed on, and Guy eyed Plum fixedly.

"You and your answers to an author's prayer! You and your

modern St. Francises of Assisi! Thank goodness we haven't got to have anything to do with the old devil. What are we seeing him about, anyway? I suppose he has some frightful Hungarian thing he wants us to fix up for fifty dollars paid in monthly installments."

Plum coughed.

"Well, not quite that. The fact is . . ." He paused. He seemed embarrassed. "You know that thing we roughed out, the one we thought of calling *Have a Heart?*"

"To follow *Eddie* at the Princess."

"Yes, that was the idea, but I'm afraid I've promised it to Savage."

"You've done *what?*"

"He's a very persuasive old gentleman. He talked me into it."

"I wouldn't let him touch it with a ten-foot pole."

Plum coughed again. His embarrassment had become more marked.

"The trouble is," he said, "I'm afraid I rather let myself be carried away and, to cut a long story short, he's got a verbal agreement, and there's no possible way we can get out of it."

· 3 ·

Colonel Savage was a man in the middle fifties, tall and thin and benevolent, his open, candid face surmounted by a handsome mop of gray hair. He walked with a slight limp, having probably in the course of his career been shot in the foot by some indignant author.

He received the visitors beamingly.

"I want to sign those *Have a Heart* contracts today," he said, all heartiness and joviality, like something out of Dickens. "Yes, Miss Stanchfield?"

Miss Stanchfield, his secretary, had entered.

33

"I've just spoken to the hospital, Colonel," she said. "Mr. Scarborough seems a little better this morning. They say he had only one screaming fit in the night. I thought you would like to know."

"Yes, indeed," said the Colonel. "I take a fatherly interest in all my authors. Poor Scarborough," he explained, "had a breakdown when we were out on the road shaping up his play for New York. He was carried off the train on a stretcher. Better, is he? That's good."

"He still keeps muttering about some scene he says you want him to fix and shuddering a good deal."

"Dear, dear."

"And he picks at the cover quite a lot."

"Well, well. These authors you get today seem very brittle. No stamina. No reserve force. Poor Cushing collapsed while we were trying out *Sari*. And look at poor Browne. There was a sad case."

"Browne?" queried Plum, as Miss Stanchfield went out. He noted uneasily that all the Savage authors mentioned so far had been qualified by the ominous adjective "poor."

"Walter Browne, who wrote *Everywoman*, one of the greatest successes of my career. He died the night the play opened. That's the second one I've had die on me, though the other was only a composer. Ah, well, here today and gone tomorrow. All flesh is grass, I sometimes say. I see," said the Colonel, following Guy's eye, which had become glassy and was fixed on a picture of a sailing vessel on the wall, "you are looking at my grandfather's ship. What a beauty! He made a lot of money out of that boat. She was a real clipper. Cargo after cargo she carried."

"Tea?"

"Slaves. And now," the Colonel went on, dismissing the subject, "about those contracts for *Have a Heart*. I like to get these business details off my mind before going ahead.

34

What figure would you suggest? Some authors, I believe, prefer to take a flat sum down—"

"Five hundred dollars?" said Guy with an unpleasant tinkle in his voice.

"Yes, I wouldn't mind going as high as that."

"We would prefer a royalty."

"What royalty were you thinking of?"

"The usual three per cent."

"Three per cent is not usual with *me*," said the Colonel emphatically. "Still, I'll tell you what I'll do," he went on, drawing a coin from his pocket. "I'll toss you for it. Three per cent if you win, one if I win. Heads or tails?" he said, flicking the coin into the air.

"TAILS! ! !" shouted the authors in unison.

The Colonel picked up the half-dollar and put it in his pocket. He seemed to have aged quite a little in the last few moments. He looked at the authors in silence for awhile.

Then he spoke.

"I suppose you boys know quite a few people in our business?" he said reflectively.

· 4 ·

Have a Heart opened on a cold winter's night— December 27, 1916, to be exact—at the Opera House, Trenton, New Jersey, not quite the best spot for the presentation of a somewhat sophisticated divorce story in which a honeymooning couple is being pursued by a lawyer bearing the tidings that their marriage is not legal.

The hero was the proprietor of a department store where the heroine worked. When the century was in its teens there was much talk of model employers and of making conditions comfortable for the workers and this was duly satirized.

The clientele of the Trenton Opera House found it all a

bit exotic. The book, lyrics and music of *Have a Heart* were integrated in a fashion then unknown, the lyrics all fitting into the story and either advancing the action or highlighting a character, and this puzzled the pleasure-seekers. Their response on the opening night was tepid, and it came as no surprise to the authors to be told by Miss Stanchfield after the final curtain had fallen that Colonel Savage would like to see them in the dining room of Teller's Hotel for a conference.

The personnel of the meeting, which began shortly after midnight, consisted of the manager, the authors and George Marion, a fine old character actor who, having yet some years to wait for *Anna Christie* to bring him his best role, eked out a poorly paid living as book director for the Colonel's musical productions.

It needed but a glance at the man up top to tell the two partners that the proceedings were likely to take some time. All through the performance he had been dictating whispered notes to Miss Stanchfield, and these, as he dumped them down on the table, looked like the manuscript of a three-volume novel.

"Let's get to work," he said.

Line by line the script was gone through. Cuts were proposed, changes discussed. The hands of the big, fly-specked clock on the wall pointed to five past two.

"What do you think of that suggestion?" asked the Colonel, turning to George Marion as Guy proposed a structural alteration.

"Let me ponder it," said George. "I would like to try to visualize it as it affects the entire dramatic structure."

He folded his arms on the table in front of him, and rested his forehead on them. Several minutes passed while the authors waited politely for his opinion.

"Go on," said the Colonel. "We'll get on to something else while George is thinking."

They got on to something else, and George continued think-

36

ing. He was still thinking when the Colonel rose and announced that he was going to bed.

"We old fellows have to take care of our health," he said.

"You approve the change I suggested?" asked Guy.

"Certainly," said the Colonel. It was plain by now that anything in the nature of a change was meat and drink to him. "And of course there will be those two new lyrics I mentioned. Start on them at once. Miss Stanchfield will meet you at eight-thirty tomorrow morning to collect the material. She will have everything typed and parts extracted by ten. You will then go over the whole thing with George and Teddy Royce, which will give you time to rewrite anything they disapprove of before you get down to rehearsal."

"May I ask a question?" said Plum.

"By all means."

"When do we sleep?"

"Sleep?" said the Colonel reprovingly. "You didn't come here to sleep. You came here to get a show ready for Broadway."

Wodehouse looked at Bolton. Bolton looked at Wodehouse. Their thoughts had flashed to George Scarborough, carried off on a stretcher at the end of the pre-Broadway tour, to Walter Browne, dying on the opening night, and—yes, there was another, that composer who had expired at the close of one of these Savage tuning-up sessions.

"I love the theater," said Colonel Savage. "I love the good old-fashioned show people to whom the stage came first whatever crisis might arise. I'd like to tell you boys a little story that will illustrate what I mean. I was a friend of Maurice Barrymore and I knew that in spite of all his peccadillos he was devoted to Georgie, his wife. I went to see him the day after she died and found him, his eyes red from weeping, with the newspapers spread about the bed in which he was lying.

" 'I've had a cruel loss, Hank,' he said. 'One I shall never get over. But I must say they've given the old girl some damn

37

good notices.' Good night, boys. Don't forget. Eight-thirty sharp."

He left them. George Marion, still bent over the table, stirred slightly.

"Do you realize," said Plum, regarding the bowed form sympathetically, "that this pondering business of George's is the only way the poor devil can get any sleep."

"Yes," agreed Guy. "We only have one tour to cope with. Poor old George goes on, from play to play."

"Well, we'd better get upstairs and work, I suppose. What do you think we ought to do about George?"

The question was decided for them by George's suddenly sitting up.

"Yes," he said briskly, "I've gone over the whole thing in my mind and I see no insurmountable obstacles. I therefore vote for the change, Colonel."

"The Colonel has gone to bed."

"Really?" said George. "I was so absorbed in the problem I didn't notice him leaving. Well, well, I'm afraid the old boy's beginning to feel his age. He's not as wide awake at these conferences as he was five or ten years ago."

The two authors went up to their room and settled down to work. By a quarter to six it was done, and Plum stretched himself wearily.

"Have you ever reflected," he said, "that forty thousand people were killed in automobile accidents last year, and not one of them was Colonel Henry W. Savage? Looks to me like mismanagement somewhere. Do you believe in heredity?"

"Why?"

"I was only thinking of the Colonel's grandfather, the slaver. Still, I believe the show's a hit, don't you?"

"A hit? Of course it's a hit. Do we ever put on anything that isn't a hit?" said Guy, making use of A. L. Erlanger's noncopyrighted material.

"But I was disappointed in the way 'Napoleon' went."

"They've probably never heard of Napoleon in Trenton."

"No, it wasn't the audience. It was the fellow who sang it."

"Napoleon" had been sung by the principal comedian, who played a brash elevator boy named Henry. It was Henry's boast that he had told more women where they could get off than any man in New York.

"He's too old. Too old and too large."

"There aren't many comics who can look like boys of sixteen."

"I know one who can. I've seen him in vaudeville. Billy B. Van. But would the Colonel engage him? He's expensive."

"Well, what's money? You can't take it with you."

"I know you can't, but nobody ever told that to Hank Savage."

"Listen," said Guy. "Let's snatch forty minutes refreshing sleep, which seems to be the most we shall ever get a night during this tour, then we'll be all rested and alert for taking it up with him before rehearsal."

Colonel Savage, approached an hour or two later, agreed that Billy B. Van would be ideal for the part of Henry.

"But his salary!" he said, a look of pain coming into his fine eyes. "I doubt if you could get him under three hundred."

"Three hundred isn't much."

"It is to me," said the Colonel, who, having only twenty-seven million dollars tucked away in blue chip securities, had to be careful. "But I'll tell you what I'll do . . ."

"TAILS ! ! !" cried the two authors, speaking as one author.

The Colonel smiled faintly and very wryly. The old wound still troubled him.

"If you and Guy will pay half his salary for the first three months, it's a deal."

Guy and Plum looked at one another. The same thought was in both their minds—viz. that for an author to pay out money to a manager instead of taking it from him was like

39

rubbing velvet the wrong way. Then they thought of Billy B. Van singing "Napoleon," and the sensation of nausea passed.

"I'm game," said Guy.

"So am I," said Plum.

So the matter was arranged. Billy B. Van was engaged and was an instantaneous success in New York, rolling the customers in the aisles with his comedy and singing "Napoleon" like a linnet. And all through the first three months Guy and Plum duly paid up seventy-five dollars per week per person, their contribution to his salary.

At the end of the third month the Colonel fired him.

Chapter Four

HAVE A HEART was one of those semi-successes in New York. It played to capacity for three months, but after Billy Van left business dropped. Old Hank didn't seem to mind. The fact that he had engaged a new comedian cheaper than Billy by a hundred and fifty dollars apparently compensated him for the loss of thousands a week at the box office. He was not, as a matter of fact, very interested in a New York run. What he liked was the road. *Have a Heart*, which had done only five months and two weeks on Broadway, played for six years outside New York, everywhere to crowded houses.

Shortly after it had opened at the Liberty Theater on Forty-second Street (now a second-run movie house) its authors received a call from Ray Comstock to come to the Princess, where *Very Good Eddie* had just passed its two hundredth performance.

For years now the Princess has ceased to be a theater, having gone the way of so many of the old theaters. Today it is not even a second-run movie house, it is a television den, God help it. The lion and the lizard keep the courts where once Ray Comstock gloried and drank deep.

It seemed to Plum, as they walked to Thirty-ninth Street, that Guy had something on his mind. He was wearing the rather dazed expression of a man who has been unexpectedly struck on the seat of the pants by the Twentieth Century Limited.

"Girl trouble," he explained briefly in answer to his friend's sympathetic query. "I had a little girl trouble last night."

"Who was the little girl?"

Guy stiffened. There came into his eye that cold, stern look which had caused him to be known in the old regiment as Chilled Steel Bolton.

"Does one bandy a woman's name in mess, old boy? If one does, Emily Post has been fooling me for years."

Plum flushed. The rebuke had been a just one.

"Forgive me, old chap. I should not have said it. Call her X and tell me what happened."

Guy was silent for a moment. His finely chiselled features twisted a little, as if the memory pained him. With men of the Guy Bolton type memories are like mulligatawny soup in a cheap restaurant. It is wiser not to stir them.

"If I told you I was about to marry an adagio dancer what would you say?"

"I should try to be sympathetic."

"Exactly. If you loved a girl you'd hate to see two men flinging her about the stage, even in this case doing the final throw with their backs to each other."

"What do you mean 'in this case'?"

"Oh, yes, I didn't explain, did I? I am—or was up to last night—engaged to an adagio dancer. I kissed her at a Christmas party, never thinking she'd take the matter seriously, and darned if she didn't construe it as a declaration of love. She rushed home and told her mother we were engaged."

"What did you do?"

"Well I went off to see her mother to explain matters to her and darned if the whole family weren't lined up waiting for me. Before I could say a word I was being kissed by the lot of them. Bottles of champagne appeared and there I was stuck fast to the fly paper."

"But last night—"

"Yes, last night I decided I must make a break for freedom. Every night for the past ten days I've had to go up to their suite for supper. The routine was first a short chat with mother while little X was removing her stage make-up and getting into something loose. Then mother would go to bed, leaving us to discuss our plans for the future. This usually narrowed down to at what age should the children begin to learn adagio dancing. Well, last night I remembered the technique for breaking off a romance, budding or otherwise. It was taught me by Jack Barrymore, an admitted expert. He said the wheeze was to engineer a violent quarrel and at its height to shout, 'This is the end! Goodbye!' and then leg it off at forty m. p. h."

"Yes, I remember hearing Jack say, 'The only way to fight a woman is with your hat.' "

"That's what I did last night. When the subject came up about the children, I said quite brutally that I wouldn't on a bet have any child of mine taught adagio dancing. X blew her top. She started to throw the crockery about which showed me how wise I was to go while the going was good. I spoke the exit line, grabbed my hat, raced down the hall and rang for the elevator."

"The happy ending."

"It was not an end, but a beginning. Just as I rang, X came dashing out of the suite and down the hall with practically nothing on. She flung herself on the floor, clasping my knees and screaming at the top of her voice. At that moment the elevator arrived, full of people."

"Embarrassing."

"Most. I disengaged my knees and stepped in. There was a dreadful silence. All that broke that silence was the sound of X's shrieks and the thudding of her fists on the elevator door. It was as the elevator started to descend that I was aware of a figure standing at my elbow, a gray-haired figure in a clerical collar."

"You don't mean—?"

"Yes. Belasco. He lives at the Marie Antoinette. He was looking at me austerely, like a clergyman who has discovered schism in his flock."

"Did he say anything?"

"He said—in a nasty, cold, disapproving voice—'Good evening, Mr. Middleton.'"

"And what did you say?"

"I said, 'Good evening, Mr. Belasco. I didn't think you would remember me.'"

Rightly shocked by this revolting glimpse into *la vie de bohème*, Plum pursed his lips.

"You and your women! Why don't you get married and settle down to a tranquil life of fruitful endeavor, like me? Don't you know that statisticians have established that in each calendar year bachelors waste between forty and forty-five full working days pursuing women and between forty-five and fifty running away from them?"

"It's all very well for you to talk. You've found the answer to the bill of requirements in Ethel. I haven't yet met the girl I'm willing to exchange my freedom for. I'm like the man George Ade wrote about, who didn't want to make his choice till he had walked the full length of the counter."

"And meanwhile you're the sort of fellow who, when he hears a sharp knock on the door of any room he happens to be in, instinctively jumps out of the window. Is that a system?"

They arrived at the Princess, and found Ray Comstock, partner with Bessie Marbury in the little theater's enterprises, seated at his desk with a bottle beside him for purposes of reference.

"That must be powerful stuff you're drinking," said Guy. "I could smell the fumes in Thirty-ninth Street."

"It isn't this bottle," said Comstock. "It's the ceiling," and they saw that it was covered by a dark stain on which beads of moisture had formed. "Whiskey," said Comstock mournfully. "The finest money can buy. I stacked it up in the loft, twenty-four cases. I forgot the steam pipes run through there. The stuff got so hot it exploded."

Ray Comstock was a thin, rangy individual who looked like

44

a boy and had almost as much charm as Charlie Dillingham. He seemed to be perpetually telephoning and had a telephone receiver that he could balance on his shoulder, thus leaving his hands free for opening letters, pouring drinks and so forth.

His mind seemed equally detachable. He could listen on the telephone and talk to visitors simultaneously. There was never any clue as to who was on the other end of the wire. His part in the conversation was mostly monosyllabic, the other person doing all the talking. He addressed all these callers as "Honey."

He had sent for Guy and Plum to tell them that the time had come to be thinking of something to follow *Very Good Eddie*. *Eddie* he proposed to move to the Casino, where there were fifteen hundred seats. It would thus become available to a public that could not afford to pay the high scale of a dollar to three dollars charged at the Princess.

This was the policy adopted from then on with the Princess shows, and a very good one, too.

He then told them something else. Bessie Marbury was out. She had withdrawn from the partnership.

"She didn't like the play."

"What play?"

"The play you boys are going to turn into a musical. Charlie Hoyt's *A Milk White Flag*."

Plum remained calm—he had never heard of *A Milk White Flag*—but Guy nearly hit the dark patch on the ceiling.

"You're crazy, Ray. You can't be thinking of making that into a Princess musical."

"Why not?" said Comstock. He spoke into the telephone. "I said 'Why not?' to somebody else, honey. 'Decidedly not,' is what I say to you."

Guy was still staring incredulously.

"I've read *A Milk White Flag*," he said. "It's about a man who pretends to be dead so as to evade his creditors and collect on his insurance. He's laid out on ice and catches cold."

45

"That's right," said Ray, laughing heartily. "I had forgotten about him catching cold. I remember now it was terrific. Every now and then there would be a sneeze from the room where the body was laid out. The family were scared pop-eyed." He laughed again at the recollection of this rich comedy, and spoke into the telephone. "No, honey, you needn't get sore. I'm not laughing at you."

"But listen, Ray. The thing that has made the Princess shows is charm. We must have charm."

"Be as charming as you like. No one's stopping you."

"Well, you can't say A *Milk White Flag* has charm, with a corpse that keeps coming on the stage without any trousers on."

"Why would a corpse have trousers on? Only the upper half of the body would be on view. No, honey, I'm not talking about the party last night. This is in a play, the new Princess show."

"And he makes a buffet dinner off the sandwiches set out for the mourners."

"We'll change it to a sit-down dinner."

"A *what*?"

"I was speaking on the telephone."

"Perhaps we'd better wait until Ray's finished phoning," suggested Plum.

"He's never finished phoning," said Guy. "As soon as he hangs up on that call, there'll be another."

"Look, Ray," said Plum. "Guy doesn't seem to like this *Milk White Flag* of yours. Why not do the piece we've been working on?"

He was referring to a fantasy which Guy had written called *The Little Thing*, a whimsical trifle about an orphan girl in a Greenwich Village boardinghouse. Every young playwright has something of this sort tucked away in a drawer, and it is al-ways something which managers refuse to consider. Shakes-peare, as he sat listening to the audience at the Globe whis-

46

tling and stamping its feet at the end of the "To be or not to be" soliloquy, was probably not congratulating himself that Hamlet was a sell-out and that if business kept up like this they would do fifteen ducats, eleven rose nobles and four pieces of eight on the week. It is far more likely that he was thinking wistfully of his masterpiece, that tragedy of Alexander the Great, which he could never get Burbage to look at.

"What piece is that?" asked Comstock.

"It's called *The Little Thing*. It's a fantasy."

"It's wonderful," said Guy.

"Terrific," said Plum. "Strikes a new note."

"Yes, honey," said Comstock. "No, honey," said Comstock. "Just as you say, honey. Goodbye, honey." He hung up the receiver. "I'm glad you like the idea, boys," he said. "A big hit in its day, the *Milk White Flag*."

Guy clutched his forehead.

"But what about the numbers?"

"Oh, hello, honey," said Comstock as the telephone tinkled. He tucked the receiver between ear and shoulder and poured himself a drink. There was nothing to indicate whether this was the previous honey, playing a return date, or another honey. "What's your trouble?" he said. "Not yours, honey. I have some authors with me."

"Who does the numbers?"

"The corpse has two daughters, and they have beaux. What more do you want?"

"But the daughters think their father is lying dead on ice in the next room. They'll scarcely be in the mood to sing."

"That's up to you. I'm not writing the show. Would you mind repeating that, honey, somebody was talking. No, I *can't* throw them out on their fannies, honey, this is business. I have to work, don't I, honey? If I didn't, where would you be? Oh, you would, would you? Oh, they do, do they? Begging you on their bended knees, are they? Well, why don't you? Darned good idea." He seemed not in the least perturbed. His tone was mild, even affectionate. "Go to hell, honey," he concluded almost lovingly and, hanging up the receiver, turned to Bolton. "What were you saying about a fantasy?"

"I was speaking of the show we've written, *The Little Thing*."

"I don't like fantasies."

"You'll like this fantasy."

"Who says so?"

It seemed to Plum that it was a case for compromise.

"Well, if *The Little Thing* doesn't appeal to you, Ray, how about *Oh, Boy!*?"

"What's *Oh, Boy!*?"

"Another show we've been working on. It's got a good story, and Jerry and I have finished half the numbers. There's one called 'Till the Clouds Roll By'—"

"Perfect for the *Milk White Flag*. One of the beaux is trying to cheer up one of the daughters. 'Too bad your old man shuffled off,' he says. 'Yes, damned shame if you ask me,' says the daughter. 'Still, nothing to be done about it, of course,' says the fellow. 'No,' says the girl. 'To hell with it. Let's wait till the clouds roll by.' And into number. Fits like the paper on the wall."

Guy rose.

"The charm dissolves apace," he said. "I quote Shakespeare."

"That's the trouble with you," said Comstock. "You've been reading Shakespeare. You've gone highbrow on me. This *Oh, Boy!* What's it a musical version of?"

"It isn't a musical version of anything. It's original. Our own unaided work."

Comstock shook his head.

"I don't want an original. I want something I've heard them laugh at. Then I know what I'm getting. Now, *A Milk White Flag*—"

"No," said Guy firmly. "Shoot, if you must, this old gray

48

head, but don't ask me to make a Princess musical with half the numbers done by a corpse with no trousers on. I'm sorry."

"I'm sorry, too," said Comstock. The telephone tinkled. "Oh, hello, honey," he said. "Haven't heard from you in some time."

· 2 ·

For some months after that a number of writers wrestled with *A Milk White Flag*. Otto Harbach made a start, but gave it up. Henry Blossom, Victor Herbert's writing partner, had a go and turned in his portfolio. It was finally taken on by a triumvirate consisting of John L. Golden, Anne Caldwell and Jack Hazzard. The music was by Baldwin Sloane, and the piece was called *Go To It*, one of those unfortunate titles which spell disaster from the outset. Offer a dramatic critic something called *Go To It*, and he is immediately struck by the happy thought of saying that it should have been called *Don't Go To It*, for these dramatic critics are as quick as lightning.

Guy held his breath. Plum held his breath. Jerry, in his Bronxville home, was also holding his breath. They realized that this was a crisis. If *Go To It* was a hit, their hold on the Princess was gone, and the chance to put on an original anywhere would vanish forever. The adapted farce would seem to every manager, as it seemed to Ray Comstock, a safer bet, and *Oh, Boy!* would not have a hope of production.

They journeyed down to Atlantic City for the out-of-town opening, and were able to breathe again. The thing was awful, just as they had predicted it would be. Not even the corpse on its bed of ice was colder than the audience. It was with uplifted hearts that they returned to the Traymore. In the lobby they encountered Freddy Zimmerman, the son of the owner of a large chain of theaters in the provinces, who invited them to his suite for a nightcap. He had come over from Philadelphia as an emissary of his father to view the new Princess show and decide whether to accept it as tenant of one of the Zimmerman houses. After the first intermission he had phoned his old man and told him to let *Go To It* go elsewhere.

In Freddy's suite they found Joe Urban. Joe, who was making history with his stage settings and even more with his revolutionary stage lighting, had done a beautiful job with *Miss Springtime*. He eyed the trio with momentary anxiety.

"This *Goes To It*—you boys did not write it?" he asked.

With considerable emphasis the boys assured him they did not.

"I am so glad," he said. "For me it is a very bad smell. It should be taken away by the grubbage collector to the city dumpings."

Joe, a charming Austrian, spoke a language of his own. He couldn't drink milk because it cuddled in his stomach; he promised that he would have his sketches ready at the drop of a bucket, and, when he grew emphatic, his favorite expression was, "just mock my words." In those days people collected Urbanisms as they later collected the quaint sayings of Samuel Goldwyn.

Joe remarked that he loved Atlantic City. The air was so embracing.

"I can remember a time when it wasn't as embracing as you would have liked it to be," laughed Freddy.

"No," agreed Joe, "I get a sock in the pants that time I shall never forget."

It had happened during the war when Atlantic City was full of volunteer spy-chasers, dollar-a-year men, proud of the federal badges they carried under their lapels and all anxious to make names for themselves by uncovering a trail of espionage. One of these had his eye on Joe. The Follies scenery had been damaged in transit and Joe had sent for his Austrian business manager, who had arrived with three Austrian scene painters, and while they worked, the manager would whisper to Joe asking how chances were for getting some money out of Ziegfeld, and Joe would whisper back that they were not good, explaining that, while fantastically generous about anything he didn't owe, Ziegfeld had a constitutional objection to paying for what he did.

It was these Teutonic whisperings that had aroused the suspicions of the spy chaser, who was lurking in the background, but what really set him hot on the trail was the signalling.

"In the mornings," said Joe, "I do always my sitting-up exercises. We are staying at the Shelbourne that time and I open the window and breathe the invizerating sea's air while I go oop, down, out, back with the arms."

"The sleuth hound was down below," supplemented Freddy, "making notes."

"What did he think you were doing—signalling to Germany?"

"To Germany no. To someone in the Bellevue-Stratford. It is you know only a stone's jump from the Shelbourne. This dumkoph think when I go oop, down, out, back it is a code—a wag wag."

It seems that the thrill of sharing a hotel with the Follies beauties had been too much for Joe. He had fallen in love. He had fallen in love with, of all girls, the gorgeous Lillian Lamont. And Joe's Austrian charm, his soft, vibrant voice breathing words of adoration, had found ready response from a heart which, like the U. S. Navy, was "open to all men from eighteen to forty."

Joe, somewhat falteringly, had suggested that if she would come up to his suite he would show her a collection of his drawings and, at the same time, they could deal with another bottle of Bollinger non vintage. Miss Lamont accepted on both counts, and they made their way to the Shelbourne. When they got in the elevator a man stepped in with them. When they got out he followed. As Joe was putting the key in the lock he felt a hand on his shoulder and a voice said:

"You are under arrest."

"I think it is someone pushing my leg," said Joe. "I say to him in my most chalant manner, 'This is no time for clown making.' He say it is no clown making but honest to level and that I must come with him. I make pleadings. I say I do not know what I have done but can he not, for a little while, let bygones be hasbeens? All he does is say like a parrot, 'You are under arrest.' "

Ziegfeld was sent for and he explained who Joe was, adding that, while the United States was important, the *Ziegfeld Follies* wasn't to be kicked around either. He needed Joe to get his scenery right. Finally a compromise was effected. The sleuth would give Joe a week before hauling him into court but, during that time, the artist must remain in his custody. Not for a single moment was he to be out of his sight.

"Everywhere I go," said Joe, "there he is dodging my feet-steps. Whenever Lillian and me went chair-riding it must be one of those big, for three chairs. Lillian has heard of a wonderful fish ghetto where they make special fine lobster humidor. This lowlife goes with us to the ghetto. He also eats lobster humidor."

When the week was up Joe was carted over to Philadelphia, taken before a judge—and cleared. He returned to New York just in time for the Follies opening.

"So it all ended happily?"

"Not so much happily," answered Joe. "I ask Lillian to have supper with me opening night, but she say she cannot. And then when I walk into Rector's after the show, what do I see? Lillian sitting handholding with the verdampte spy-chaser!"

· 3 ·

Go To It duly opened at the Princess. All the critics—except one, who headed his review with the word "Why?"—said that it should not have been called *Go To It* but *Don't Go To It*.

Jerry Kern had a call from Comstock soon after breakfast, asking him to come at once to the office and bring Guy and Plum. In the Comstock office there was a hushed, funereal atmosphere. The customary row of actors sat in the waiting room, looking rather more animated than usual. One gathered that the newspaper each one held contained a message of hope for the artist who was resting. They would soon be casting again at the Princess.

Ray Comstock was at his desk, the receiver wedged against his ear.

"Come in, boys," he said. "Yes, honey, it's a flop. . . . So am I, honey. . . . Thanks, honey. . . . Goodbye, honey." He hung up. "Now, boys," he said with, for him, a surprising briskness, "we've taken a kick in the pants, as I'm sure you know. I blame you fellows, partly. Oh, hello, honey. If you'd tackled the job as I asked you to, things might have been different. You've got something—maybe it's this 'charm' you talk about. No, honey, I'm not talking to you, I'm talking to the boys. I saw *Miss Springtime* the other night. It's a swell show, a clever show, plenty of laughs, too."

"It isn't in it with *Oh, Boy!*," said Guy.

"That's what I wanted to see you about. I'll give you a contract for *Oh, Boy!* right now."

"But you haven't read it."

"I don't need to. You fellows know what you're doing. I'll see it opening night. The only question is how soon can we get into rehearsals?"

Guy reflected.

"A month for writing, a couple of weeks for casting—we should be ready by December."

"Okay, boys, go to it." Comstock coughed apologetically. "Sorry, it slipped out. I shall try never to use those words again."

"You really mean that you'll buy the show without reading it or hearing a note of music?"

53

"That's right. Tell your agent to draw the contracts, seven per cent, no more. You choose the directors and the cast. If they'll fit in the budget you can have anyone you name."

"I'd like Robert Milton to stage the book," said Guy.

"Isn't that the red-headed Russian who talks about 'pear-shaped tones'?"

"Yes, but he's clever just the same, and he's begging for a chance to do a musical."

"That's what I like," said Ray, "people begging. It's when you got to beg *them* that things get expensive. Now run along. Don't waste time talking. Go to —" He checked himself. "Get busy," he amended.

The three rose. Plum pulled a cigar from his pocket and held it out.

"Have a cigar, Ray," he said. It was the first and perhaps the last time an author ever gave a cigar to a theatrical manager. Ray took it with a slightly dazed air.

"Thank **you**, honey," he said mechanically.

Chapter Five

THERE WERE TWO SMALL FEMALE ROLES in *Oh, Boy!* which still remained to be filled after the rest of the cast—Anna Wheaton, Marie Carroll, Edna May Oliver and the others—had been signed up: and one morning Comstock asked Guy and Plum to look in at his office. They found him telephoning as usual.

"Can you fellows . . . Get the hell off the line, honey, we're casting. And don't ask if there's anything for you, because there isn't . . . keep a secret?" he said.

They thought they could.

"Well, I don't promise, but I think I'm going to steal the two top Follies beauties away from Flo Ziegfeld."

"You don't mean—?"

"That's right. Marion Davies and Justine Johnstone."

"You're kidding, Ray. Why would they leave Flo? Look at the publicity he gives them."

"They want to be actresses."

"Ah!"

"And I caught them at just the right moment. They're sore about the dressing room sketch."

"What's the dressing room sketch?" asked Plum.

"I know all about that," said Guy. "It's a thing Gene Buck wrote for the *Follies*, but it has never been used. It never will be, either. It's much too valuable to Flo for him to waste it on the public. You see, every year Flo has this same trouble with some of the girls getting ambitious. They tell him they won't sign up unless they're given lines to speak. So up pops the dressing room sketch. The girls get their parts, and every-body's happy."

"And then he says it's so bad it must come out?"

Guy was amazed.

"*Flo*? You think Flo would do anything as crude as that? Of course not. He tells them the sketch is great stuff and they're going to knock the customers endways. He says he never realized before how wonderful they were and thanks them for making him give them the opportunity of showing what they could do. But, come opening night at Atlantic City, he's all broken up to find that the costumes, owing to some-body's inexcusable carelessness, have been left behind. He yells and storms at the wardrobe mistress, but there's nothing to be done about it, of course, till tomorrow night. And be-fore tomorrow night they've found out that the show is an hour too long and he's all broken up but the dressing room sketch will have to go. Meanwhile, the girls have signed up for another year."

The following afternoon when Guy and Plum approached the Princess, there were two town cars parked at the curb, a pair of uniformed chauffeurs standing by them. The Delage bore no identifying insignia, but on the door of the Pierce Arrow were two J's intertwined back to back like the double L's emblazoned on the royal coach of the Sun Monarch.

"It must be the girls!" said Guy.

They went on up the stair and found the outer office in a state of flutter.

A ripple of laughter greeted them as they entered Ray's office, that and a heady scent—what was it? Coty's "L'Origan"? "Quelques Fleurs"? Whatever it was it breathed the word "romance."

The girls were quite breathtakingly lovely. Marion was eighteen, Justine a year and a half older. Both wore mink coats that even a masculine eye could see were the best that the mink family had to offer. Both wore a spray of orchids as if orchids

56

were an everyday affair—which for them they were. Diamonds sparkled at their wrists and glistened more discreetly through the sheer black silk stocking that covered Marion's slender ankle.

Bob Milton, a mature and serious man, sat on the sofa beside Marion, gazing at her as Bernard Berenson would gaze on a Botticelli Venus.

"Don't waste your time with them," he said, as Guy and Plum were "presented." "They're only writers. I'm the man that's going to make you into an actress."

"Yes, b-but they'll have to write the w-words I'm to say." Marion had an ever so faint and ever so attractive stammer.

Justine Johnstone was, if anything, even more likely than her friend to provoke the long low whistle. Daughter of a Norwegian sea captain, she had that touch of aloofness, that faintly haughty carriage that seem to characterize the beauties claiming Viking ancestry.

Robert Milton caressed the sleeve beside him. "Beautiful mink," he commented. "Russian, isn't it?"

"Yes. The poor things lived in Siberia and never saw a single bright light or ever went into a smart restaurant until they met me."

She laughed infectiously.

"How do you girls get such things?" enquired Comstock of the world at large.

Someone answered, "Don't you know? Girls get mink the same way the minks do."

"The girls are ready to sign up with us," said Ray after the chorus of masculine laughter had faded, "as long as they get parts."

Guy assured them they would have parts.

"And names," said Justine. "Not just 'first girl' and 'second girl.'"

"Of course you have names. Yours is Polly Andrews."

"Is that a play on polyandrous?"

"Good heavens, no."

"It sounds like it."

"What does polyandrous mean?" Bob Milton enquired. He was a Russian whose real name was Davidoff and a surprisingly short time before he had known no English words at all.

"It means the same thing about a woman that polygamous does about a man."

"You're too well-educated," said Marion. "I just say snuggle-hound—that's what I hear Ray is. I hear he's the worst old snuggle-hound on Broadway."

"I'm not a patch on Guy. A flick of the finger, a broken heart—that's Guy Bolton."

"Really?"

"He once kissed a girl on Broadway, and she shot clear up to the top of the Woolworth Building."

"You don't say?"

"I'm telling you. Just closed her eyes with a little moan and floated up and up and up."

"And he looks so good. Are you married, Guy?"

"Not yet."

"But you are?" said Marion to Plum.

"Oh, yes," Guy told her. "Plum is very happily married and he's constantly telling me I should be too."

"You get married," said Marion, "and first thing you know you have a baby. Then in a few months—there's another baby. Mind you, I like babies, I like them a lot, but I'm glad I haven't one now."

Then, as if it were an afterthought, she leaned over and rapped the top of Ray's desk. The laugh that rewarded her carried her to the door.

"Write me some funny stuff, boys," she said. "I want to be a comic."

She went out.

"Marion will say anything to get a laugh," Justine commented in her low, Ethel Barrymore voice, "but really she's a perfectly good girl and lives at home with her mother."

She gave a little gurgling laugh as if she too had said something funny, then raised her hand in the straight forearm salute associated with royalty. Her hand fluttered a farewell. "Goodbye, boys."

She followed Marion out. Through the open door they could see the actors craning their necks after her. There was a buzz of comment. Plum, who had been the little gentleman to spring up and open the door, closed it behind her.

"I feel as if I had stepped back into good King Charles's golden reign," he remarked. "Saucy Nell must have been very like Saucy Marion."

"Yes, Charles would have made them both duchesses," agreed Guy.

"They'll get us a lot of publicity," said Ray. "But, great Godfrey, how the rest of the women in the show are going to hate them!"

· 2 ·

The rehearsal period passed swiftly and uneventfully. It seemed no time before a day arrived when the company was gathering on a platform in Grand Central, with the usual collection of dogs, fiancés and anxious mothers that appear whenever a theatrical troupe is setting off "on the road."

The manager in charge was a young man named Jefferson Perry. He was new at the game, but anxious to learn all he could about it before embarking on some private ventures of a highbrow nature beside which *Oh, Boy!* seemed trivial indeed. His wife was a severe looking young woman with glasses, who wore a small brooch on which the letters "D.A.R." appeared in red-white-and-blue enamel.

Schenectady was the first stop, and there the authors were plunged into the depths of despair by a dress rehearsal at which all the things that can go wrong at dress rehearsals did.

The shoes, for instance. The gentleman from I. Miller sitting stolidly out front was a constant object of attack.

"These are my own shoes, Mr. Comstock. The shoes from Miller don't fit."

"You need them larger?"

"Larger on the inside—yes."

The prop department had its share of blame.

"I'm supposed to have a letter to read but no one's given it to me."

Then, most nerve-wracking of all—the stage wait. "What's the matter? What's supposed to be happening?"

"Miss Wheaton says she can't make the change. There'll have to be more dialogue."

The two Ziegfeld lovelies appeared on the stage for a brief scene that lit the depressing gloom with a moment or two of comic relief. Marion, it seems, had suffered an attack of stage fright and, in an effort to dispel it, had downed a glass or two of champagne. This had the unfortunate effect of increasing her charming little stammer to a point at which she was unable to deliver her lines.

To cope with this situation the girls had arranged between them that Justine should speak not only her own lines but Marion's as well. The remarkable monologue ran as follows:

"Oh, so you're here? Yes, I'm here—what about it? You won't leave George Budd alone. That's my business. You don't stand a chance with him. Why not? He's in love with that little Carter girl. He isn't. Yes, darling, he is. I don't care. I'll tell you something else, darling. They're married. They're *not*. Yes, they are—secretly married."

Some effort at verisimilitude was made by Justine's changing her voice on each alternate line, speaking first in a piping treble then in her own rich contralto. On the treble lines Marion kept moving her lips as if she were actually speaking. Alas, the guiding hand of Edgar Bergen was not there. Mouthing and sound were a very poor fit.

The scattering of dressmakers, scene painters, music arrangers, house managers, not to mention the gentleman from I. Miller, burst into shouts of laughter.

"Keep it in, Guy," said Comstock grimly. "At least you'll be sure of one laugh."

The climax came with the sudden appearance of a reporter and a press photographer shepherded by the show's press agent. There was a whispered exchange with Ray Comstock, who shook hands with the newcomers and then called Milton over.

"Stop the rehearsal," he said. "We're going to get a spread in the papers."

The actors gathered together in little groups as the newsmen made their way on to the stage.

"Who do you want first?" asked the stage manager.

"We only want Miss Davies and Miss Johnstone."

"You mean you're not going to take any pictures of the rest of the company?"

"No, that's our orders—just Miss Davies and Miss Johnstone."

The company had come out front and sat watching the girls as they moved from pose to pose. The expression on the faces of the female members of the cast were much the same as those of the *bonnet rouge* leading the mob in Delacroix' famous painting of the storming of the Tuileries. One heard the mutterings of the crowd coming from the seats where the chorus had grouped themselves.

"They're just a bunch of amateurs." Guy and Plum sitting together, numb and despairing, heard it without knowing who said it. Then someone added:

"Like a college show."

Finally the picture-taking was finished.

"Let's get on with the rehearsal," Comstock called from the back of the theater.

"Sorry, Mr. Comstock, Miss Wheaton and Miss Carroll

have gone. They said they'd have no voices tomorrow if they sat around in this cold theater any longer."

Comstock rose. "Send 'em all home," he said. "No use going on. You'll just have to trust to luck tomorrow—and God knows you'll need plenty."

He turned to Jerry Kern, ignoring the pair seated behind him, and delivered the *coup de grâce*.

"I thought *Go To It* was bad," he said. "But it was a sweetheart compared to this turkey."

· 3 ·

The two who had planned and written the atrocity made no reply. They slipped out of a side exit to avoid meeting anyone either on the stage or in the lobby. No conference was called. The thing was beyond conferences. The scribbled notes of errors detected earlier in the evening seemed too trivial to mention. To have wasted time on them would have been like cleaning spots off the deck of a vessel about to founder.

There was a bitter wind blowing, and when a bitter wind blows in Schenectady it is a matter of civic pride with the citizens that no other upstate city can claim a bitterer. Guy and Plum turned up the collars of substantial overcoats that felt as if they were fashioned of gossamer.

The empty streets were dark as were their thoughts. It was very late. The Schenectadians were abed, dreaming no doubt of the treat that awaited them tomorrow evening at the Gaiety Theater.

Guy and Plum rounded a corner and were met by a blast that seemed to say, "You thought it was cold on Main Street, did you? Now we'll show you what Canal Street can do." They bowed their heads and pushed forward like Robert Peary and his Eskimo companion on April 8, 1909.

A figure suddenly appeared beside them. It was the red-headed boy who played the waiter at the country club in Act Two, a part of less than a dozen lines.

"How was I?" he asked, barring their path.

"You were fine, Eddie." It was hard to speak without losing your breath. "You were wonderful."

"I'd like to have a little chat about my part," said Eddie. "I guess some of the things you wrote have more meaning than I'm putting into them."

"Not a bit, old man."

"If I could go over them."

"But for God's sake, Eddie—not here."

"Okay. Just one thing, though. That last exit of mine. I'd like a laugh, if you could give me one."

"We haven't a laugh in us, Eddie."

"I thought of something myself. I'd like to tell it to you, if you won't get sore."

"We won't get sore, but we may get pneumonia. I feel like the corpse on ice in *Go To It*," said Plum.

"Yes, it's a bit chilly tonight, isn't it?" said Eddie, as if he had just noticed it. "But this won't take a minute. Of course, it's pretty fresh of me to be trying to put a line in a wonderful show like *Oh, Boy!*"

"You think *Oh, Boy!* is wonderful?"

"I sure do."

"Then," said Guy, "we're at your service until hell freezes over. And that, I should think, is liable to happen most any minute."

"Well, you know the situation," said Eddie, getting down to it. "Miss Wheaton has just got a flash of Sheriff Simms through the window. He's been looking for her ever since she escaped from that raid in the speakeasy and so—"

"Yes, yes, we know the plot," interjected Plum, stamping his feet and beating his hands on his chest.

"Well, she runs to the Ladies Room just as I'm going off on

63

the other side, and I thought maybe I could call to her: 'When you come out would you mind bringing me my umbrella?' Would that be okay?"

"Absolutely okay," said Guy. "And if you'd like to rewrite the rest of the show you're more than welcome."

· 4 ·

The next night it was a riot. Everything went like clockwork. The hand-props were there. I. Miller's shoes were there. When it came to the quick change, Anna Wheaton was there. Most important of all, the laughs were there, and none topped that put in by Eddie, the red-headed waiter.

Ray Comstock beamed. "I knew it was all right last night," he said. "You could feel success in the air."

They moved on to Syracuse, Rochester, Buffalo and Albany. Everywhere the reception was the same, though a lady in Buffalo turned in a minority report. "I like a show with some *jokes* in it," she was overheard to say as she came down the balcony steps. Apparently even Eddie's line about the umbrella had not pleased her.

As the tour proceeded, the authors kept cutting and polishing. Two vital changes were made in the cast, as often happened in those pre-Equity days. Tom Powers was brought in for George Budd, the hero, and Hal Forde for his friend, playing opposite Anna Wheaton, and the results were magical. These two were exactly what the piece needed to make it a hundred per cent. Old-timers will remember how perfect Tom in particular was in his part. Anna Wheaton, Marie Carroll and Edna May Oliver had been perfect right along.

The company, after the manner of theatrical touring companies, soon became one big, happy family. No team, no clique, no sworn band of blood brothers has such a tendency to gang up as a company of travelling actors. They move like Xenophon's Ten Thousand through an alien country, speaking a different language. They think of nothing but the show. Even newspapers lose their interest. The important question is "How's the play going to go tonight? They say the audience here is a lot tougher than they are in Syracuse."

But even in big happy families things do not always run smoothly, and the *Oh, Boy!* company had its disturbing experiences. The trouble, as might have been expected, was the Girls. Not that they weren't nice to everybody, not that they weren't good troupers. They were all that and more. But they were much too pretty and they lived on a scale which caused jealousy to rear its ugly head among the less fortunately placed.

Those hotel suites, for instance.

These started quite modestly. Marion would have a small sitting room, which she openheartedly shared with Justine, a bedroom and a bath. But as the company progressed westward the suites became larger and the flowers with which they were bedecked appeared in more luxurious profusion. Somebody—possibly her mother—was intent on seeing that while on the road Marion got all the comforts of home, and this mother—or it may have been an aunt—was plainly a woman of spacious ideas. In the old Hollenden Hotel in Cleveland what Marion drew was a reception room, a large sitting room, a small sitting room, a dining room, two bedrooms, two baths, a clothes-pressing room, maid's room and maid's bath, not to mention a refrigerator bursting at the seams with delicacies of every description.

Invited to share this little cubbyhole, Justine looked dubious.

"Where do I put my maid?" she asked.

"That's all right," Marion cheerily reassured her. "We'll tell them to tack on another room and bath."

· 5 ·

It was in this cosy little chummery that the famous party was given, but before the party came the arrival of Ethel

Wodehouse and before the arrival of Ethel Wodehouse came the contretemps.

Mrs. Jefferson Perry, the wife of the company manager, was, here in Cleveland, treading her native heath. Her mother, still extant, was of the *crème de la crème* of Cleveland society. And in those days there was no nonsense about "café society." As Ward McAlister could tell you, you were either born to it or you weren't.

Mrs. Jefferson Perry, Mrs. Jefferson Perry's mother, Mrs. Pell, and the Kerns were having supper following the Cleveland opening of *Oh, Boy!* the reception of which had been all that could be desired. At another table in the Hollenden dining room the Girls were the guests of Guy and Plum. Their meal was the first finished and the quartette filed out, passing the Kern-Perry-Pell table. A pause was indicated.

"Went well, didn't it?" said Guy, and turned to Mrs. Perry who with downcast eye was busying herself with a Nesselrode pudding.

"You don't know Miss Davies and Miss Johnstone, do you, Mrs. Perry?"

"No, and I don't care to," said Mrs. Perry.

This devastating rejoinder broke up the little gathering.

The one big happy family was no longer one and no longer happy. The story quickly went the rounds and produced varying reactions. Most of the company sided with the Girls but there were exceptions. At least two of the members of the company laughed when they heard the story and said "Good." This was duly reported to the Girls by one of those little birds that goes around poking his bill into other people's business. Also Eva Kern continued to be seen about with Mrs. Jefferson Perry. It made of her a marked woman.

It had reached the point where certain members of the company were not speaking to each other, and at which unpleasant words were muttered half audibly as some member of the opposing camp passed by, when the party was augmented by the arrival of Ethel Wodehouse. She loved the show, but was appalled by the "atmosphere."

"It's the best way to get a failure," she said. "You can't have a company bickering and quarrelling. People can't work together unless there is harmony."

"Nonsense," rejoined her husband. "Look at Gilbert and Sullivan, they were like a dose of Paris green to each other but they worked together all right."

"There may be exceptions, but that doesn't alter the fact that in most cases dissension destroys the team spirit."

"What can we do about it?"

"You must give a party, you and Guy—Jerry too if you like. A real bang up 'get-together.' And when they're all there and have had plenty to drink you must make a little speech about the importance of harmony."

"My instinct is against it, but I know from experience that once you make up your mind to giving a party neither man nor elemental power may stay your course."

"I'm only doing it for you and Guy. You neither of you seem to think it important to have everyone pulling together, but I feel sure that it is."

"What do you think, Guy?"

"I think if Ethel wants us to give a party we'll give a party."

"It needn't be anything elaborate. Lots of beer and a few bottles of whiskey."

"And sandwiches?"

"Yes, and a few other odds and ends. 'Picnic style' I'd call it. Songs round the piano. By the time it's over they'll all be one big happy family."

· 6 ·

Two evenings later the party took place. Ethel assured Plum and Guy that she would take care of everything. Ray Comstock, she said, had promised to find a room of suitable size. Everyone was coming, chorus as well as principals.

"It's going to set us back a bit," said Plum.

"But it's making Ethel happy. She feels that this party may save the shattered *esprit de corps* and—who knows—perhaps she's right."

The two hosts were the first to arrive. Ethel had said that they would find her there but she wasn't visible.

"Anybody here?" called Plum.

"Only us tables and chairs."

"And a hell of a lot of expensive looking flowers."

They peered into adjoining rooms. In the dining room was a U-shaped table with American Beauty roses strewn about artistically between the places. Standing at one end of the room was a marvellous buffet of cold dishes that included a big salmon encased in ice. There was a platter of Chicken Jeannette and another of some small birds that looked like quail in aspic.

Guy pointed to it. "Picnic style," he said. "For the love of Pete, what has Ethel been up to? The show will have to run six months for us to break even."

"Gosh, yes, look at this—there are music stands. She's engaged an orchestra."

"And what about these champagne buckets? There are bottles and bottles."

"What kind of champagne is it?"

"I'm afraid to look."

"Suffering Pete—Bollinger 1911."

Max Hirschfeld arrived with three or four of his musicians. He said that Ray Comstock had told him there would be dancing. The musicians started in to play the music from the show. Some of the girls and boys came trooping in and took the floor. Then came the magnetic Anna Wheaton and her opposite number, Hal Forde. Marie Carroll and Tom Powers followed, then the Kerns accompanied by the Perrys and the inevitable Mrs. Pell.

"Say, what *is* all this?" exclaimed Jerry. "Putting on the dog a bit, aren't you?"

"What about yourself? What about those beads Eva is wearing?" countered Plum. "Pearls unless my old eyes deceive me."

"Aren't they lovely?" said Eva. "Jerry said he'd get them for me when he was sure the show would be a big hit."

"Expensive, of course," said Jerry. "Seven thousand, five hundred, no less."

As he spoke they became aware of a sudden hush in the room. All eyes had turned to the door. It was the Girls. They paused just inside the door waiting for the lovely ermine wraps to knock 'em dead. They looked ravishing in sheathlike dinner dresses that showed off the flowing lines of their young figures. They both wore sprays of orchids and pearl necklaces. The other women, looking them over with microscopic carelessness, knew that they might as well pack up and go home. They'd had it.

The two hosts went forward and greeted them. "Let's dance," said the Girls simultaneously.

As Guy danced with Justine, she asked him what it was Jerry was saying when they arrived. "Something about a pearl necklace."

The music stopped and Plum suggested they come in to supper. Four waiters had appeared. The champagne had begun to flow.

"Don't look now," said Plum to his fellow-sufferer, "but I think the stuff in those crocks the waiters are passing is caviar."

It was caviar—the big gray kind that nowadays never gets farther than the tables of particular friends of the boys in the back room of the Kremlin.

Then at last, pale and scared, Ethel Wodehouse appeared. She drew the hosts aside.

"I've been looking everywhere for Ray Comstock. I gave him my lists, but left the ordering to him. He's changed everything."

"You didn't order caviar?"

"Good Heavens, no."

"How about Bollinger '11?"

"I asked for whiskey and beer as I said I would—everything Bohemian and informal."

"And the performers on sackbut and psaltery?"

"No, I told Ray to make sure there was a piano for Jerry and whoever else might play."

"Ray thinks it's a joke, I suppose. He's always making cracks about all the money we have rolling in."

Save for the bad moment when the Girls had appeared, Mrs. Jefferson Perry was having a good time.

"I adore caviar," she said. "I've never had enough, but I'm really making the most of my opportunity tonight. And this champagne is the last word."

"I love the peeled hothouse peaches in the glasses," chimed in her mother.

Ethel closed her eyes and drew a long breath. "Hothouse peaches," she murmured.

The Girls, seated across the table from Jerry, Eva and the Perry contingent, were engaged in a conversation about jewelry.

"Lillian Lorraine has a new pearl necklace," said Miss Johnstone casually.

"What, another one?"

"Oh, this isn't like her real one. It's just something to wear when she's slumming. It only cost seven thousand, five hundred."

"I wouldn't be seen dead in a thing like that," said Miss Davies disdainfully. "My motto is don't have it if you can't have it good."

"You're so right, darling," agreed Miss Johnstone. "Of

70

course it's one of those cultured Japanese jobs. The Japs tease the oyster into making the pearl by pushing a bit of grit into his shell. He makes a pearl, of course, but apparently his heart isn't in the work."

"Serves them right," said Miss Davies. "Why should an oyster be annoyed like that just to make second-class pearls for cheap necklaces? Left alone he might some day make a really good pearl—something an oyster could be proud of."

It was at this point that Eva said that she had a headache and thought she'd go to bed. Mrs. Jefferson Perry downed a final glass of Bollinger and said if Eva was going she would go too.

"Oh, not before the dessert," protested Marion. "I ordered Nesselrode pudding especially for you. I know how fond you are of it."

"*You* ordered it?" cried Mrs. Perry. "I was told this party was being given by Mr. Wodehouse and Mr. Bolton."

"Not *this* party, dear," said Marion. "*This* party is mine. I believe their party is in one of the banquetting rooms on the second floor."

"But we were told to come here."

"Yes, Ray thought you might all enjoy coming to my party first." She turned her charming smile full on Mrs. Perry. "Perhaps he knew how fond you are of caviar."

"Well thank you very much," said Jefferson Perry lamely. "It was very nice of you to ask us."

"Not at all. And now you've found the way, come again."

Two pink spots gathered in Mrs. Perry's cheeks as she searched for her wraps.

"And be sure to bring Mrs. Pill with you," added the hostess cooingly.

"Pell," corrected Jefferson Perry in a shocked undertone.

"Are *we* invited to your party?" asked Marion, turning to the authors.

"Of course," said Plum, fastening his gaze on Ethel. "Ours

is for everybody—a get-together. The entire big happy family."

"That's lovely," said Marion, "but anyone who wants to stay here can. How are you doing, girls?" she asked, addressing herself to a group at one end of the table which included all the female principals. "Are they giving you plenty of champagne?"

It was the day of the gold mesh bag. Each of the girls was carrying one. Marion opened hers.

"Oh, dear," she said, turning to Justine. "Have you a loose hundred dollars on you, darling? I want to leave something for the waiter."

Chapter Six

THE DEFINITION of a smash hit in the theater is one that has varied a good deal from age to age. In Shakespeare's time anything that ran two nights was good, and if you did three you went out and bought a new fur coat. In the nineties authors became offensively conceited if they broke the hundred mark. Today a musical comedy which runs less than five years is presumed to have had some structural weakness in it. It ought to have been fixed up out of town, people say, even if it meant calling in Abe Burrows.

It is difficult, therefore, to estimate the degree of success which *Oh, Boy!* achieved. One can only say that it was sufficient to make one chuck one's chest out quite considerably when it happened. It did not run five years, but it did do four hundred and seventy-five performances in New York, and during its Broadway run there were four companies out on the road, one playing Chicago, another Boston, a third the one-week cities and a fourth the one-night stands. It cost $29,-262.56 to produce, this including a seven-week tour during which two authors, a composer, a book director, a dance director and a manager had to be supported in luxury, and it made a profit of $181,641.54.

For those days it was a socko, and it left Bolton and Wodehouse—the latter now better known as the Sweet-Singing Thrush of Thirty-ninth Street—sitting on top of the world and loving it. It seemed as though Fate had decided that there was nothing she could deny to these favorite sons of hers. They were in. As they sauntered past Cain's Storehouse of a morning, taking snuff from their jewelled snuff boxes and sneering at the lower orders whom they jostled off the sidewalk, there was never a thought in their minds that the time was coming when that gaunt building would play an impressive part in their lives and that before many more suns had set its proprietor, when asked by friends how business was, would be saying, "Quiet at the moment, boys, a little quiet at the moment, but it'll pick up. Bolton and Wodehouse have a couple of shows coming on." Like most young authors who get a run of luck, the unhappy saps had taken on much more work than they could do even fairly well. They had so many irons in the fire that they put the fire out.

Writing musical comedies is like eating salted almonds—you can always manage one more. Every time the two partners met, they vowed that they would go on the musical comedy wagon, but nothing ever came of their good resolutions. Somehow they found themselves in Charlie Dillingham's office, and there was the box of cigars on the desk and Mr. Ziegfeld in a chair by the window and Mr. Dillingham saying, "Wouldn't it be fun to get up some theatricals?" and Mr. Ziegfeld saying, "Yes, wouldn't it?" and then a voice through the smoke cooed, "Sign here, boys," and the boys woke up and found that they were booked to do a colossal revue for the Century Theater.

And after that . . . Cain's hospitable storehouse.

Cain's Storehouse, like so many monuments of the past, no longer exists. One is not quite sure what happens now to the scenery of shows that have failed to attract. According to Moss Hart, in his play *Light Up the Sky*, you have to cart it out into the wilds somewhere and set fire to it with matches. But in the days of which we are writing Cain's was a great institution, a sort of Sargasso Sea into which the wrecks of dramatic Hesperuses drifted automatically. Or you might call it a morgue. To this morgue it was inevitable that sooner or later Bolton and Wodehouse would be contributing a corpse or two. In actual fact, they contributed three, one after the other.

There was once a manager who, examining his books, made the discovery that his box-office man had been cheating him for years. He sent for the culprit.

"How much do I pay you a week?" he asked.

"Sixty dollars, sir."

"It's raised to seventy-five."

"Oh, thank you, sir!"

"Or, rather, a hundred."

"Oh, thank you, sir! !"

"No, wait. That's not enough. A hundred and fifty. And when I say a hundred and fifty, I mean, of course, two hundred."

"Oh, *thank* you, sir! ! !"

"Just one thing more," said the manager, beaming at him like a Cheeryble Brother. "You're fired. You see," he explained to a friend when telling him of the incident later, "I wanted to fire the son of a what-not from a really *good* job."

It is in a precisely similar way that Fate likes to work, waiting with the brass knucks and the sock full of sand until its victims are at the peak of one of those boom periods when life appears to be roses, roses all the way. As Shakespeare, who often hits off a thing rather neatly, once said:

This is the state of man: today he puts forth
The tender leaves of hopes; tomorrow blossoms,
And bears his blushing honors thick upon him; the third day comes
*   a frost, a killing frost;*
And when he thinks, good easy man, full surely
His greatness is a-ripening, nips his root . . .

It was just like that with Guy and Plum. They couldn't have put it better themselves.

The first V-shaped depressions to darken their lives after the unbroken fine weather in which they had been basking came along, ironically, in the season when they had set a mark for all other authors to shoot at by having five shows running simultaneously on Broadway . . . or, in Guy's case, six, for Belasco had taken sufficient time off from his picture hanging to produce the Bolton-Middleton comedy, *Polly with a Past*, starring Ina Claire, and it had settled down to a long and prosperous run.

These were the five:

Oh, Boy!
Leave It to Jane
The Rose of China
The Riviera Girl
Miss 1917

Oh, Boy!, as we say, was a smash hit, and so to a lesser extent was *Leave It to Jane*, a rather free adaptation of George Ade's *College Widow*.

But the others . . .

(1) *The Rose of China*

The writing of this blot on the New York theatrical scene was due entirely to too much rich food, too much potent liquor and the heady effect of Oriental music on top of these. The consumers of the food and the liquor were the pair so shortly to become the toast of Cain's Storehouse, and the music was that of Armand Vecsey, rendered by himself in the Oval Room of the Ritz-Carlton Hotel, where he was the *chef d'orchestre*.

In one of America's folk songs we are told that

> *Young Herman von Bellow,*
> *A musical fellow,*
> *Performed on the 'cello each night*

76

At a restaurant where
All the brave and the fair
Would look in for a chat and a bite.
He played tunes that you know
From Wagner and Gounod
To give the gay building a tone,
But the place started swaying
When he began playing
A sweet little thing of his own.

It was precisely the same with Armand Vecsey, except that his instrument was the violin. He played superbly, and when he dished out the Chinese suite he had composed, the brave and the fair curled up like carbon paper and the Messrs. Bolton and Wodehouse, puffing their cigars and taking another beaker of old brandy, told each other emotionally that this was the stuff. Not realizing that practically anything sounds good after a well-lubricated dinner, they agreed that a musical play written around these marvellous melodies could not fail to bring home the gravy. A week later they were writing *The Rose of China.*

It just shows how overwork can dull the senses that neither of the gifted youths realized what was bound to happen if they started getting mixed up with things of that sort. The advice that should be given to all aspiring young authors is: Have nothing to do with anything with a title like *The Rose of China* or *The Willow Pattern Plate* or *The Siren of Shanghai* or *Me Velly Solly*—in fact, avoid Chinese plays altogether. Much misery may thus be averted.

What happens when you write a Chinese play is that before you know where you are your heroine has gone cute on you, adding just that touch of glucose to the part which renders it unsuitable for human consumption. She twitters through the evening saying, "Me Plum Blossom. Me good girl. Me love

77

Chlistian god velly much," and things of that sort, like the heroine of Sammy Shipman's *East Is West*, by which, one supposes now that the agony has abated and it is possible to think clearly, the Bolton-Wodehouse opus must have been—if that is the right word—inspired.

It is the view of competent critics that—with the possible exception of *Abie's Irish Rose* and *Grandma's Diary—East Is West* is the ghastliest mess ever put on the American stage, but this is an opinion held only by those who did not see *The Rose of China*. It was of *The Rose of China* that Ring Lardner, one of the scattered few who caught it during its New York run, said, "Cain's horses are *snorting* for this one," and how right he was. It was the sort of piece where the eyes of the audience keep wandering to that cheering notice at the top of the program: "This theater can be emptied in three minutes. Look around, choose the nearest exit to your seat and walk (do not run) to that exit."

Without referring to the script, a thing they are naturally reluctant to do, the authors cannot say after this length of time whether or not the heroine of *The Rose of China* turned out in the end to be the daughter of an American missionary, kidnapped by Chinese bandits in her infancy, but it would seem virtually certain that she did. All heroines of Chinese plays turn out in the end to be the daughters of American missionaries, kidnapped by bandits in their infancy. This is known as Shipman's Law. There is no reason to suppose that in this instance there would have been any deviation from the straight party line.

(2) *The Riviera Girl*

By all the ruling of the form book this one should have been all right, for it was a Klaw and Erlanger production, put on with Joseph Urban scenery at the New Amsterdam, and the score was by Kalman, the composer of *Sari* and *Miss Springtime*, with additional numbers by Jerome Kern.

78

The Kalman score was not only the best that gifted Hungarian ever wrote but about the best anybody ever wrote. After thirty-odd years it is still played constantly on the radio, and last year it was revived, with another libretto, in Paris, and pulled in the cash customers in their thousands. Which seems to place the responsibility for its deplorable failure on Broadway squarely on the shoulders of the boys who wrote the book. They feel, looking back, that where they went wrong was in being perhaps a little too ingenious in devising a plot to replace that of the original Viennese libretto, which, like all Viennese librettos, was simply terrible. And the odd thing is that—till the critics got at it with their little hatchets—both authors thought highly of it. "Boy," Guy would say to Plum, his eyes sparkling, "you could take that plot down to the bank and borrow money on it!" and Plum, his eyes sparkling, too, would agree that you certainly could.

A brief outline for anyone who is interested:
An Austrian Count has a son. Call him Hildebrand. Hildebrand wants to marry an actress. The Count says he will disinherit him unless he marries a woman of title. Hildebrand and the actress, thinking fast, see a way out. They will hunt around for a broken-down aristocrat and pay him to marry the actress, after which he will, of course, let her divorce him. She will thus acquire a title and be free to marry Hildebrand.

Time out while you brood on this.
But their plans are overheard by a Louse. (And if you have never seen a Viennese louse, you don't know what lice are.) He tips the Count off to what is cooking and suggests a foul scheme. He says he knows of a derelict who could credibly *pose* as a nobleman, and they will pay him to marry the actress and then refuse to let her divorce him. This will put her out of circulation as far as Hilde-

79

brand is concerned. But what neither of them knows is that the derelict really *is* a nobleman, come down in the world, and has loved the actress from afar for years.

Are you still with us?

Approached by the Count and the Louse, the derelict agrees to take on the job. He is cunningly thrown in Hildebrand's way, and Hildebrand feels that here is the very man he wants. He signs him up. End of Act One. The position now being that Hildebrand thinks the derelict is a nobleman and is in his pay, while the Count and the Louse think the derelict is not a nobleman and is in their pay. And all the time the derelict, who really is a nobleman, is in nobody's pay. He is in business for himself.

Aspirin will relieve the severest headache.

A lot of guff to fill in before the big moment, and then the marriage takes place. Directly the knot has been tied, the Count and the Louse start turning handsprings. They reveal their plot. The actress, convinced by what they say that the husband she has married is an impostor and is not going to release her, grits her teeth and goes into the Act Two Finale at the top of her voice. She calls the bridegroom a cur. She says she hates him. He says he hates her. She strikes him with her glove. He hurls a purse filled with bank notes at her feet and strides out. And there you have it. Quite a mix-up. But, believe it or not, before the third act is over she has realized that he is the man she loves. Hildebrand gets the gate. She falls into the hero's arms. They sing a reprise of the big waltz number. Curtain and a certain amount of sporadic applause from the ushers, in which those who have paid for their seats rather markedly do not join.

That is the plot of *The Riviera Girl*, and we still think it's good. However, let us pass on to

(3) *Miss 1917*

This was the one mentioned earlier, into which the authors were lured by the combined persuasiveness of C. B. Dillingham and Florenz Ziegfeld, Jr., the former of whom alone was capable—for there never was a more genial man than Charlie Dillingham—of luring an author into anything. The two had gone into partnership in the previous year to produce a mammoth revue at the Century Theater called *The Century Show*, and they now wanted another, equally mammoth, to follow it. The Century, long since pulled down, stood at the bottom of Central Park West and was the last word in theaters, its girders made of gold, and thousand-dollar bills used instead of carpets. It was built by a syndicate of millionaires. At least, they were millionaires when they began building it.

The thing that turned the scale and decided the Bolton-Wodehouse duo to sign on the dotted line was the fact that the latter a few years earlier had collaborated on a revue for the Empire Theatre in London and had found it the most delightful experience. As he told Bolton, all the author of a revue had to do was put his name on the thing. The dialogue was written by the artists, worthy fellows who asked nothing better than to write their own stuff, while publishers vied with one another to contribute songs. Doing the Second Century Show, he said, would be a nice rest.

The bitter awakening came with the discovery that the New York method of assembling a revue differed from that in vogue in London. The authors found that they were expected to do the work themselves. It was an unpleasant shock, but they rallied from it and sat down to think what sort of a masterpiece they should give the customers.

On one thing they were resolved—there should be a real, coherent, consecutive story. Not like that show last year. They were frightfully contemptuous and superior about that last year's show. They called it a mere vaudeville entertainment and other harsh things.

The first jarring note was struck when they learned that the cast of principals as selected—and given contracts—to date consisted of three classical dancers, three acrobatic dancers, a Spanish dancer, forty-eight buck and wing dancers, two trained cows, a performing seal and Harry Kelly and his dog Lizzie. (Does anybody remember Harry Kelly and Lizzie? "She's a hunting dog. Sometimes she hunts here, sometimes she hunts there." Harry would say, "Roll over," and Lizzie would take not the slightest notice, and Harry would say, "Good dog," and the act would proceed.)

This did not seem what you might call a balanced cast for a plotty show, but the management urged them to go ahead and fear nothing. They said they would see to it that performers were provided, and they certainly were. Scarcely a day went by without the addition to the cast of some new juggler or trapeze artist, and the gallant little plot swallowed them all like a frog swallowing flies, till at last, in a heroic attempt to absorb the performing seal, it burst and died, regretted by all.

You could find fragments of it splashed about all over the final version of the Second Century Show, gruesome fragments like the remains of the man who died of spontaneous combustion in Bleak House. Guy was at the sick bed to the last, hoping for the best, for he loved that plot. He would pick it up and nurse it back to consciousness after some frightful blow had stunned it, but just as it was beginning to recover, along would come somebody and cram Van and Schenk down its throat, and all the weary work to do again.

Plum was more occupied with the lyrics. Occasionally a sharp scream from the tortured plot would make him wince, but it was the lyrics that etched those lines on his face and were responsible for the dark circles under his eyes.

A revue lyric of that period was a monstrous freak with one verse and twelve refrains, each introducing a separate girl in some distinctive costume. The lyric was written round the dresses. On arriving at the theater in the morning, the sensitive

poet was handed a pile of costume designs. One would repre-
sent a butterfly, another the Woolworth Building, a third a
fish, a fourth a bird, a fifth a fruit salad and the others the
Spirit of American Womanhood, Education Enlightening the
Backward South, Venus Rising from the Sea, and so on, and
Mr. Ziegfeld says will you please have it ready for tomorrow's
rehearsal, as the girls are threatening to walk out because they
have nothing to do. ("Walking out" was the technical term
when a show girl stepped into her Rolls Royce, said, "Home,
James," to the chauffeur and drove off, never to be seen again.)

When the bard had finished twelve refrains, cunningly introducing the butterfly, the Woolworth Building, the Growing
Unrest in the Balkans and Venus Rising from the Sea, the
management decided that they didn't want to use those costumes after all, and handed him another batch. Critics have
often commented on the somber gloom which permeates all
Wodehouse novels like the smell of muddy shoes in a locker
room and have wished that, fine as they are, there was not quite
so much of the Russian spirit of pessimism and hopelessness
in them, but now that it has been revealed that he wrote the
lyrics for *Miss* 1917, they will understand and sympathize.

The harassed authors had a few, very few, moments of
gaiety during the concoction of this lamentable mishmash.
One such occurred when an Italian tenor known as "the Neapolitan Nightingale" auditioned for the management.

He had inevitably selected "Ridi Pagliaccio" with which to
show up Caruso, and he planted his feet in that firm-rooted
fashion peculiar to Italian tenors about to give their all.

He had emitted but a few smoldering tones when the revolving stage of the Century started off at its number three speed
and swept the singer away into the wings.

Why he didn't jump off or, at least, why he didn't stop singing is a question. True, as singers often do, he had started the
aria with his eyes closed and, being intent on his job, may not
have noticed what was happening. Or, possibly, he supposed

the spinning turntable was part of the test and that, in the revue, there was to be a scene featuring a wandering minstrel. If that was the idea, he was letting them know that his voice could be heard even when traversing the back stage behind an Urban drop.

Suddenly he burst into view on the opposite side from which he had made his exit, putting up a swell performance. He was seen but briefly before he was off on his second journey. Either they couldn't stop the thing or, which was more likely, Charlie Dillingham had told them to pretend they couldn't. Canio had reached the sobbing bit as he made his next appearance.

"Ridi, Pagliaccio . . . e ognuno applaudira!"

He was right. They were applauding rapturously. Ziegfeld and the lovelies that clustered about him were yelping with laughter, while Charlie Dillingham, seated with the authors, roared delightedly. Plum and Guy had an uncomfortable remembrance of the stage tradition that laughter at rehearsal is a bad sign.

"A pity we can't keep it in," said Plum.

"Yes, tell Guy to fit it into that plot of his," said Charlie Dillingham.

Alas! The superstition was right. No such laughter was to be heard again in the Century during the brief run of *Miss* 1917.

What other mirth there was during the period of rehearsals of this historic floperoo was occasioned by the activities of Bertie the performing seal, who like all his species was a hardened comic, always hamming it up, his motto "Anything for a laugh."

Well, no harm in that, you may say. A laugh does us all good, does it not? But though he went like a breeze with the company and stage hands, the authors were inclined to look askance at Bertie. On days when things went well, his cheerful face and broad comedy helped to raise their spirits, but the trouble was that there very seldom were days when things went well, and it is not pleasant for worried literary men, conscious that Mr. Ziegfeld is looking at them with a brooding eye, wondering what fatal weakness led him to entrust the preparation of an important revue to two such pinheads, to glance round and see a seal a couple of feet away balancing a bottle on its nose or giving imitations of footlight favorites. On these occasions the only thing that kept them from breaking down was the thought of the clientele.

It was an axiom in the theater of those days that if you had a clientele you could not fail to bring home the bacon. The Empire had its clientele. So had the Princess and one or two other houses. But the real clientele boys, head and shoulders above all the rest, were C. B. Dillingham and Florenz Ziegfeld. With the two of them joining forces, it seemed obvious that *Miss 1917* must be a success. But it was not. In the immortal words of whoever it was, the clientele didn't come to that one.

Have you ever been distressed and mortified at the unexpected refusal of your dog to accept the proffered morsel? You are enjoying a quiet meal, when Towser intimates by every means at his disposal that he wishes to come in on the ground floor. You offer him a bit of the delicacy you are consuming, and he sniffs at it and then turns away with an expression on his face that suggests that you have wounded him in his finest feelings, leaving you piqued, chagrined and frustrated. Just so does an author feel when the public, who have been pawing and whining at him for some particular brand of entertainment, turn away on being offered it and leave it untouched.

If there was one thing it was certain that the New York public wanted at this time, it was a large, lavish revue crammed with lovely girls, and this was what they had been given. Nothing could have been larger and more lavish than *Miss 1917*, and there were lovely girls in every nook and cranny of it. And yet it was withdrawn after thirty performances. Which was perhaps just as well, come to think of it, for it was discovered later that it was so large and lavish that if it had played to absolute capacity with two rows of standees every night, the weekly loss would have been between three and four thousand dollars.

There was only one thing about *Miss 1917* that is of historic interest. The boy who played the piano at rehearsals was a young fellow named George Gershwin.

Chapter Seven

FOR TWO ARDENT YOUNG MEN who have made it their mission in life to raise the lighter American musical drama to new heights there are few things more unpleasant than a resounding flop. Let them have three such flops in rapid succession, and they begin to feel like a couple of lepers who have been expelled from their club for cheating at cards. After *The Rose of China, The Riviera Girl* and *Miss 1917* the guilty pair were afraid to walk past the Lambs Club lest they run into some reproachful ham who had appeared briefly in one or other of these outstanding turkeys. A jocular boulevardier induced in them a strong distaste for all jocular boulevardiers by saying to the jocular boulevardiers with whom he was drinking synthetic Scotch that he felt nervous about leaving town for the week end these days because he might be missing a Bolton-Wodehouse show.

It was the tragedy of *The Rose of China* that they found hardest to bear. The other two had been commissions, and nobody could have been expected to turn down a commission for a big musical from Klaw and Erlanger and what had seemed like an even bigger musical from two pre-eminent managers like Dillingham and Ziegfeld. But they had gone into *The Rose of China* entirely on their own initiative, just because a fiddler had hypnotized them with his violin at a moment when their better judgment had been clouded by a good dinner at the Ritz-Carlton.

They were not eating at the Ritz-Carlton now but at the Columbus Circle Childs. There were three reasons for this—

the first the prices on the right-hand side at the former of the two hostelries, the second an understandable shrinking from being pointed out as the pariahs of Broadway, and the third, most potent of all, a desire never again to lay eyes on or lend ears to the Ritz-Carlton's *chef d'orchestre.*

At this very moment, they felt, as the waitress slammed down their buckwheat cakes and coffee, Armand Vecsey was probably tying himself in knots as he rendered some excerpt from *The Rose of China* designed to show the luncheon patrons that its failure was not the fault of the composer.

They were just squaring their elbows and getting at the wholesome foodstuffs when Plum gave a start and sat rigid, the buckwheat cake frozen on his fork. The expression on his face was that of someone passing a sewer excavation.

"What's that noise I hear?" he asked in a low, toneless voice. "I don't mean the waitresses throwing used dishes down the chute, I mean that music. It's Chinese music!"

"Nonsense. You're hearing things."

"Don't tell me. That's Chinese music. Listen."

"Do you know, I believe you're right."

They hailed a waitress, who explained that the music was indeed Chinese music and was filtering through the ceiling from the Far East restaurant immediately above.

"We shall not be coming to this Childs again," said Plum coldly.

"Decidedly not. Even here we can't escape it. And do you realize," said Guy, "that if a certain man had not happened to walk down a certain street in a certain Hungarian town on a certain evening *The Rose of China* would never have happened?"

"What do you mean?"

"It was owing to this son of a Hungarian that Armand Vecsey got his musical education. I had it from Armand himself. It seems that he began life as a poor boy in a farming district near Budapest called the Puszta. He wanted to be a violinist, but his family wouldn't hear of it, so one day he ran off with his fiddle and what little money he had managed to save to a place with the impossible name of Papa. It's the Heidelberg of Hungary, I gather, and there is a famous Conservatory of Music there."

"How do you spell Papa?"

"P-a-p-a."

"The students, no doubt, refer to it as their Alma Pater."

"Please! Not now. Well, in next to no time, of course, Armand ran out of money, and his landlady said that if he didn't pay his back rent, she would kick him out and keep his violin."

"So he packed it in his trunk and tried to sneak away?"

"Exactly. And he had got it as far as the front door when this man came along. Seeing that Armand was in difficulties, he stopped and asked if he could give him a hand. Armand explained the situation, and they started down the front steps, carrying the trunk. At this moment the landlady appeared."

"Embarrassing. I suppose Armand was nonplussed."

"He was. But the man wasn't. He told the landlady that he was a friend of Armand's, and Armand had inflamed him with his stories of what a delightful dump this of the landlady's was, so here he was with his trunk and he would like, if possible, a room with a southern exposure."

"Ingenious."

"Yes, he was one of those quick-thinking Hungarians. Well, the landlady not unnaturally blew her top. 'I don't want any friends of this little so-and-so in my house,' she said, speaking of course in Hungarian. 'You take that trunk and get out of here!' Which they did. Are you laughing heartily?"

"Very."

"Well, save it up, because there's a lot more coming. When they were out of sight of the house, they put down the trunk and sat on it. Armand thanked the man, and told him all about his ambition to become a violinist, but how on earth he was ever going to become a violinist he didn't know, he added, because he lacked the cash to study at the Conservatory, and if you're a musician and don't study at conservatories, you haven't a hope."

"Like that line in *Leave It to Jane*. 'If you don't get an eddication, you can't be a lawyer.' "

"Exactly. Well, when he heard this, the man pricked up his ears. 'Now, that's a funny thing,' he said. 'I've been sent to the Conservatory to study, and I want no piece of it. What I like is pottering around and having a good time. I've not been near the place yet. How would you react to the idea of going there and studying in my place?'

"Armand felt that this must be some beautiful dream.

" 'You're offering me a musical education? Your education?'

" 'Why not? I don't want it. I hate music. But my grand-mother told me to come here, and her word is law. She has supplied me with ample funds to see me through the Conservatory, so it seems to me our path lies clear before us. We split the money, you taking one quarter, me three-quarters, and you go and study till you're blue in the face, leaving me to continue pottering around and, as I say, having a good time.' "

"Gosh! This thing's beginning to shape. Armand, who of course takes the other fellow's name, is a great success at the Conservatory and writes a diploma number that enchants one and all, and the grandmother comes hotfooting to applaud the young genius—"

"And the chap who knows nothing about music has to play for the old lady, so he sits at the player-piano and—"

"—halfway through he gets absentminded and gets up—"

"—and the piano goes on playing. . . . There's a show there."

"If we were going to write any more shows."

"But we aren't."

"No. Still, it's a good story."

"Very good."

"The only thing wrong with it," said Guy broodingly, "is that, to make it dramatic, after a start like that Armand should have finished up as a world-famous composer instead of sawing a fiddle in a New York hash house. In which event he wouldn't have intrigued us with a lot of pseudo-Chinese music and we wouldn't have written a prize bust called *The Rose of China.*"

· 2 ·

Despondency continued to grip the two. After three failures in a row it seemed impossible that they would ever again find a manager with confidence enough in their moth-eaten talent to entrust them with a commission. And it was just when Guy was saying that, come right down to it, there was no life like the architect's and Plum had begun to mutter that if he had it to do all over again he would certainly think twice before he gave up a steady job at three pounds a week that Ray Comstock brought the sunshine back into their lives by asking them to look in and discuss a new piece for the Princess. They were in his presence twenty minutes after the receipt of the telephone message, not even stopping to wonder how Ray could have staved off the honeys long enough to be able to give them a call.

In the familiar surroundings of the Princess their flagging spirits revived. True, the actors on either side of the waiting room eyed them distrustfully as they appeared at the wicket and one of their number rose, pocketed his *Variety* and left, glancing at them in a meaning way as he passed through the door.

"There's a fellow doesn't want to be in anything of ours," said Guy, as they went into the inner office and found Ray with the receiver propped on his shoulder as usual. The conversation he was conducting had apparently reached its end, for he said "Goodbye, sugar," and hung up.

"*Sugar?*" said Plum, startled. It seemed very unorthodox.

"He's giving the South a play," said Guy.

Ray smiled his Sphinxlike smile.

"Where have you boys been keeping yourselves?" he asked genially. "Time you stopped loafing and got down to work."

They exchanged glances. Was this tact, or had he not noticed certain things that had been happening around the corner on Broadway?

Presumably he had not, for his faith in them appeared to be unimpaired.

"Another *Oh, Boy!* is what we want," he said. "Oh, hello, honey."

"How do you like *Oh, Lady, Lady* for a title?" asked Guy. It was a phrase which Bert Williams, the Negro comedian, was using at the moment.

"H'm . . . Go jump in the lake, honey . . . Yes, good. Well, if you boys want contracts, you can have them now, and an advance of a thousand apiece. I'm adding a half per cent to your royalty. Every time you give me a hit, the next time . . . I said, 'Go jump in the lake, honey' . . . will be a half per cent more."

The two partners were so moved by the thought that somebody still considered them capable of writing hits that they nearly broke down. As they left the office, they agreed that there was no manager like Ray Comstock and no theater like the Princess.

"I shall be practically next door to it, which will be convenient," said Plum. "Ethel's taken an apartment for the winter in the Beaux Arts."

This new abode was a handsome studio apartment recently vacated by the well-known artist, Leon Gordon. It was here that Guy and Plum met one morning to work on *Oh, Lady, Lady*. Ethel had gone out, leaving them to get on with it.

But they had struck a snag. A story was shaping itself, but they could not decide where the action was to be laid. Also, what to do with the second love interest was bothering them.

Bill, the hero, and Molly, the heroine, would take care of the main plot, but running parallel with it there had to be a second love interest, and it had to be funny. And to make the process of composition tougher, they had run out of tobacco, without which it was impossible to think properly. Guy said he would go out and buy some.

"I wish you would," said Plum. "I ought not to leave here. There's a lady decorator coming to collect that settee there."

"A bastard piece," said Guy, surveying it. "Early American top with Victorian legs."

He went out, and in the lobby encountered Audrey Munson, New York's leading artists' model, whose acquaintance he had made in a friend's studio. It is Audrey Munson whom the passer-by sees when he walks down Fifth Avenue and arrives at Fifty-ninth Street, for she is the lady on top of the fountain in the Plaza, who seems to be awaiting, from the other side of Fifty-ninth Street, the imminent arrival of General Sherman, rather inconveniently chaperoned by an angel. She may also be seen in the Modern Room of the Metropolitan as Phryne dropping her cloak at the trial, as Hagar driven into the wilderness, and as an unnamed female strolling in the nude along a presumably unfrequented beach.

"What are you doing?" asked Guy after the customary greetings and civilities had been exchanged.

"Oh, I'm making the rounds of the artists' studios, seeing if I can't drum up a little trade," said Audrey. "In my line you've got to make the most of what you've got while you've still got it."

Guy went on his way, and Audrey looked in on a few likely prospects. None of them wanted a model at the moment, but one of them suggested she try Leon Gordon. To the Leon Gordon studio she went, and in response to her ring Plum opened the door.

"Oh, come in," he said cordially. He waved a hand toward the settee. "There's the old sofa."

Miss Munson interpreted this as an invitation to be seated.

"I'm Audrey Munson," she said. "Have you any work for me?"

Plum had not paid much attention to the name of the lady decorator when Ethel had mentioned it, but it seemed to him that it had been something like Munson. (Actually, it was McFarland.)

"Oh, rather, quite a bit of work," he chirruped brightly, and, remembering his instructions, added: "And more to come later, if your figure is all right."

Miss Munson bridled slightly.

"My figure is generally supposed to be all right."

Plum knitted his brow, trying to remember just what Ethel had told him about that settee. The back and the arms were okay, if he recalled, but . . . Ah, yes.

"It's the legs that are the problem."

"You need have no anxiety about those."

"That's good. And how much will it be altogether?"

"You want the altogether?"

"Oh, while I remember, the seat. It should be covered with a piece of chintz. To hide the legs, if they show too much sign of wear and tear."

Miss Munson smiled indulgently.

"I guess I'm being kidded," she said. "You fooled me at first with that deadpan stuff." She rose and glanced about the room. "Do you have a screen?"

"I don't believe so. Should we, do you think?"

"It doesn't matter. I can manage. You want to work now, right away?"

"Yes, I've got to get to work."

"Fine," said Audrey. She walked over to the bedroom door. "Anyone in there?"

"No, I'm all alone."

"Good. I'll only be a minute."

Plum told Guy later that it did occur to him as a trifle odd

94

that a lady decorator should have accompanied the foregoing remarks by starting to unfasten the buttons of her dress. However, he knew that lady decorators, like adagio dancers, had their own way of doing things. Assuming that she had gone into the bedroom to inspect something Ethel had asked her to inspect in there, he dismissed her from his thoughts and turned back to the lyric he had been working on for *Oh, Lady,* a trio for Bill, the hero, Hale, his friend, and Cyril Twombley, the aristocratic private detective subsequently played so per-fectly by Reginald Mason. It was entitled—appropriately in view of what was so soon to happen—"It's a Hard World for a Man."

He had just written the last line when the door of the bed-room opened and Audrey Munson emerged in an advanced state of nudity. And as he stood gaping, with the feeling that this was pretty eccentric even for a lady decorator, there was a ring at the bell and there entered another strange young woman.

"I've come for—" she began, then stopped, having caught a glimpse of what should have been covered with a piece of chintz disappearing up stage left. "Perhaps it would be more convenient if I were to look in some other time," she added frigidly, and Plum observed that behind her there was stand-ing a man in overalls, obviously one of those sons of toil whose function it is to heave furniture about. Quick on the uptake, like all the other Wodehouses, he saw that this new arrival must be the authentic female decorator. Who the other had been, he could not say. Probably just one of the neighbors making a social call.

"Oh, good morning," he said, and was about to add that that was the settee over there and, as he had been saying only a moment ago to the lady who has just left us, the legs didn't match with the upper part, when his visitor withdrew, taking the man in overalls with her. The latter, he noticed, seemed reluctant to leave, as if he were feeling that by doing so he might be missing something of more than passing interest. His eyes, as they rested on the bedroom door, were protruding some inches from the parent sockets.

It was a few minutes later that Guy returned with the tobacco. Plum welcomed him warmly. He was glad to have at his disposal the advice of this seasoned man of the world.

"Listen, old boy," he said. "I have a problem, and one that seems to me to call for sophisticated handling. There's a girl in there."

"A girl!"

"Yes, it's a girl, all right." It was a point on which no room had been left for doubt. "She came in while you were out and after a few civil remarks had been exchanged took all her clothes off."

"Took her *clothes* off?"

"Yes. It struck me at the time as peculiar. And the problem, as I envisage it, is—taking into consideration the fact that Ethel will be back at any moment—what do we do for the best?"

Even as he spoke, the inspiration of Puvis de Chavennes and Homer St. Gaudens came out, fully clad, and Guy was able to effect the introductions. Plum apologized gracefully to Miss Munson for having proved so distrait a host, and Audrey, as good a sport as ever sat on a model throne, apologized for having made it necessary for him to apologize to her. They sketched out for Guy's benefit the story of the recent misunderstandings, and it was just after Miss Munson had left that Guy leaped from his chair as Archimedes leaped from his bath when he made that historic observation of his—"Eureka!"

"That's it," he said. "There's our scene."

"What scene?"

"The comedy scene we want for the first meeting of Bill's friend Hale and our soubrette—May Barber, or whatever we were going to call her. Bill must be an artist, and he leaves Hale with instructions about the settee, and in comes May, who's a model. The thing will write itself, and it gives us our setting—Greenwich Village. I can't remember a Greenwich Village set in a musical comedy, so it'll be brand new. There ought to be a Greenwich Village lyric."

"There will be," said Plum, and next day he was able to hand it over to Jerry, complete.

Way down in Greenwich Village
There's something, 'twould appear,
Demoralizing in the atmosphere.
Quite ordinary people,
Who come to live down here,
Get changed to perfect nuts within a year.
They learn to eat spaghetti:
(That's hard enough, as you know)
They leave off frocks
And wear Greek smocks
And study Guido Bruno.

For there's something in the air
Down here in Greenwich Village
That makes a fellow feel he doesn't care:
And as soon as he is in it, he
Gets hold of an affinity
Who's long on modern Art but short on hair.
Though he may have been a model,
Ever since he learned to toddle,
To his relatives and neighbors everywhere,
When he hits our Latin Quarter
He does things he shouldn't oughter:
It's a sort of,
Sort of kind of,
It's a sort of kind of something in the air.

97

Oh, Lady, Lady! opened out of town in Wilmington, Delaware, three days before Christmas, and the authors thought highly of it.

The integration of book and music was better than in *Oh, Boy!*, the story—for a musical play—exceptionally strong, so much so that Plum was able later to use it for a full-length novel, *The Small Bachelor,* and the score one long succession of those Kern melodies of his early youthful days that were so gay and carefree compared with his maturer style. After *Show Boat* he turned to more serious things, and the light duets and trios of the Princess era were no more for him.

But it was the cast for which the authors have always remembered *Oh, Lady* gratefully.

The story called for an eighteen-year-old heroine and a mild young man to play opposite her. If Vivienne Segal was available, they all felt, from Comstock down to the humble lyric writer, she would be ideal for Molly. She was extraordinarily pretty, she had a wonderful voice, she was as light as a feather on her feet, she had lots of comedy, and, best of all, she looked, and probably was, just about eighteen. She had been one of the few redeeming features of *Miss 1917.* Fortunately she turned out to be available and was signed up immediately.

The mild young man, who had to be able to sing a little and dance a great deal, was a bigger problem. It began to seem to the authors as if they would have to fall back on one of the thousand brash, singing-and-hoofing juveniles who were such familiar figures of the Broadway landscape, hoping that the director would be able to tone down his brashness sufficiently to make him at least something remotely like the Bill they had in mind, but feeling all the while that to have somebody of that sort playing the part would be murder in the first degree.

And then one morning in walked Carl Randall looking for

a job and hoping there might be a spot in the show for a specialty dancer. He had never played a part before, had never even considered playing a part, but it occurred to some genius —Bob Milton, probably—that here was the man they wanted. He looked exactly like Bill and his dancing, was, of course, supreme, so what did it matter if he just mumbled his lines? All shortcomings would be forgiven by the audience once those feet of his began to move.

And, amazingly, there were no shortcomings. Nobody could have played the part better than he did. He gave exactly the right value to every line and sang quite as well as was needed.

Harry Brown, a straight actor who had never thought of using his fine baritone voice in a musical show, confining himself to singing at parties, was Hale, and could not have been better. Nor could Carroll McComas as May Barber, Edward Abeles as Spike Hudgins, the reformed burglar, Florence Shirley as Fainting Fanny, the very much unreformed pickpocket and shoplifter, Reginald Mason as Cyril Twombley, the detective, Margaret Dale as Molly's mother and Harry Fisher as the janitor. They had all had years of experience on the legitimate stage. The tiny part of a maid in Act One was played by Constance Binney, who later became a prominent star in Hollywood.

It was probably the first—one might almost say only—occasion on which a musical play had in the matter of cast an absolutely full hand.

But in spite of the excellence of the players and the tunefulness of the score, *Oh, Lady* ran into trouble at the start. Three days before Christmas is not the best time to produce a new show.

The Wednesday matinee fell on Christmas Eve, and the number of Wilmingtonians who preferred to finish their shopping was in considerable excess of those who visited the Dupont Theater. Guy and Plum sat surrounded by a vast acreage of empty seats. What audience there was was in the first two rows, and the authors hardly knew they were there.

For the paying customers did little to draw attention to themselves. In theater parlance they "sat on their hands" and were pretty defiant toward any attempt to make them laugh. The best that could be said of them is that they were not the barking seal type. They were quiet.

So quiet that half way through the first act Bolton, forgetting their existence, rose and addressed Harry Brown, who was playing his opening scene with Carroll McComas.

"That's wrong, Harry," he said. "You'll kill the laughs if you keep pointing to the settee. Carroll would be bound to know what you were talking about."

His voice trailed off into silence as he became aware of thirty-six blank faces which had turned and were regarding him with astonishment from rows one and two. Plum came to the rescue.

"Ladies and gentlemen," he said, "We must apologize. We're down here trying to get this show right for New York, and Mr. Bolton has just spotted something that is wrong. Would you mind if we fixed it?"

Some civil person said, "Not at all. Go ahead," and Guy, encouraged, found his voice.

"There are so few of you," he said, "and you were keeping so quiet that I had quite forgotten you were there."

This got a better laugh than any of the lines in the show, and Guy said:

"We're all a little dizzy these days, and I thought we were having a rehearsal. If you don't mind, we'll have one now."

It was one of the most successful rehearsals in the history of the stage. The audience listened with rapt attention as the authors made their corrections. Many of them contributed suggestions. When the performance ended, the cast came down to the footlights and signed the programs that were handed up to them.

"If only we could have you people with us for our first night in New York," said Vivienne Segal.

"They certainly liked it," said Plum, as he and Guy crossed the corridor that separates the theater from the hotel. "There was a delightful woman with a face like a weasel who called it a gem."

"If they call this a gem," said Guy, "can you imagine what they'd say about *The Little Thing?*"

"You know what," said Plum. "I almost hope *The Little Thing* is never produced. Then you'll always have something to look forward to."

· 4 ·

Oh, Lady, Lady turned out to be what Comstock had asked for, another *Oh, Boy!*. All the New York critics—there were about twenty of them in those days—were enthusiastic and complimentary. One burst into song:

> *This is the trio of musical fame,*
> > *Bolton and Wodehouse and Kern:*
> *Better than anyone else you can name,*
> > *Bolton and Wodehouse and Kern.*
> *Nobody knows what on earth they've been bitten by:*
> *All I can say is I mean to get lit an' buy*
> *Orchestra seats for the next one that's written by*
> > *Bolton and Wodehouse and Kern.*

And Dorothy Parker, never easy to please, wrote:

Well, Bolton and Wodehouse and Kern have done it again. Every time these three gather together, the Princess Theater is sold out for months in advance. You can get a seat for *Oh, Lady, Lady* somewhere around the middle of August for just about the price of one on the Stock Exchange. Only moving picture artists and food profiteers will be able to attend for the first six months. After that, owners of munition plants may be able to get a couple of standing rooms.

If you ask me, I will look you fearlessly in the eye and tell you in low, throbbing tones that it has it over any other musical comedy in town. I was completely sold on it. . . . But then Bolton and Wodehouse and Kern are my favorite indoor sport, anyway. I like the way they go about a musical comedy. I like the way the action slides casually into the songs. I like the deft rhyming of the song that is always sung in the last act by two comedians and a comedienne. And oh, how I do like Jerome Kern's music. And all these things are even more so in *Oh, Lady, Lady* than they were in *Oh, Boy!*

All of which was as rare and refreshing fruit to two battered wrecks who had just groped their way out of the ruins of *The Riviera Girl*, *The Rose of China* and *Miss 1917*. Life began to animate the rigid limbs again, and Cain's Storehouse became once more merely a number in the telephone book.

Oh, Lady had a very long run at the Princess, and was actually played simultaneously at the Casino by a second company. It also had the distinction of being put on at Sing-Sing with an all-convict cast.

One of the most popular numbers in it was the duet between Spike Hudgins, the ex-burglar, and Fainting Fanny, the shoplifter, which ran as follows:

SPIKE

Since first I was a burglar, I have saved in every way
Against the time when some nice girl should name the happy day.
When I retired from active work and ceased at nights to roam,
I meant to have enough nice things to furnish up the home.
* And I achieved, as you will find,*
* The object that I had in mind.*

Our home will be so bright and cheery 6
That you will bless your burglar boy:
I got some nifty silver, dearie,
When I cracked that crib in Troy:
And I got stuff enough in Yonkers
To fill a fairly good-sized chest,
And at a house in Mineola
I got away with their victrola,
So we'll have music in the evenings
When we are in our little nest.

FANNY

I've made a nice collection, too, to add, my love, to yours
Since I began professionally visiting the stores.
I've been a prudent little girl, and I have saved, like you:
I never started squandering as girls are apt to do:
Each time I stole a brush and comb,
I said "There's something for the home."

Our home will be so bright and cheery
With all the stuff I swiped from Stern's
And all the knick-knacks from McCreery
And from Bloomingdale's and Hearn's.
And I've got stacks from Saks and Macy's
Of all the things that you'll like best,
And when at night we're roasting peanuts
Upon the stove I pinched from Greenhut's,
Although it's humble, you won't grumble,
You'll love our cosy little nest.

This number was, as they say, "well received" up Ossining
way, where it must have brought nostalgic memories to many
a first-nighter. Playwrights who nowadays console themselves

for a flop on Broadway with the thought that "they liked us in New Haven" know nothing of the thrill of being able to say, "They liked us in Sing-Sing."

One odd thing in connection with the piece was that the song "My Bill," subsequently so popular when sung by Helen Morgan in *Show Boat*, was written for *Oh, Lady,* tried on the road and cut out before the New York opening.

Chapter Eight

EXPERIENCE BRINGS WISDOM. The two alumni of Cain's Storehouse had learned their lesson. The vital thing for brain workers, they saw now, is to husband their energies and never attempt to do too much. That way disaster lies.

"We must have been crazy," said Guy as they walked down Fifth Avenue one morning about a week after *Oh, Lady* had opened. "We just said yes, yes, yes to everything anybody offered us, not realizing that if the machine is not to break down it must have constant intervals for rest and repose. The reservoir needs to fill itself. But never again. At least six months must elapse before we consider writing another show. It will be embarrassing, of course. Managers will come pleading with us to accept contracts, but we shall be firm . . . resolute . . . and—what's the word?"

"Adamant?"

"Yes, adamant. We shall say, 'Sorry, boys, but nothing doing. We are husbanding our energies and filling the reservoir. We hate to disappoint you, dear old chaps, but in a word—' "

"No!"

"No!"

It was at this point that Colonel Henry W. Savage suddenly appeared on the steps of a brownstone church which they were approaching.

"Just the boys I was looking for," he said, beaming. "Would you like to write a show for me for W. C. Fields?"

"Yes!" said Plum.

"You betcher!" said Guy.

"Then what I would suggest is that you come for a few days run in my boat, the 'Dorinda.' A yacht is a perfect place for conferences."

"A yachting trip? We'd love it."

"Good. The 'Dorinda' has been lucky for me as a workshop. It was aboard her that poor Browne and I laid out *Every-woman*."

The reference to "poor" Browne coupled with the ominous phrase "laid out" cast a momentary chill, but the Colonel's pleasure at the prospect of having them as guests on his luxury yacht was so evident that the unfortunate allusion was soon forgotten. The following Friday—Friday the thirteenth, they realized later—was fixed for the start of the cruise.

"And now I must be getting back to my trustees' meeting," said the Colonel. "The church has had a handsome offer for its property, but they want me to see if I can't get a bit more. They seem to think I'm a pretty good bargainer."

There was silence for some moments as the two authors continued on their way down the avenue.

"Yes, I know," said Guy, speaking a little defensively. "But one can't husband energies and fill reservoirs when one's offered W. C. Fields. And, anyway, you said 'Yes' first."

"And I'd say it again," said Plum. "W. C. Fields! The greatest comedian there is. And W. C. Fields plus a yachting cruise . . ."

"Have you ever been on a yachting cruise?"

"No, but I know what it's like. I've seen it in the movies. Deep cushioned chairs on the afterdeck, stewards in white coats handing round cocktails and canapes . . . You realize what has happened, of course? Remorse has been gnawing old Hank because he did us down over that Billy Van thing. Quite possibly he heard an organ playing a hymn his mother used to play on the harmonium in his childhood, and it softened him. 'I must atone,' he said to himself, 'I must atone,' so regard-

less of expense he gives us this yachting trip. It does him credit,
I say."

"Great credit," agreed Guy.

Friday was a springlike day and the yachts at the Columbia
anchorage made an attractive picture. They found the Colonel
in the clubhouse attired in an ancient serge suit and a yachting
cap which the passage of time had changed from blue to green.
He greeted them warmly, but seemed surprised by the spruce-
ness of their appearance.

"You lads look rather dressed up," he said, "but I think
I've some dungarees aboard that will fit you."

"Dungarees?"

"You'll need dungarees," said the Colonel, and he never
spoke a truer word.

The "Dorinda" was a large boat—seventy-three feet six on
the waterline, eighteen foot two beam, four master cabins and
two baths—but its crew consisted of an engineer called Peasemarch, a name Plum registered for future use, a cook called
Palmer, quickly christened Palmer the Poisoner by the guests,
and a captain, Henry W. Savage. The thing that struck Guy
and Plum immediately was that what it needed was a couple
of deckhands to do the dirty work, and this, events were to
prove, it got.

"I thought of asking Jerry along," said the Colonel as he
showed them to their cabins, "but he's such a little chap."

This puzzled the two pleasure-seekers. Why Jerry's delicate
physique should rule him out as a reveller aboard the
"Dorinda" they were unable to understand.

"We thought we might have Bill Fields with us," said Guy.

"Bill Fields?" The Colonel spoke the name a little blankly,
as if it were new to him. "Ah, yes," he said. "Bill Fields. No,
no, too fat and lazy."

The guests had rather expected that the course would lie
north to Spuyten Duyvil and through that waterway to the

Harlem and Long Island Sound. The northern shore of the Island with its charming harbors and the great houses of Morgan, Mackey, Otto Kahn and Mrs. Belmont would make an ideal cruising ground, and then they could slip through the Shinnecock Canal to the romantic south shore lagoons or perhaps cross the Sound to Newport and Narragansett, then in the Indian Summer of their glory.

But the Colonel had other plans. Erect at the wheel, he steered down the bay past Guttenberg and Weehawken and, hugging a shore lined with factories, foundries and coal yards, through the oily waters of Bayonne to the narrow inlet that separates Staten Island from the mainland.

"Afraid lunch will be a bit late," he said. "I want to hit the Raritan canal on the incoming tide. Tide's quite a help until you get to the locks."

Locks! That magic word. Visions of Boulter's Lock on Jerome K. Jerome's Thames with its punts and skiffs, its girls with parasols and its young men in club blazers rose before the eyes.

When the locks on the Raritan and Delaware rose before the eyes, they proved to be somewhat different. The traffic consisted mostly of barges laden with gravel or coal. One that was preceding the "Dorinda" had a cargo of fish destined, the Colonel explained, for a glue factory on the Delaware River. Only the riper and more elderly fish are used for manufacturing glue, and those aboard the "Shirley B" were well stricken in years and almost excessively ripe.

As they approached the first lock they brought the matter up.

"Think we might slip past 'Shirley'?" asked Plum.

"The barge ahead?"

"That's the one. It reminds me of Cleopatra's. 'Purple the sails and so perfumed that the winds were love-sick with them.'"

"We find 'Shirley' a little on the nifty side," said Guy.

The Colonel was unsympathetic.

"Come, come, you lads are a bit finicky, aren't you? You aren't here to sniff dead fish. You've work to do. There's a lot of handling needed in the locks."

There were three boats swung outboard on davits, a launch, a dory for fishing and a dinghy, and these had to be swung inboard before the "Dorinda" was able to enter the lock.

"First get the boats stowed and then when we're in the lock go ashore and secure the hawsers. You'll have to remove a few sections of the rail first," said the Colonel, and his guests at last realized what all that stuff about dungarees and Jerry Kern's lack of robustness had meant. The scales fell from their eyes. For all practical purposes, they saw, they might have been aboard the Savage grandfather's slave ship.

"Morning, Cap'n," said the Colonel genially to the master of the "Shirley B." "Carrying fish, eh?"

"Ah."

"I've got two dudes aboard who don't like the way you smell."

"Sissies," said the old salt briefly.

After an eternity of removing sections of rail, stowing boats and securing hawsers and trying not to inhale, they were past and the "Dorinda" drew away down the long straight waterway. Guy cautiously lowered the handkerchief from his nose.

"Goodbye, 'Shirley'! Thank heaven we've seen the last of the lady."

"Lock ahoy!" called the Colonel.

The work began again. The boats were hauled inboard, the lock gates opened, the amateur deck hands seized the hawsers as Peasemarch threw them and made the "Dorinda" fast. They stood waiting expectantly for the lock gates to close and the water to be poured in. Nothing happened.

"What's the matter, Colonel?"

"Lock master's waiting for the barge. He doesn't like to work the lock for one vessel."

Presently the "Shirley B" bore slowly down on them, preceded by its noisome effluvium. There are—or were—eleven locks on the New Jersey canal system, and in every one of them "Shirley" snuggled in cosily beside the "Dorinda."

"Got any fresh fish, Cap'n?" inquired the Colonel on their third encounter.

"My God, he wouldn't!" muttered Plum, aghast.

They were spared. The barge captain shook his head.

"Never eat it."

"You should. Healthiest food in the world."

"I guess maybe I'll try a piece sometime," said the barge captain.

They tied up for the night at the side of the canal. When they sat down to dinner they noticed that the table was laid for four. The extra place, it appeared, was for Palmer.

"I always have him in for dinner," said the Colonel.

"Like Cesare Borgia," said Plum. "He used to have the cook dine with him and always made him eat a bit of each course before he sailed into it himself. So if it was poisoned, all that happened was that he was a cook short."

"Ha, ha!" laughed the Colonel merrily. Then, as Palmer entered bearing a dish of boiled potatoes and another of turnips, the smile faded from his lips. "What, two vegetables?" he said, frowning like someone austere contemplating one of those orgies that preceded the fall of Babylon. "Oh, well," he said resignedly. "I suppose this *is* something of an occasion."

Palmer was a weedy young man with a pale face and large horn-rimmed spectacles. He deposited the turnips and potatoes and went back for the *plat du jour*, a dish of brined herring. When this had been distributed, the two authors got down to business.

"We've roughed out a tentative idea for the Bill Fields play," said Guy.

"Oh?" said the Colonel.

"Let's hear it," said Palmer, closing his eyes and putting the tips of his fingers together.

"We thought Bill might be a phoney magician with a travelling medicine show. He has a pal, a crook, whom he sends ahead of him to the various towns. The crook steals things there and hides them. Then Bill appears and goes into a trance and tells where they can be found. Naturally this gives him a tremendous lift with the townspeople. They think he's wonderful. . . ."

"Why must there always be crooks in these things?" said Palmer. "Can't we sometimes have a little uplift?"

"We're writing for a comic. We want to get laughs."

Palmer shook his head.

"I doubt whether that sort of stuff will make much of an appeal to the more advanced appreciators. Amusing, but scarcely for the *avant garde*. In writing a play," said Palmer, "the scale of values should be at once objective and rational, hence absolute but authentic. One aims to achieve in these days of mere impressionism a newness—if I may use the term —which is continually intended and essentially correct. You agree?" he said, turning to Plum.

"You take the words out of my mouth," said Plum. "But I can only repeat what Guy has told you. We're trying to be funny."

"One's explorations should be vital. Eruptive, vital and intense," said Palmer firmly.

Guy tried again.

"Well, if that idea doesn't attract you," he said, as the Colonel still toyed aloofly with his herring, "we have another. Bill is a pawnbroker, the last of a long line. His family have been pawnbrokers for centuries, and one of them was the fellow who loaned the money on Queen Isabella's jewels when she hocked them to finance Columbus. She signed a document to say that the pawnbroker should get ten per cent on whatever Columbus discovered."

"And, as I daresay you have heard," said Plum, "he discovered America."

"And this old Spanish grant suddenly turns up," said Guy, "so there is Bill Fields in the position of having an ironclad legal claim to ten per cent of America. Then some crooks get hold of him—"

"Those crooks again!" sighed Palmer. "Thematic archaism. And just as I was beginning to think that you were groping for something esoteric and foreign to the debauched conception the public of today has of the theater. I've made a steam pudding," he said, rising. "I'll go and get it."

He disappeared in the direction of the galley.

"That's an odd cook you've got, Colonel," said Guy.

"Yes, not any great shakes at his job, I'm afraid. Of course it doesn't matter to me. I was shipwrecked once and lived for three weeks on dog biscuits. Ever since then I find everything wonderful."

Palmer returned with the pudding, a large glutenous lump that tasted not unlike a pair of old boiled slippers. The authors declined it and shortly afterwards went out on deck. The air was still vibrant with the scent of dead fish.

The next morning they were roused at daybreak. The moorings had to be dealt with and after that there were more locks ahead. They came out on deck to find rain falling in a manner which Palmer would no doubt have described as eruptive, vital and intense. They negotiated the last of the locks and the "Dorinda" sailed on down the Delaware, slipping into the Chesapeake and Delaware Canal and thence through the Elk River into Chesapeake Bay. As Plum and Guy sat huddled under a tattered and inadequate awning, Palmer popped out of the galley and bore down on them.

"Good morning," he said. "Have you ever studied the dominant impulse of the unconscious as exemplified in the plays of Pirandello?"

The two stared at him.

"You seem to know a great deal about plays," said Guy.

"Well, naturally. I'm a playwright."

"I thought you were a cook . . . well, when I say a cook . . ."

"Oh, no, I'm a playwright really. The Colonel's got a play of mine which he's going to do as soon as he finds the right star. It's called *Ophelia*. *Hamlet* from the woman's angle. Meanwhile, he's given me this job. He doesn't pay me anything, of course. But I must be getting back to my galley. I'm doing you a bouillabaisse for lunch. An experiment, but I think it will have significant form."

"Hold on a moment," said Guy. "How long has the Colonel had this *Ophelia* of yours?"

Palmer considered. "Let's see. This is my fifth trip to Florida on the 'Dorinda' . . ."

"Florida? You mean we're on our way to Florida?"

"Of course. Didn't the Colonel tell you?"

"He didn't say a word about it. He just suggested a cruise."

"We haven't brought any clothes for Florida," said Plum.

"Oh, *you're* not going to Florida," said Palmer, reassuring him. "He'll put you ashore somewhere round here. That's what he has always done before."

"What do you mean, 'before'?"

"With the other authors he's brought along to work the 'Dorinda' through the locks. As we've passed the last of the locks—the Inland Waterway is at tide level—I should imagine he will be landing you shortly. Excuse me, I must be looking after that bouillabaisse. If all goes well, it should be an entertaining little *morceau*. I think you will be amused by its naïveté."

The two authors made their way to where the Colonel, clad in glistening oilskins, stood at the wheel.

"You didn't tell us you were going to Florida, Colonel," said Guy.

"Didn't I?" said the Colonel mildly. "Stupid of me."

"If you had warned us before we started—"

"Of course, yes, I ought to have done. It slipped my mind,

I'm sorry. I'll land you boys after lunch. You can get a train from Annapolis. It will give you a chance to look around the Naval Academy."

"You realize," said Guy, "that we haven't discussed the play yet?"

"The play? Ah, yes, the play. I'm sorry about that. I didn't want to cloud your enjoyment of the trip by telling you before. That's off. I'm not doing it. Fields wants too much money."

It was as they sat in the drafty station at Annapolis, waiting for their train to arrive, that Guy observed that Plum was scribbling on the back of an envelope.

"What's that?" he asked. "A lyric?"

"No, just an idea I've had for a mystery thriller. It's a little out of my usual line—but I think it will be good. A corpse has been discovered with its head bashed in by a blunt instrument, and the police lieutenant has come with his sergeant to the scene of the crime.

" 'A foul and brutal murder,' he says. 'Cost what it may, we must spare no effort to bring the perpetrator of this hideous outrage to justice.' (You know how these police lieutenants talk.) Has the identity of the deceased been ascertained?'

" 'It has,' says the sergeant. 'The stiff is a theatrical manager—Colonel Henry W. Savage.'

" 'Oh, well,' says the lieutenant, 'in that case, let's not bother.'

"And they go off to lunch. It will run a bit short, I suppose, but it should have a wide appeal."

"Very wide," said Guy. "You've got a winner."

Chapter Nine

ANOTHER RESULT of the substantial clicking of *Oh Lady, Lady* was that Abraham Lincoln Erlanger—who during the bleak *Riviera Girl* days had shown a tendency to be as aloof to the authors of that musical gumboil as in his incarnation as Napoleon he would have been to a couple of marshals who had lost an important battle—abandoned his resolve to have them shot at sunrise and invited them to do a piece for the New Amsterdam with Ivan Caryll, the composer of a long list of shows at George Edwardes' London Gaiety Theatre and of that historic success of 1911, *The Pink Lady*, the "Beautiful Lady" waltz from which is still sung even now in many bathtubs both in England and America, mostly off key.

Caryll—he was a Belgian, and his real name was Felix Tilken—was widely known as Fabulous Felix. He had made a great deal of money in the theater, and whatever else you might say about him, you could not say that he did not do himself well. He lived *en prince*, as much *en prince* as if his first name had been Flo and his second Ziegfeld, having apartments in both London and Paris, as well as a villa containing five bathrooms, overlooking the Deauville racecourse. A man, as he sometimes said, or if he didn't, he should have done, needs plenty of elbow-room, and if he has five children, as Fabulous Felix had, how can he possibly do with fewer than five baths, one for each child to sing "Beautiful Lady" in?

When visiting New York, he did not actually charter a private liner, but he took most of Deck C on whichever was the best boat crossing, and on arrival settled down with his five children, his wife Maud and a cohort of nurses, tutors, governesses, valets and ladysmaids in a vast suite at the Hotel Knickerbocker. Then, instead of calling on the managers like the rest of the *canaille*, he would send word to them that he was, so to speak, in residence, ready to receive them and consider offers. And they came trotting round like rabbits.

It has never been decided whether or not Fabulous Felix did it with mirrors, but he had a hypnotic effect on all the big musical comedy impresarios of Broadway. Harry Kelly's dog Lizzie could have picked up some useful hints on technique from the way these normally hardboiled characters rolled over with their paws in the air in this man's presence. Some authorities claim that it was his beard that did the trick, and it may be that they are right. It was one of those long, black, square-cut, bushy numbers, as worn by Ozymandias, King of Kings, and other prominent Assyrians, concealing the whole face with the exception of the eyes and lending to its proprietor's appearance a suggestion of some dangerous creature of the wild peering out through a jungle. It is not surprising that sensitive managers, raised from childhood among composers who shaved daily and pink-cheeked authors smelling of witch hazel, should have been as wax in his hands.

What happened on these occasions was that Felix would say he had found a wonderful play in Paris which would make an ideal musical and, being an impulsive sort of fellow who had taken a sudden fancy to the manager whom he had selected to be the goat, was prepared to let him have this and to write the score for the customary composer's royalty of three per cent. No need for you to read the thing, my dear boy—it was, he assured his dear boy, superb, and he had the contracts here, all ready to sign.

"You couldn't give me some idea of what it's about?" the manager would say timidly.

"It's about a man who's in love with a girl."

"I see. Yes, that sounds fine."

"And there's another man. He's in love with a girl, too. It's tremendous. There's just one point. The French authors' royalties. These French authors come high. I doubt if I could beat them down below seven per cent."

And just as the manager was about to say "Ouch!" or "Zowie!" or whatever managers say when they are asked to part with seven per of the gross to a bunch of French authors, he would catch sight of that beard, quivering a little as though what was inside it was crouching for the spring, and his nerve would fail him. Quaking, he signed on the dotted line.

And what Felix in the rush and bustle of the conversation had completely forgotten to mention was that, as he had bought the French authors out for a few thousand francs before leaving Paris and was sole owner of the property, the entire seven per cent would be added to his personal take-home pay. No wonder he could afford to launch out a bit in the matter of bathrooms. He must have been astounded sometimes at his moderation in confining himself to five.

This time he had deviated from his normal routine. What he had sold to Erlanger was not a French play but a mere idea of his own which had occurred to him on the voyage over. It concerned the Parisian ladies who during the First World War had adopted army "godsons" to whom they wrote letters and sent cigarettes and books and food. It seemed to Felix that out of this pleasant custom there might grow a romance.

The thing presented possibilities. Guy and Plum felt that they could do something with it, making the lady a star of the Paris stage and the "godson" a struggling playwright who had written a play and wanted to get acquainted with her in order to persuade her to act in it. With this end in view, he exchanges identity books with the star's actual "godson," an army cook, and presents himself at her home in the country. Add a comic husband, whom the star has caught cheating and

is determined to punish in kind; a rich uncle who, finding the
star and the playwright in each other's arms, assumes the latter
to be the husband; and bring the playwright's fiancée on the
scene, she being a co-worker with the star in an army canteen;
and you have something which, if not literature, is certainly
a French farce. And it was a French farce on which Felix insisted, for his *Pink Lady* had been founded on one and he
believed in sticking to a formula.

So gradually *The Girl Behind the Gun*—it became *Kissing
Time* when produced in London—took shape.

· 2 ·

Rehearsals began in the middle of September, and one morning, a week later, Plum, arriving at Guy's apartment, nearly
collided with a strikingly handsome brunette in a very exotic
costume who was coming out. She beamed upon him in
friendly fashion.

"Are you Mr. Wodehouse?"

Plum said he was.

"How do you do? I'm Marguerite Namara."

"Of course, yes. I recognized you at once."

Marguerite Namara was a well-known opera singer. She
had appeared recently in a Schubert operetta, *Alone at Last*.

"I'm so glad to meet you," she said. "Guy has told me so
much about you." She looked at her wrist watch. "Oh, dear,
is that really the time? I must rush. We shall be seeing one
another again at dinner tonight."

She hurried off, and Plum went in and found Guy settling
down to work.

"Oh, there you are," said Guy. "Did you see Marguerite?"

"We met in the doorway. She says we're dining tonight."

"Yes."

"Will she be joining us in that Czechoslovakian costume?"

"It isn't Czechoslovakian. It's Greek. That thing she was wearing is called a peplum."

"Will she expect me to wear a peplum?"

"A peplum is a feminine garment. If you wore anything, it would be a *sakos* or possibly the *esorroko* or *palto*."

"Does she always dress like that?"

"Generally."

"Slightly cuckoo is she, by any chance?"

Guy stiffened.

"You are speaking of the woman I love."

"I thought you loved them all."

"Not as I love Marguerite. You're the one who has kept telling me I ought to find myself a wife. Well, now I've done it."

"You aren't married?"

"We're going to be."

"A thousand congratulations. This means that your lightest wish is law to her. Ask her not to wear those Greek reach-me-downs tonight."

"Why not?"

"I don't like them."

"Very well. I think they're charming myself, but perhaps they are more suited for the privacy of the home."

Marguerite, the soul of amiability, cheerfully consented to substitute for the Greek costume something simple and inconspicuous. When Guy called for her that night, she was wearing a bright scarlet dress trimmed with astrakhan and a matching *shlyapa*, or, as we would say, hat. Around her neck was a collar decorated with silver bells similar in design to those seen in paintings of troikas pursued through the Siberian woods by wolves. Short red Russian boots completed the costume, each having a large bell hanging where one would have expected a tassel. The *tout ensemble*, though perfect for Old Home Week at Nijni-Novgorod, was not so good, Guy felt, for the Ritz-

Carlton, where he had been intending to dine. Didn't she think, he said, that the Ritz-Carlton was a bit stodgy, and wouldn't a Bohemian place be more fun?

"Oh, yes, let's go to Mouquin's. We'll see all the people from the Met."

Guy could think of no reasonable excuse for avoiding an encounter with the Metropolitan Opera personnel. At any rate it was better than braving the stares of the aristocratic feeders at the Ritz-Carlton's Oval Room. He telephoned Plum to meet them there with a flask and to order some "set-ups" if he got there first.

He did get there first and was seated sipping something that had been sold to him as bourbon, when he was startled by what sounded like a troika with a bevy of wolves after it. The jingling appeared to be coming from his immediate rear, and, turning, he found himself confronted by what might have been The Spirit of the Volga in one of the twelve refrains of a number for the girls in *Miss 1917*.

His imitation, a very close one, of the late Sir Henry Irving in his most famous role ("Eah! daun't you hear . . . the sund of bell-ll-s?") was interrupted by the converging on the table of a maître d'hôtel, an assistant headwaiter, two ordinary waiters and a bus boy, for Marguerite was an established and popular patron at Mouquin's. Wine was brought—in a teapot —and the soup had just been served when several new arrivals came through the swing doors that faced Sixth Avenue.

"SCOTTI!!" screamed Marguerite in that carrying voice of hers which had so often given the back rows of the Paris Opera Comique their money's worth. "Scotti, my ANGEL!!!"

Guy and Plum, the latter a little unsteady on his feet, for he was feeling as if he had just been hit by something solid between the eyes, rose as the great Scarpia of the Met came over, and stood politely while an animated conversation took place in Italian. Finally, after Scotti had delivered a long speech, accompanied by passionate gestures, they were at liberty to resume the soup at which they had been looking long-ingly for the last ten minutes.

"What was all that excitement?" asked Guy.

"No excitement," said Marguerite. "Antonio was just saying he doesn't like the steam heat in New York. I love Antonio."

"Charming chap," agreed Plum, "but he made it a little difficult to concentrate on soup. I often say that it is fatal to let soup—"

"PAVEL!!!" shrieked Marguerite. "Pavel, my DEAR!!!"

The new arrival was Pavel Solokolov of the Ballet Russe. He had known Marguerite in Moscow when she had appeared at the Malenskia Theater with Isadora Duncan and her troupe of dancers. Guy and Plum once more rose politely, but contributed little to the conversation. It was in Russian, and their Russian was a bit rusty. They were inclined to be peevish as they resumed their soup, and Guy was just saying that when the next one came along he was going to fix three of these straws together and get his standing up, when Marguerite interrupted him.

"FEODOR!! Feodor, my PET!!"

This time it was something spectacular, the great Chaliapin in person, looking, as he always did, like a benevolent all-in wrestler. Both Guy and Plum had often admired him, but never more so than now, for his first act was to thrust them back into their seats with a hamlike hand and insist jovially that they get on with the serious business of the evening.

"Zoop is zoop," he said, speaking in English with an accent in which a spoon would have stood upright, and they felt he could not have phrased it more neatly.

"These are two playwrights that I am dining with," said Marguerite, performing a belated introduction.

"We do musical comedies," said Guy, pegging away at his soup.

"A low form of art, of course," said Plum, pegging away at his.

Chaliapin would have none of this self-depreciation.

"*Not* a low form of art," he insisted vehemently. "When I am a student at the gymnasium, I too write a musical comedy. In it there is a scene which I will give to you, Mr. Bolton, as a present. It is a bum scene and very phoney."

It seemed to Plum that the great man was too modest.

"Oh, I'm sure it isn't," he said politely.

Marguerite interpreted.

"Bomb scene. Very funny."

"Yes, so phoney you will laugh off your heads," said Chaliapin. "You are to imagine that I am a cruel governor and you two are revolutionists who have come to blow me up with a bum. But I catch you, and my men they tie you to a bench and I put the bum beneath the bench. It is a time-bum and it goes tick-tock, tick-tock. I laugh. It tickles me like a horsehair undervest. Because it is a fine torture for you to hear that tick-tock, tick-tock, tick-tock."

"Like someone reading the minutes at a meeting," said Guy brightly. "What happens then?"

"I tell you. The bum is going tick-tock, tick-tock, when a noise outside distracts my attention, and I turn my back for a moment. You have one hand free, and you take the bum and slip it into the pocket of my *palto*, my big overcoat. There are more noises outside and I go out to ask, "What the hell?" and the bum she goes with me."

He illustrated this bit of action by turning away and squeezing past a party of two elderly ladies and a deaf old gentleman who were taking their places at the next table.

"But wait," bellowed Chaliapin from a distance of several yards, his organ tones ringing through the restaurant. "You have not seen the last of me. I come back now to gloot over you."

He began to creep back, his face wearing a hideous and menacing scowl. The two ladies at the next table stirred uneasily.

"Remember I have the bum in my pocket." He patted his pocket. "I am coming back to laugh, to gloot over you. The bum is ticking—any minute now she is going off—and I am glooting. Pigs! Children of pigs! In a little moment you will be sausage meat. You will be buttered all over the walls. It makes me laugh to think of it. Ha, ha, ha, ha."

It was a good laugh, and it sent the two elderly ladies scurrying to the door, leaving their deaf escort to his fate. People were standing up, trying to see what the commotion was about. There was a sense of relief, mingled perhaps with a certain disappointment, when Chaliapin, reaching the table, sat down and helped himself to wine from the teapot, his face wreathed in smiles.

"Phoney?" he said.

"Very phoney," agreed Guy faintly.

Chaliapin looked about him, inspecting the table closely. He seemed puzzled.

"Where is the other gentleman? There were two gentlemen, two musical comedy writers, drinking zoop. Now there is one gentleman."

"Mr. Wodehouse had to leave hurriedly," Guy explained. "A sudden seizure. He gets them sometimes. I understand he hears buzzing sounds—"

"Like a bum going tick-tock tick-tock tick-tock?"

"Exactly. Accompanied by an occasional cowbell."

As Guy was going to bed, the telephone rang.

"Sorry about running away like that," said Plum.

"I don't blame you. Heaven deliver us from opera stars with comedy scenes."

"How did it end?"

"The bum scene? I couldn't tell you."

"You mean that ruddy basso left you without giving you the finish?"

"He never mentioned it. He went on to speak of other things. Why, are you interested?"

"Interested! I shall dream about it for weeks. You and me tied to a bench and Chaliapin coming back and forth, glooting over us, and the bum going tick-tock tick-tock."

"I'll get Marguerite to call him up and ask him to tell us who blew up who in the end. Oh, by the way. Marguerite. Charming, don't you think?"

"Very charming. And I'll tell you something else I think—something you probably know already. I think you're going to have a wonderfully exciting married life."

· 3 ·

The Girl Behind the Gun opened in New York in November, settling down at once to a long run, and the authors were able to concentrate on the next show for the Princess, on which they had been working for some time in their intervals of leisure.

It seemed to both Guy and Plum that these Princess shows were running too much to type and that the formula was becoming evident. They begged Ray to strike out in a new direction with *The Little Thing*, but he insisted that the pattern be followed just once more. Even if this one were not so successful as its predecessors, there was, he argued, plenty of slack to take up.

This one—they called it *Oh, My Dear*—was certainly not another *Oh, Boy!* or *Oh, Lady*, but it did quite well when, a few weeks after *The Girl Behind the Gun* had opened at the New Amsterdam, it made its bow on Thirty-ninth Street. It was a lively musical farce, the scene of which was a sanatorium in the country, where a young man who thought he had inadvertently committed a murder found it convenient to hide out. It was the first comedy to bring the psychiatrist to the stage and also the only Princess show to have a non-Kern score. Jerry was busy elsewhere, and Lou Hirsch, composer of "The Love Nest," a song still heard after all these years, wrote the music but without—unfortunately—contributing another "Love Nest." It was one of those pieces which are quite all right—business excellent—nothing to complain of—but not sensational. It was the *Ruddigore* of the series.

· 4 ·

A couple of weeks after the *Oh, My Dear* opening the two authors met for lunch.

"I suppose you're spending your Christmas with Marguerite?" said Plum.

"No," said Guy. "On Christmas Day Marguerite will be appearing in the Bull Ring in Mexico City with Titta Ruffo."

"Become a lady bullfighter, has she?"

"She's singing *Carmen*, ass."

"I trust she won't wear that red dress."

"There are no bulls in the Bull Ring while they are singing."

"A pity. It would make the thing so much more exciting. So she's in Mexico City, eh? Your fiancée does get about, doesn't she? How's the romance going?"

"It's in a state of suspended animation."

His partner asked him to elucidate. Had there been a lovers' quarrel? No, nothing like that, only Marguerite had doubts as to whether their divergent tastes, their disparate careers could be welded into a workable marriage.

"It'll probably end in her going her way and you going hers."

"It'll probably end where it is right now," replied Guy pessimistically.

Plum looked at him.

"The thing you need is a holiday," he said. "You pack your traps and come off to Palm Beach with Ethel and me."

"Don't you have to be a Cabot or a Biddle or something?"

"Not at all. Theatrical managers and other lower type Fauna Americana are migrating there in flocks."

"You call consorting with managers a holiday?"

"There is other companionship. It is a spot favored by members of the Follies ensemble to rest up after the ardors of a New York run."

"I don't want Follies girls either."

"That remark alone proves you are far from being yourself."

At the moment they were comparatively idle. Plum had just published *A Damsel in Distress* and in his spare moments was at work on *The Indiscretions of Archie*. Guy was collaborating on two comedies, *The Five Million* with Frank Mandel and *Adam and Eva* with George Middleton. Still, these things were not being written to order. There was no deadline to meet. Though Guy was still inclined to demur, Plum remained firm. They bought straw hats and pongee slacks. They bought bathing suits. They bought tickets to Palm Beach.

Chapter Ten

Anyone in those days arriving for the first time in America's number one winter playground would have had to be very blasé not to experience a thrill. There was magic in the place. Nowadays you are deposited at a shabby Florida East Coast station situated in the least glamorous section of Palm Beach's frowsy namesake on the wrong side of the tracks, but when Guy and Plum opened their eyes shortly before eight that December morning they found their train crossing a blue lagoon fringed with royal palms and a little later were deposited in a shining, white-painted terminus festooned with brilliant-hued bougainvillea. Colored bellboys and porters, all in spotless uniforms, stood lined up, awaiting them. On the pathway that ran along the shore of Lake Worth the hansom cab of Palm Beach, the open basket chair with the driver mounted behind, sped by, carrying a couple attired in, of all things, evening dress.

"Must have been some party," commented Guy.

"Probably spent the night at Bradley's," said a fellow traveller who was sorting out his baggage beside him. He pointed to a large frame building on the opposite side of the palm-lined avenue, and they looked with interest at the most famous gambling casino in America. One of the unobtrusive corps of guards, armed with a sawed-off shotgun, was strolling round between the big flowering bushes that dotted the lawn.

Back in New York it had been snowing, but here the sun shone brightly. Little puffy white clouds like dabs of whipped cream moved lazily across a sky of the deepest blue. The two mounted the steps that led from the station through a covered way into the longest hotel in the world, the fourteen-hundred-foot Royal Poinciana, with one employee for each foot. Shops lined the way, New York's top couturiers, Charvet of Paris, Beale and Inman of London, bag shops, flower shops, jewelry shops. Plum waved a hand at one of the last named.

"Remind me to tell you a story about Arch Selwyn."

"Who's Arch Selwyn?" asked Ethel.

"New York manager."

"Then don't tell me about him," said Ethel. "I'm trying to forget that there is such a place as New York. Why can't we stay forever in this paradise?"

Their rooms overlooked the golf course. To one side were a couple of spurs running from the railway. On these, packed closely together, stood the private cars which had brought the wealthy down from Manhattan. One of them, which had been attached to the back of their train, was being shunted into place. The owner strolled out on to the spacious lounging platform. There seemed something familiar about his appearance.

"Good Lord! It's Flo!"

"Gosh, so it is. What does it cost to travel in one of those?"

"I can tell you," said Plum. "I asked. Not because I was toying with the idea of booking one for the homeward journey. I wanted to use it in a story. The tariff is ninety fares."

"You mean ninety times what we paid?"

"That's right. Flo must be feeling rich."

"Flo Ziegfeld always feels rich. The trouble is, it's just a feeling. The most extravagant man of our time. The arch-squanderer. . . . That reminds me. What was that about Arch Selwyn?"

"Oh, that? It was something Ray told me. It seems that last year Arch made his first trip to Palm Beach, and the night of his arrival found him at Bradley's plunging with the best of them. Birdie tried her best to stop him—"

" 'Birdie'?" queried Ethel.

"His wife—but when she saw him scooping in the counters—"

"Oh, he won?"

"A packet. Couldn't go wrong. He was so loaded with the stuff when he left that he had to lean on her all the way home. She said 'My hero!' or words to that effect, and next day steered him into one of those shops downstairs. He bought her a georgeous diamond clip costing about two thousand."

"Nice man."

"Yes. Well, the next night he went back to Bradley's, and you can guess what happened. First he lost the price of the clip and after that the price of his shirt and underpants. The next night it was the same, and the next and the next, and all the time Birdie was chirruping around showing her clip and saying what a thing it was to have a generous husband. And when Arch dropped hints about marriage being a partnership in which the loyal little comrade should share the downs as well as the ups, she didn't seem to get it.

"Finally Arch pleaded with her to put the clip away somewhere. He said he couldn't bear to look at it.

"Then one evening it disappeared. It wasn't insured, and Birdie kept the loss to herself. It was only when they were back in New York that Arch happened to ask her why she never wore that diamond clip he had bought her in Palm Beach. She explained what had happened.

"When Arch at last gathered that the clip had been stolen, he nearly had a fit.

" 'Why in heaven's name didn't you notify the hotel detective, the police?'

" 'How could I? It would have got into the papers. It would have looked terrible—ARCH SELWYN STEALS WIFE'S JEWELS.'

"Arch tottered.

" 'You thought *that* of me? You really supposed that I would stoop . . . my God!'

"Arch was properly indignant, but he admitted to Ray privately that the thing that made him really so sore was to think of all those weary hours he had spent hunting everywhere for the clip after Birdie was asleep, and all the while some dirty crook had beaten him to it."

· 2 ·

They swam and lay in the sun. They played a round of golf on that odd little course where the hazards were palm trees and the greens—in those days—were of sand.

That night they went to Bradley's and Sam Harris, of Cohan and Harris, who came in with Charlie Dillingham, took them into the office and introduced them to the Colonel and his brother.

"Two writin' fellers, Colonel," said Charlie. "They want membership cards."

"Can they afford to lose?"

"Up to a point, and I guess you know what that is."

The Colonel told his brother to make out the cards.

"I don't like to win money from people who can't afford it," he said. "I think that's pretty well known . . . too well known, perhaps. At any rate, I got caught nicely the other day. Man came in and started to play big. In less than an hour he'd dropped seventeen thousand dollars. I went myself and watched him at the end. Seemed to me he looked kind of upset, and it worried me. Then the next day his wife came in and asked to see me. She was terribly wrought-up. Said her husband must have been crazy. What he'd lost, she said, was the money they had been saving up for years to buy a home in Florida. A real tear-jerker it was. Well, I did what I've done quite a few times when this sort of thing has happened, I gave her back half the money and told her to tell her old man that if he ever tried to come sneaking into my place again, I'd make it my business to kick him out personally. That woman was certainly grateful. Tears coursed down her cheeks. She grabbed my hand and kissed it. She said she wished there were more men like me in the world."

"I'll bet she did," said Sam Harris. "I've known a lot of gamblers in my time, from Dick Canfield down, but you're the only one that would hand back eighty-five hundred dollars just because a dame cried at you."

"You haven't heard the pay-off," said the Colonel, and his brother, sitting at the desk, started to laugh. "Spite of my warning, darned if the husband didn't come in again that very same night, and sat down calm as a codfish and began to high-roll all over the board. I was hopping mad. I sent one of my table men to fetch him to the office, and when he came in I started to lay him out. 'Didn't your wife tell you I said you weren't to come here?' I yelled at him. He looked sort of surprised. 'My wife, Colonel?' he said. 'I haven't got a wife!' I said, 'You mean you haven't got a wife who came in here this morning and told me you'd lost the money you had been saving for years to buy a home?' 'Certainly not,' said the fellow. 'Why would I buy a home?' he said. 'I'm lousy with homes. Homes are what I've got nothing else but. I own the biggest hotel chain on the West Coast.' "

"Women aren't gentlemen," said Charlie Dillingham.

"But Ed hasn't told you the real snapper," said the Colonel's brother. "The fellow he'd been so bighearted about had a run of fool's luck that night. He nicked us for close on eighty thousand dollars."

They went into the gambling rooms, which were filled with men in dress clothes and women laden down with jewels. Europe, in the winter of 1918, had not yet regained its prewar popularity, and everyone was coming to Palm Beach. The recently established tax on income, crushing though it was—four per cent, if we remember rightly—had not removed any of the gilt from the gilded set. The two writers, who had but recently acquired the feeling of solvency, shrank back into the ranks of the underprivileged as they saw the walnut-sized diamonds and the piles of green twenty-dollar chips strewn across the roulette tables.

There were a few faces that they recognized . . . Otto Kahn with his neat white moustache . . . General Pershing accompanied by his friend, Coleman Dupont . . . Willie K. Vanderbilt, Junior . . . Mrs. O. H. P. Belmont . . . the impish-faced Margaret Lawrence with her husband, Orson Munn. Most of these they knew from having seen their photographs in papers and magazines, but there was a leavening of characters from their own bailiwick . . . Arch Selwyn, Condé Nast, Addison Mizner.

"Take a look round," said Plum, "and tell me—who, if you didn't know who any of them were, would you say was head man, most assured, most at home?"

Guy could answer that without a moment's hesitation.

"Ziegfeld."

"That's right. He's got an air. You feel that hundred dollar bills mean no more to him than paper matches to a cigar store."

"And half the time he hasn't enough to buy a knitted waist-coat for a smallish gnat."

Ziegfeld was standing by a table with a handful of the costly green chips, dropping them carelessly on the numbers and turning to talk to the woman next him without watching the wheel. He won, but went on talking, leaving the chips where they lay. He won again. It was quite a win, but only when his companion squealed excitedly and pointed to the piled-up counters did he motion languidly to the croupier to push them toward him.

"The lady seems more thrilled at his win than he is," said Guy.

"So I notice. 'Blasé' about sums it up."

"Know who she is? I just heard someone say. Mrs. Edward B. McLean of Washington."

"Do you mean to say that that blue thing she's wearing round her neck is the Hope diamond?"

"That's it. The stone Tavernier stole from the idol Rama-Sita. Fifteen violent deaths laid to its account."

"Is that really the score?"

"So far. You wouldn't catch me playing roulette with that thing alongside me."

But the Hope diamond seemed to have lost its malignant power tonight. Ziegfeld continued to win. Then, apparently bored, he pushed his counters over to the table man and received a slip of paper in exchange. Two famous beauties from the Follies came up to him, Helen Lee Worthing and Olive Thomas. He fished some loose chips from his pocket and handed them to the girls. He caught sight of Guy and Plum and came over to them. He asked them how long they had been in Palm Beach. They told him they had arrived that morning by the same train as himself.

"Why didn't you come in my car?" he said. "It's a lot more comfortable than those stuffy drawing rooms."

They did not mention that they had travelled down in humble "lowers."

"You didn't bring Jerry with you?"

"No."

"He's coming. I reserved a room for him at the Breakers. He and I have been talking about a show for Marilyn Miller."

This was news. Presumably Jerry had not mentioned this because there was another librettist involved.

"You ought to have a huge success with her," said Guy. "She's got the same sort of quality Maud Adams had. A wistful charm that goes right to the heart."

"Have you settled on a story?" asked Plum.

"Practically settled. It's a musical version of *Be Calm, Camilla*, that Clare Kummer comedy. Clare will do the book and lyrics."

"Isn't that the play in which the heroine breaks her ankle in the first act?" enquired Plum innocently.

"That's it."

"I shouldn't have thought it would be an ideal vehicle for a dancer."

Ziegfeld stared at him for a moment, then he laughed.

"Jerry and I ought to have our heads examined."

"However, that's the only objection." Plum's smile was benevolent. "It's a very charming play otherwise."

Ziegfeld eyed them thoughtfully.

"Have you fellows got a story?"

"Guy has. Scheherazade had nothing on that boy. He's full of stories."

"We must get together when Jerry arrives and have a talk," said Ziegfeld. He turned away, but came back as if struck by an afterthought. "You boys like yachting?"

With the hint of an *arrière pensée* the boys said they did.

"I've chartered the 'Wench,' Len Replogle's boat. We might take a cruise through the Indian River and possibly run up the Loxahackie in one of the launches. You'll see alligators and orchids growing wild."

"That should be quite a saving for you, gathering a few wild orchids," laughed Plum. Ziegfeld was famous as an orchid-giver.

"Are there any locks?" asked Guy.

"Locks? No. Why?"

"I was just thinking of something. How many do you carry as crew?"

"Fourteen, including the captain."

Guy drew a deep breath.

"We'd love to come, wouldn't we, Plum?" he said.

An immediate conference seemed to be called for. Watching millionaires winning and losing fortunes had its thrills, but it was not so thrilling as the contemplation of a show for Ziegfeld with Marilyn Miller as star. They left Bradley's and climbed into one of the chairs lined up at the entrance. They told the colored owner to take them where he pleased. A full moon was shining. The air was soft and balmy. Though wearing dinner jackets without overcoats they had no sense of chill, even when they turned down the broad cedar-lined way that led to the ocean.

No motor vehicles were allowed on the island in those days. Bicycles and the bicycle-chairs were the only means of transit on pathways that wound through the semi-tropical clusters of palm, cedar and banyan.

They agreed that a show for Ziegfeld would be the biggest thing that had happened to them. Quite aside from New York, his name on the road was dynamite. *The Ziegfeld Follies* were the top drawing card of America. And a show for Ziegfeld *with* Marilyn Miller. . . . You couldn't beat that for a combination.

Inevitably Guy suggested *The Little Thing*. Plum was dubious. It seemed to him that the setting and costumes would strike Flo as giving insufficient opportunity for glamor.

The first scene of *The Little Thing* was the back yard of an actors' boardinghouse, the heroine a little drudge who loathed washing dishes and longed to be a ballet dancer like the great Esmeralda, one of the boarders. Esmeralda, now an old woman with nothing left of her days of glory but an imperious temper, was certainly not a Ziegfeld type, nor was Mr. Tolly, the old actor who had loved Esmeralda when she was the toast of Broadway and who had surreptitiously fastened a gold star to the door of her hall-bedroom. Not much there for Flo, said Plum.

"But can't you just see Marilyn in that scene with the writer who'd do the article on the old-timers?"

"Which scene do you mean?"

"He says, 'What's your last name, Sally?' 'Rhinelander.' 'Oh, a society lady?' 'No, that was just the telephone district. I was found in a telephone booth wrapped in an old shawl. I go and put flowers in it every Mother's Day.' "

"Yes, yes." Guy, once started on the subject of *The Little Thing*, was not easy to stop. "Yes, I remember."

" 'The last time I saw Mother,' " Guy went on, " 'one of her hinges was broken and she had a sign on her "Out of Order." It's kinda sad, don't you think?' "

"What I remember most clearly about *The Little Thing*," said Plum, "is the lyrics. You secured a very gifted man to write those, some name beginning with W."

"You are thinking of 'Joan of Arc'?"

"No. Good, but not W at his best. 'Church Around the Corner' was more up to the W mark. Church Around the Corner—did I ever tell you Ethel and I were married there?"

"No. Were you?" Guy sighed enviously.

"We were. We had a hundred and twenty-six dollars between us in the world, and we were standing there waiting for the parson to appear and beginning to wonder if he had stood us up, when he came bounding in with a six-inch grin across his face. 'I've just made ten thousand bucks on the Stock Exchange,' he yodelled. I was as sick as mud. Ten thousand! There ought to be a law."

They lapsed into silence as their chair turtled along beside a sea spread out like a dark blue counterpane lace-edged with white where it touched the shore. Presently Plum spoke.

"By and large not a bad world," he said.

· 3 ·

Jerry Kern arrived, and after a talk with Ziegfeld said:

"Well, boys, it looks as if you'd done Clare Kummer out of a job."

Guy disagreed.

136

"All we did was point out that a play where the heroine spends the entire evening on crutches with a plaster cast on her leg might not be just right for Marilyn Miller. But Clare Kummer is so clever that I'm sure she will be able to think up something that will give a dancer more scope."

"Come off it. You two hi-jackers are after the thing for yourselves."

"Naturally we would like the job. But only if Clare Kummer turns it down."

"She has turned it down. She's at work on a play called A *Successful Calamity*. She might have managed an adaptation, but isn't equal to inventing a new story, starting from scratch."

"Well, tell Flo we are in residence, ready to receive him and consider offers."

"Eh?"

"I was thinking of Fabulous Felix," said Guy.

But Ziegfeld, having raised their hopes, did nothing to sustain them. They ran into him every day, but on the subject of shows for Marilyn Miller he preserved a proud silence. His conversation was of golf, of gossip, of gambling. He talked quite a lot, but he did not talk turkey. One morning, meeting them pottering round the Country Club course, he told them that the yachting trip was set to start next Sunday morning.

"Do you boys like terrapin?" he asked in that curious, melancholy way of his.

Jerry Kern said he was crazy about it. Plum and Guy, neither of whom had ever tasted it, said they were, too. (As he later admitted, Jerry had never tasted it, either.)

"Well, don't eat too much breakfast," said Flo. "We'll have terrapin for lunch that beats any you've ever eaten. The ship's cook has a special way of preparing it."

The "Wench" was something very different from the "Dorinda" of evil memory, a real dream boat with a cocktail shaker for every porthole. Confident this time of finding a steward in a white coat deferentially serving refreshments, the

visitors found three stewards in white coats, each more defer-
ential than the last. Everything capable of glistening glistened.
Everything fashioned to glow glowed. The deck chairs were
lower, deeper and more luxuriously cushioned than those of
any other vessel to be seen about the yacht club pier. Each
single item was the best money could buy, from the giant
Havana perfectos to the three long-limbed young ladies
stretched at their ease under an awning of the famous Ziegfeld
rose-pink. Their costumes were to the last degree what Palmer
would have called *avant garde*. In a day when girls were
arrested if they appeared on a bathing beach without stockings,
the three nymphs justified Will Rogers' famous crack, "I
never expected to see the day when girls would get sunburned
in the places they do."

The other men of the party were Messmore Kendall, the
theatrical manager, Paul Block, the newspaper owner, and
Walter Chrysler. Just before they were ready to sail, Arthur
Somers Roche, the novelist, came aboard with his bride, Ethel
Pettit, who had played the heroine of *Miss Springtime* in the
Chicago company and later, when Sari Petrass, the Hungarian
prima donna, retired from the New York company, took her
place. In this gathering of millionaires and Follies girls it was
pleasant to meet one of the gang.

The "Wench" turned through the inlet and headed up the
coast past the tall red column of Jupiter Light standing at the
end of the island which had been the home of Joseph Jefferson.
Messmore Kendall had known one of the Jefferson sons—four
of them, all actors—and this younger Jefferson had told him
that when his father had moved there, Jupiter Island had had
only one other inhabitant, a hermit who had not exchanged a
word with another human being for thirty years. The story ran
that he had had his tongue cut out by a tribe of Seminoles,
he having told a lie about one of them. (Seminoles are touchy.)
He was held up as an awful warning to the younger Jeffersons.

The legend lost considerably in impressiveness when it was

discovered that not only could he talk, but that once started it was impossible to stop him. Conversation, the accumulation of thirty years of silence, poured from him in an unending stream. He attached himself to the Jeffersons, and nothing they could do would rid them of him. Finally they accepted the inevitable and he became old Joe's constant companion on his fishing, hunting and painting expeditions. One day Joe asked him if it was true that he had remained silent for thirty years.

"Yeppy, that's right."

"Why?"

"Weren't nobody worth talking to."

Old Joe said he considered that one of the highest compliments ever paid him.

Jerry sat down at the little yacht piano that had been moved out of the saloon for the occasion and began to play.

"What's that?" asked Ollie Thomas.

"It's a delicious melody," said Ethel Pettit. "Are there any words?"

"You bet there are words, and I'd love to hear you sing them. The song was written for *Oh, Lady,* but we took it out."

Jerry asked Plum to scribble down the lyric for Ethel and told them something more of the song's origin. The melody was one of several that Jerry had assembled to play to Charles Frohman back in 1906 or thereabouts. He wanted to get in on the writing of those extra numbers which were interpolated into the scores of the Austrian composers. These at that time were always supplied by some member of the "English school" —Lionel Monckton, Paul Rubens, Howard Talbot and the rest, Frohman having that odd passion of his for anything English.

Frohman refused to see Jerry, sending word that he bought all his material in England, and anybody but Jerry would have accepted the situation meekly and given up the struggle. But the fellow who said, "You can't keep a good man down"

must have been thinking of Jerome D. Kern. He scraped together his few pennies and went to London. There he suc-
ceeded in selling a number called "Won't You Come and Flirt
with Me?" to George Edwardes, who put it into one of his
productions. It had girls in swings that swung out over the
audience displaying black-stockinged legs and frilly petticoats,
and was the hit of the show.

On the second night, when Jerry was standing at the back of
the circle glooting, as Chaliapin would have said, over his success, Charles Frohman came up. He told Jerry that he had
been pointed out to him as the composer of the number. He
was enthusiastic.

"When it comes to this sort of thing," he said, "you English-
men are in a class by yourselves. We haven't anyone who can
do it on the other side."

He asked Jerry if he would consider coming to America.
Jerry thought he might be able to fit in a trip, and they sailed
back on the same ship. As the boat went up the bay, C. F.
pointed out the various objects of interest to the bit of im-
ported English talent at his side.

"The highest building of all is the Manhattan Life. The one
with the gold dome is the World Building. This is the Hudson
River, navigable by quite large vessels for a hundred miles."

"Coo!" said Jerry. "Really? A hundred miles? Lord-love-a-
duck! Makes a chap think a bit, that sort of thing, what?"

At this point a lady, a poor sailor, who had remained in her
stateroom during the voyage, espied Jerry and came up to him.

"Why, Jerry Kern!" she cried. "How did you like London?
Weren't you homesick? After all, there's no place like dear old
Newark, is there?"

"What did Frohman say?" asked Paul Block.

"He behaved like the sport he always was," said Jerry. "He
laughed and laughed, and finally I was sufficiently reassured
to join in. We became great friends, and the next time C. F.

went abroad, he asked me to come with him. There were a couple of new musicals in London and he wanted my opinion on them. Well, naturally I jumped at the invitation, and the night before we were to sail a bunch of my friends gave me a farewell party, at which I did a thing I don't often do. I got pie-eyed. I was just sober enough to ask whoever it was that brought me home to set the alarm clock for seven, and when seven came there was a little croak from the clock, but it was enough to wake me up, and I staggered out of bed and started getting dressed. The boat was sailing at ten, and I wanted to have plenty of time.

"I made myself a cup of coffee and got my clothes on. It was a miserable day, and all the time it kept getting darker, until I thought there must be a terrible storm coming up. By the time I got into a taxi, the sky was almost black. I said to the driver, 'What on earth's happening? Is there going to be a thunderstorm?' He said he didn't think so. 'Then what's making the sky so dark?' I said. 'Why wouldn't the sky be dark?' he said. 'It's close on eight-thirty.'

"And suddenly I got it. It was eight-thirty at *night*. I'd slept right through the day. The alarm clock hadn't waked me, and that croaking sound which I had finally managed to hear had been the little bit of alarm left for the next time the hour it's set at comes round."

"So of course you had missed the boat by hours?" said Chrysler.

"Yes. And do you know what boat it was? The 'Lusitania, sailing May the second, nineteen-fifteen."

· 4 ·

Plum handed the lyric he had been writing out to Ethel Pettit, but before she had a chance to sing it one of the stewards announced luncheon. They all filed through the big lounge

141

into the dining saloon. The meal started with grapefruit au Kirsch, caviar having already been served with the cocktails. Then came the terrapin.

"Wait till you taste this," said Ziegfeld.

But after the first mouthfuls and the appreciative "Oh's" and "Ah's," he shook his head.

"There's something wrong," he said. "This isn't it. It's not bad, but nothing like what I promised you." He turned to the steward. "Did Shimo cook this?"

He was told that Shimo had not cooked it, having been fired by the captain for impertinence. Ziegfeld nodded moodily, but said nothing.

While they were still at lunch, the "Wench" put into Port Pierce. A steward went ashore with a sheaf of Ziegfeld telegrams. This was routine. Few hours of the day passed without Ziegfeld sending a telegram to someone.

It was on the return journey, when the sky had begun to glow with one of those magical Florida sunsets, that Ethel Pettit sang the song that had been dropped from the score of *Oh, Lady, Lady.*

> *I used to dream that I would discover*
> *The perfect lover*
> *Some day:*
> *I knew I'd recognize him if ever*
> *He came round my way:*
> *He'd have hair of gold*
> *And a noble head*
> *Like the heroes bold*
> *In the books I'd read.*
>
> *Then along came Bill,*
> *Who's not like that at all:*
> *You'd pass him on the street and never notice him.*
> *His form and face,*
> *His manly grace,*

Are not the sort that you
Would find in a statue:
I can't explain . . .
It's surely not his brain
  That makes me thrill:
I love him because . . . oh, I don't know,
  Because he's just my Bill.

"I've got to have that song," said Ziegfeld. "What do you boys want for it?"

"It's not for sale," said Jerry. "It's a valuable adjunct to a show."

"I'll have Fanny Brice sing it and give it a big set-up—plenty of schmaltz."

"It's no good for a revue, Flo. It needs a situation back of it. It needs a guy named Bill and the girl who loves him." He turned to Plum. "Am I right or am I right?"

"Of course you're right. I wrote it for Molly to sing about Bill in *Oh, Lady*. The whole point is the audience has seen Bill and has been wondering what a girl like her can find to love in a chap like that. . . . And she tells them. It's no good except for a book show."

"Well, I'm going to do a book show—plenty of them before I'm through," said Flo. "I'm starting next season with one for Marilyn Miller."

"Okay, we'll put it aside till we see who you offer us to sing it."

"Ruth Etting suit you?"

"Yes, Ruth Etting would suit us fine. So would Ethel Pettit."

"Sorry, I've retired," said Ethel. "Though I admit," she added, "if anything would tempt me back, it would be a song like that."

"Nora Bayes, Elizabeth Brice, Fanny . . . there's plenty who could sing it," said Jerry, "but let's get the show first."

"We'll get a show."

"If that song is in it and Ollie Thomas, I'll back it," said Chrysler.

"You'll have a little competition, Walter," said Paul Block. "I'm already elected to back Flo's show for Marilyn, and I may say I don't mind having Ollie in it either."

That's how simple it was to get backing in those days when big musicals cost fifty thousand to put on and not three hundred thousand . . . a well-staged party with a few pretty girls . . . Irving or Jerry, Lou Hirsch or Rudy Friml . . . and one lady guest carefully chosen for her voice.

When the "Wench" came into the yacht harbor, there was a Jap standing on the clubhouse pier. Ziegfeld went over to the captain.

"I'm told you fired Shimo because he was fresh," he said. "You were quite right, but I wired him that he's hired again. He won't be the ship's cook. He'll live in a hotel and come aboard only when we're having terrapin. That's all he's for— just terrapin."

Chrysler laughed.

"You and Paul and I," he said, turning to Messmore Kendall, "have quite a piece of change between us, but it takes a Ziegfeld to do a thing like that."

· 5 ·

The two partners had one more encounter with the Glorifier before they left. It was on the golf course that had been laid out between the Breakers and the Royal Poinciana. There were only nine holes, and though it was quite late in the afternoon Plum thought he would be able to make it before dark. Guy, who had blistered his hands in a country club match the day before, was walking round with him. On the first tee they found Ziegfeld, who was likewise accompanied by a non-player, Freddie Zimmerman. It seemed only fitting that the two active members of the quartette should team up.

"What'll we play for?" asked Flo. "Five dollars?"

"All right," said Plum, getting ready to drive. "And if it gets too dark to finish, we'll give the ten bucks to Freddie to hold for tomorrow."

"I meant five dollars a hole."

Plum was actually swinging as Flo said it. He foozled his drive. Flo, however, following his almost invariable custom, foozled his, and Plum won the first hole. As he addressed his ball on the second tee, Ziegfeld called out, "Double or quits," which caused his opponent to slice, and the ball, striking a palm tree, returned almost to the starting point. In these circumstances a protest regarding the wager would hardly have been sporting, so Plum agreed and Ziegfeld sent a topped shot a matter of eighty yards down the fairway. Once more Plum won the hole, and once more Ziegfeld said, "Double or quits."

By the time they holed out at the seventh, Plum again winning, two things had begun to gather—darkness and a gallery. Guy and Freddie, working it out with pencils and bits of paper, announced that the contest for the short eighth would be for six hundred and forty dollars.

The eighth was a mashie-niblick shot on to a narrow green surrounded by bunkers.

"You shoot first," said Plum. "It may change your luck," and Ziegfeld proceeded to make a shot Francis Ouimet might have been proud of. The ball rose in a beautiful arc against the still faintly glowing western sky. It dropped a yard from the hole, and there was a round of applause that was probably as gratifying to the master manager's ear as any earned for him by his artists.

It was unnerving for Plum to have to follow such an effort, and he topped his shot badly. The ball took off on a flat trajectory, whizzed across the green, hit one of the private cars in the siding behind it, came whistling back, ricochetted off a caddy, soared into the air, fell ten inches from the cup and trickled in.

Plum was relieved. It had been a near thing.

"Thought for a moment I'd missed it," he said.

"Double or quits," said Ziegfeld.

"Or suppose we make it an even thousand?"

"Okay. Mind if I shoot first again?"

"Go ahead."

The shades of night were falling fast now. There was just enough visibility for the spectators to be aware that this time Ziegfeld meant business. They could see him only vaguely, a dim form in the darkness, but even that glimpse was sufficient to tell them that there stood a man who intended that his stance should be right, his grip right, his body still, his head unmoved, and his eye on the ball; a man who proposed to come back slow, bring the arms well through, roll the wrists, let the club-head lead and pivot on the ball of the left foot, being careful not to duck the right knee. A man, in short, whose driver would travel from point A to point B along dotted line C, winding up at point D, as recommended in all the golf books.

And so it proved. It was a superb drive. It was unhurried. It had rhythm. The arms were straight, the wrists cocked at the top of the swing, the elbows close to the body, the weight shifting at precisely the right moment from leg to leg, the wrists uncocking to give the final snap, the whole winding up with a perfect follow-through. A ball hit by a man doing all that sort of thing has to go places. Ziegfeld's did. It shot from the tee as if Walter Hagen were behind it, and was immediately swallowed up by the night.

"Watch it!" yelled Flo, apparently crediting those present with the patent double million magnifyin' gas microscopes of hextra power which Sam Weller claimed not to possess in place of eyes, and the caddies ran ahead, the gallery following. The hunt was up. Ziegfeld, his caddy, Freddie Zimmerman,

Guy, Plum and perhaps twenty pleasure-loving followers of sport were searching hither and thither about the fairway, striking matches and lining up in arm-linked squads. They combed the ground in every direction, but the ball was nowhere to be found.

Plum, meanwhile, having given up the search, had holed out, using his putter, not trying for distance but being content with smooth, wristy shots that travelled from eighteen inches to two feet. Ziegfeld, joining him on the ninth green, pulled out a roll of bills and extracted one. It was a beautiful thing with a yellow back on which was a portrait of President Garfield and a printed promise that it could be redeemed at the U. S. Treasury for one thousand dollars. The two authors gazed at it respectfully. It was the first thing of the sort they had ever seen.

They walked back to the Poinciana.

"What I like about show business is that you meet such interesting people," said Plum, taking out the thousand dollar bill and fondling it. "Flo Ziegfeld, to name but one."

"Yes, and Felix, Ray, Arch Selwyn, Charlie Dillingham, Hank Savage and the rest of them. I suppose that's why the theater draws one like a maggot, as Joe Urban would say."

They came to the hotel. Enquiring at the desk for mail, they were handed a cablegram. It was from Fabulous Felix, urging them to come to London. *The Girl Behind the Gun*, its title changed to *Kissing Time*, was to go into rehearsal in a week or two with a cast of stars—George Grossmith, Leslie Henson, Phyllis Dare, Yvonne Arnaud, Tom Walls, Stanley Holloway —a breathtaking roster of talent.

"*Kissing Time!*" said Guy. "My God, what a title! We'd better get over there quick and change it."

"It may not be so bad for London. 'Kissing Time' was the hit song of *Chu Chin Chow*."

They cabled Felix that they would come, but a few days later Guy had developed doubts.

"Suppose Flo suddenly comes through with the Miller show?"

"One of us could always jump on a boat and come back."

"One of us, yes. I suppose one would also be able to look after things in London."

Guy had personal reasons for not wanting to go to England at this time. He had hopes that he might be able to convince his prima donna that if Jack Spratt and his wife could make a go of it with such contrary tastes, why couldn't they? She was still in Mexico and there was no hint of an early return. Unless things were taken in hand their romance seemed destined to dwindle to extinction in a dismal and occasional exchange of picture postcards.

"All right," said Plum. "You stay here. You can keep in touch with Flo, and I can do anything that needs to be done in London."

A week later he and Ethel sailed for Southampton on the "Majestic."

· 6 ·

Guy went to see them off, joining the crowd at the end of the pier and waving as the queen of the White Star fleet turned from the pack of bustling tugs and moved slowly down stream. A couple unrecognizable at the distance were waving. They looked like Plum and Ethel. Guy waved back, then turned away disconsolately. When he returned to his Fifty-seventh Street apartment, he was conscious of a lost feeling. For the first time since he and Plum had met and formed their partnership he faced the ups and downs of their strange theater world alone, and he could not help feeling that it was the end of a phase—a period. Something told him that there would be no more Princess shows. Jerry had drifted away and was writing with other librettists, while Plum, he knew, was in process of capturing a public with his books and short stories that would give him a more secure position, a more solid standing than the theater ever could.

It depressed Guy to think that this separation might mean the end of a writing partnership which had been so pleasant and so successful. He knew that Plum had been feeling the need of refreshing his view of the English scene. England was the background of his stories, and he had said while they were waiting for the boat to sail that he might settle there for awhile. How long was "awhile"?

However, there was work to do, as always, and Guy got down to it and finished *The Five Million* and *Adam and Eva* and went on to tinker with a comedy George Middleton had written called *The Cave Girl*. He and George also wrote a rather strange play about the Oberammergau Passion Players, *The Light of the World*. He was steering away from musical comedy. He started work on a serious play all his own with a wartime background, *The Dark Angel*.

Letters passed back and forth between him and Plum. *Kissing Time*—the London management had insisted on keeping the title—had opened at the Winter Garden and was the success it was bound to be with that galaxy of stars. It ran for nineteen months.

Several times during that period Guy was on the point of boarding a liner and joining Plum, who had settled down in Kensington, but something always happened to stop him. Marguerite was singing with the Chicago opera, and he journeyed there and back between rehearsals and bouts of intensive writing at Atlantic City.

She still held off on their marriage, arguing that, for his own sake, he should find himself a wife who would fit into the pattern of his life without having any conflicting pattern of her own. It was on this note that they parted when, the Chicago Opera season ended, Marguerite started off on a tour with the St. Louis Symphony Orchestra while Guy returned to New York for the *Adam and Eva* rehearsals.

Then, with the seeming inconsequence associated with feminine decisions, came a letter saying that she had changed her mind. She told Guy she was ready to get married as fast as he could get himself out to San Francisco where her tour was ending. They would be free then to buy a car and spend an enchanting honeymoon roving the Pacific coast. Only pausing on his way to Grand Central to pay a quick visit to Tiffany's, Guy boarded the Twentieth Century.

The four-and-a-half-day journey seemed endless, but the Overland Limited, to which he had changed in Chicago, finally ambled through vast fields of artichokes into the delightful City of Hills. It was early and San Francisco was wrapped in its pearly morning mist. To Guy's surprise Marguerite was waiting on the platform.

"Come on," she said. "We've got time to go over to the Cliff House for breakfast."

" 'Got time'? What do you mean? Where are we going?"

"You're going back to New York on the noon train."

"What are you talking about?"

"You've had a wire from Jerry Kern and heaven knows how many from Ziegfeld. They want you at once for the Marilyn Miller show."

"Are you coming back with me?"

"I can't, darling. I've got two more concerts."

"Well then I shall chuck it."

"Oh, no, you won't. I'm not going to have you looking at me some morning when I've a cold in the head and saying: 'It was for that that I turned down the biggest opportunity of my life.' "

They took a taxi and breakfasted at a table looking down on the seal rocks. Guy saw in the seals a symbol of separation.

"Those aren't loving couples," he explained in answer to her question. "These are all females. The males never bother with California. They are up in the Misty Islands where the fishing is better."

"And don't these wives of theirs suffer from the same qualms as I do? Wondering whether the old boy isn't playing house with some little Misty Island chorus seal."

"Not a chance. The bull seals are sick to death of women once the mating season is over." Marguerite laughed.

"There's an idea there," she said.

She looked at the diamond wrist watch that had occasioned the stop at Tiffany's. It was time to go back to the station.

A little later Guy was staring out of the train window wondering who the heck it was that ate all those artichokes.

· 7 ·

The Marilyn Miller show was to be called *Sally*. Ziegfeld had originally planned three shows, one for Marilyn, one for Leon Errol and the third for Walter Catlett, but after *Sally* was completed he decided to have Errol co-star with Marilyn. This necessitated a complete reconstruction, and not more than a week after it was finished he sent for Guy and asked him to "put in" a part for Catlett which would be equal to Errol's but must take nothing away from it as Errol had already seen the script. Just one of those simple little rewrite jobs that are so common in the world of musical comedy. Guy, as he toiled away, found himself thinking enviously of Plum, who about now was probably writing a serial for the *Saturday Evening Post* which would be accepted, paid for on the nail and printed without the change of a comma. These novelists, he felt, had it soft. It was some slight consolation to him, as he courted brain fever in the effort to make the Catlett part screamingly funny but not so funny as to provoke growls of anger from his fellow-star, to reflect that it would hardly be possible not to reap a small fortune from a Miller-Errol-Catlett show with Kern's music, Ziegfeld's girls and Joe Urban's scenery to help it along. Ziegfeld authors might wind up sticking straws in their hair and cutting out paper dolls, but they could afford expensive nursing homes in which to do it.

Plum having written that it was impossible for him to leave England at the moment, Guy was working alone. He shipped a script over to his partner in London, and a certain amount of long distance collaboration took place. Plum wrote two or three lyrics, at the same time urging Guy to use "Bill" and extract "Church Around the Corner" from *The Little Thing*. He did use the latter, and the final scene was built around it, but Marilyn's tiny voice was incapable of singing "Bill," which needed—and finally got—a Helen Morgan. Two more lyrics were taken from a musical adaptation of *Brewster's Millions* which Jerry and Guy had started but abandoned. These— "Whip-poor-will" and "Look for the Silver Lining"—were by Buddy de Sylva. Two other lyrists, Clifford Grey and Anne Caldwell, also had lyrics included. It was all pretty haphazard and very different from the Princess days.

The script called for a funny woman to play opposite Catlett. Guy suggested Ada Lewis. Flo wouldn't hear of it.

"Make her young and cute," he said. "I hate women comics."

He gave the role to little Mary Hay, and again overruled the author in the matter of the casting of the elderly society matron who was mixed up with Sally's fortunes. Guy presented the names of several of the leading theatrical *grandes dames*, but Flo refused to consider them. He engaged Dolores, the lovely six-foot-one amazon who had been the central figure of the Ben Ali Hagan tableaux in the Follies.

"I don't want any old people in my shows," he said. "What you look at is just as important as what you listen to."

One argument, however, Guy did win. Ziegfeld wanted a "star" entrance for Marilyn, and Guy had introduced her as one of the six orphan girls who came on early in Act One in a line, all dressed alike in cotton frocks and laced-up ankle boots, to be inspected by the restaurant owner, who had applied to the orphanage for a dishwasher.

Ziegfeld hated the idea. So did Jerry Kern. But, of all people in the world, Guy found an ally in Marilyn, who might have been expected to be the first to recoil in horror at the suggestion that she should make an entrance like that.

"It's fine," she said. "Just right for my eccentric dance."

"We'll try it in Baltimore," said Flo grudgingly. "But be prepared to rewrite it for New York."

It did not have to be rewritten. It was an immediate success. A delighted gasp went up all over the theater when the last of the row of orphans was yanked out of the line by the restaurant owner and revealed herself as Marilyn. Charlie Case, the vaudeville comedian, used to tell a story in his act which culminated in the line, "He tore off his whiskers, and it was Jim!" Marilyn's entrance had much the same effect, not only in Baltimore but two weeks later when she made it at the New Amsterdam.

But Flo had been right about Dolores. Not only was she lovely to look at, she was the perfect foil for Errol, the Balkan Grand Duke who had been thrown out of his country by a revolution and was making a living as a waiter. When the pair emerged together from "The Little Church Around the Corner," they were greeted with a storm of applause. The finale was the number that Plum had written for *The Little Thing*.

> *There's a church around the corner that's waiting for us:*
> *It's just above Madison Square.*
> *I'll borrow a dollar and buy a clean collar,*
> *And then I'll be meeting you there.*
> *There'll be crowds in the pews and excitement and fuss,*
> *For I mean to be married in style,*
> *And the girls will go dizzy and whisper "Who is he?"*
> *When I start to step up the aisle.*

153

Dear little, dear little Church Around the Corner,
   Where so many lives have begun,
Where folks without money see nothing that's funny
   In two living cheaper than one.
Our hearts to each other we've trusted:
   We're busted, but what do we care?
     For a moderate price
     You can start dodging rice
      At the Church Around the Corner,
      It's just around the corner,
      The corner of Madison Square.

Few who were there on that opening night will ever forget the reception that was accorded the little star when she came down the steps of the church in the lovely lace bridal robe that Ziegfeld had dressed her in. Many things contributed to the magic of that night—Jerry's wonderful score; the Follies beauties in their lovely costumes; the Urban scenery and still more the Urban lighting; the two comedians, each turning in the best performance of his career. But it was Marilyn that really mattered, Marilyn who gave to the play a curious enchantment that no reproduction in other lands or other mediums ever captured.

· 8 ·

"Church Around the Corner" had a significance that carried beyond its role in *Sally*. It served as admonishment and happy omen for a real life wedding. Marguerite and Guy got married with Jerry as best man in lieu of Plum.

"How are the mighty fallen," said Jerry when he and Eva were sipping champagne with the newly-married pair. " 'Marriage means giving up your comfort and your ideal of woman, in trying to be some woman's ideal of man.' Line by Guy

Bolton. 'Marriage isn't a process for prolonging the life of love but for mummifying its corpse,' a further comment on the institution from the same source. 'Marriage is the net in which the jade snares the jaded.' 'Marriage—' "

"Listen," said Guy. "Just because I write of a cynical woman-hater is no reason I should subscribe to his views. My opinion of woman as the priceless pearl of creation is well known."

"Let us trust," said Marguerite, "that I'm the last bead on the string."

"I wish to propose a toast," said Guy. "Here's to the author of 'Church Around the Corner.' "

"You'll be seeing the old boy soon."

"Let's hope," said Guy.

Actually it was five weeks later that they sailed for England on the "Olympic," a delay occasioned by discussions with Max Marcin concerning a comedy melodrama which he and Guy were writing together. Among their fellow passengers were Charlie Chaplin and Eddie Knoblock, the author of *Kismet*.

At the ship's concert Marguerite sang and Chaplin did a pantomimic act in which he portrayed an out-of-work actor applying for a job. As the manager, played by Knoblock, described each aspect of the character, Chaplin became successively humble, aggressive, charming, ultra-aristocratic. Told he was too short for the role, he seemingly grew several inches taller. Questioned as to his romantic qualifications, he hurled himself into the manager's lap. Finally he is asked to run through a scene in which he is supposed to come home and find his wife in the arms of his best friend. In a frenzy of jealous rage he is called on to kill his betrayer. The manager shakes his head and says he fears Charlie can never be sufficiently convincing in the scene, whereupon the actor, determined to win the coveted role, seizes the manager by the throat. When he at last relaxes his grip and turns away to get his hat and stick, the manager is a corpse on the floor. Charlie, turning back with an ingratiating smile to receive his applause, was Chaplin at his best. His surprise on seeing the empty chair, his consternation on discovering the body that has slipped down under the desk were done as only Chaplin could do it. And then his famous shuffling exit, looking back over his shoulder and raising his hat to the corpse. It made a perfect finish.

This was the star item, and after it was over the chairman of the concert committee rose to make the usual report of the amount collected for the seamen's charities and to thank the artists who had given their services. He was a rubicund north-country cotton man. His wife, fat and jolly like himself, sat in the front row.

"This is my fourteenth crossing," he began. "Best crossing I ever had. Best crossing, finest bunch of people."

Applause.

"Of course, thirteenth crossing was mighty fine, too, eh, Mother?"

"Was that," agreed his wife.

"And, by goom, there was nothing wrong with the twelfth crossing. Remember twelfth crossing, Mother?"

Mother said she did.

"And eleventh crossing," he went on. "Never will forget eleventh crossing. What a crowd! What fun we had! Good old eleventh crossing."

There was a pause. The audience saw that his face had lost its jovial smile and was twisted in what appeared to be agony.

"But tenth crossing. . . . Tenth crossing." His voice broke. "Do you mind tenth crossing, Mother?"

His round red face suddenly crumpled up, and tears began to fall from his eyes. His wife got up and went to him. He was led away sobbing. Everyone stared at everyone else, aghast.

"What the hell do you suppose happened on that tenth crossing?" said Eddie Knoblock. "Shall we ever know?"

Mother came wheezing back to where she had left her bag.

She took out a ball of wool and started knitting composedly.

"It wasn't tenth crossing," she said. "It was ninth. Ollerenshaw never could count straight."

· 9 ·

Two days later they steamed up the Solent, Guy, a confirmed Anglophile, going into ecstasies over the greenness of the grass and the soft gray-blue of the sky. Even the sea gulls, he insisted, seemed friendlier than other sea gulls. American sea gulls, he said, acted as if they didn't give a damn whether you landed or whether you didn't, but English sea gulls kept circling round mewing a chorus of welcome.

The first thing Guy and Marguerite did after depositing their bags at the Berkeley was to go in search of Plum. But when they reached the South Kensington block of flats where the Wodehouses had spent the winter, it was only to discover that they were no longer there. Also they had apparently left no forwarding address.

"Where's the nearest book shop?" said Guy.

It was unquestionably the place to enquire. Plum could live five years in a spot and be unknown to the liquor store, the garage, the milkman and the policeman on the beat, but he would be the buddy of whoever ran the book shop. As Charles Lamb said of Godwin, he had read more books not worth reading than any man in England.

As Guy had surmised, the woman at the book shop had the dope. Mrs. Wodehouse was in the country looking for a house in which to spend the summer. Mr. Wodehouse was, however, still in town and had been in that very morning and bought a couple of Edgar Wallaces, which seemed to suggest the intention of spending a quiet evening at home curled up with them. He was living in some service flats, having taken over the apartment of a friend who had gone to Edinburgh to get married. She was not able to supply the number nor the name of the owner. All she could say was that Mr. Wodehouse was there somewhere.

It was dusk by the time they arrived at journey's end. The building was a large one, and they stood on the pavement looking up at its unresponsive façade. As they did so, there came fluttering down, falling at their feet a small white oblong object. It was an envelope, stamped and sealed. Guy picked it up and turned it over. He looked at the address and emitted a cry such as the ex-Mrs. Arden gave when she thought she saw Enoch's dead face peering through the window.

The letter was addressed:

> Mr. Guy Bolton,
> 12 East 57th Street,
> New York, U.S.A.

"Do you see what I see?" gasped Guy. " 'The Miracle of Lowndes Square.' One can't explain it, of course, except so far as to say in a broad, general way that it must have something to do with the fourth dimension. I believe spiritualists call these things 'apports.' They flutter down from the ceiling at seances. But where are you going?"

"Upstairs," said Marguerite. "There's a lighted window on the top floor, the only one that is."

They went in again and rang the end bell, which was labelled "McPhail"—just the sort of name a man would have who had gone to Edinburgh to get married. They toiled up four long flights of stairs. The door of the flat was standing open. Plum was sitting at a desk, writing a letter.

There were great celebrations. To both members of the firm it seemed an age since they had parted on the White Star pier. It was only after much picking up of the threads that Guy said:

"Oh, by the way, I got your letter." He pulled it out of his pocket and showed it. "What an extraordinary thing, it falling out of the window just as we were standing there."

"It didn't fall out. I threw it out."

"*Threw* it out?"

Plum seemed surprised that this should be considered in any way unusual.

"I throw all my letters out of windows. If you'll excuse me for a moment, I'd like to get this one off. It's rather important. I've only got to stick it in its envelope."

He did so, stamped it and tossed it through the window.

"You see," he explained, as he did so. "Someone always picks it up and posts it. It saves me sweating up and down four flights of stairs every time I want to mail a letter."

"But suppose somebody stole the stamp and threw the letter away," said Marguerite.

"Oh, they wouldn't."

"No," said Guy. "The English have their faults—they go about calling plays *Kissing Time*, to give an instance that springs to the mind—but they are honest. You hang your gold bracelet on a tree and come back a year later and it's still there."

"Really?" said Marguerite, impressed.

"It's some time ago that Guy's talking about," said Plum. "Ninth century. King Alfred."

"Look," said Guy, "I wish you would write me a letter while I'm here. I would like to show it to people at home as a proof of English honesty."

"Where are you living?"

"At the Berkeley right now, but we're taking a little flat of some people we met on the boat. It's in South Audley Street."

It was the second day after Guy and Marguerite had moved into the flat that the buzzer sounded. Guy pressed the button and waited for the caller to arrive. It was two and a half flights up, and the man who appeared at the door was somewhat out of breath.

"Are you Mr. Bolton?"

"Yes."

"Letter for you," said the man. "I picked it up in Lowndes Square. Oh, no, sir. I don't want anything, thank you, sir, I was coming right by here anyway."

When he had gone, Guy went to the telephone and called Plum.

"I have your letter," he said.

"What!" said Plum. "Already? That's what I call service. I only threw it out of the window twenty minutes ago!"

Chapter Eleven

G UY WAS HAVING a busy honeymoon. He had hoped to be able to buy a car and tour the British Isles at his leisure, but a playwright's program is always subject to changes without notice. Work fell on him out of the skies, like Plum's letter. Gilbert Miller was putting on *Polly with a Past* at the St. James, and he suddenly decided to advance the opening date and called on Guy to attend rehearsals.

Miller had assembled a brilliant cast for *Polly*—Edna Best, a newly-arrived star who had made a great success in a play called *Brown Sugar*, Edith Evans, Claude Rains, C. Aubrey Smith, Henry Kendall, Helen Haye, Donald Calthrop and a young man named Noel Coward. Altogether quite an array of talent and one that would be on the expensive side today.

"The London theater is wonderful," said Guy. He had dropped in to pay a morning call on Plum.

"Surely not as vital as New York?"

"I'm worried about New York—not the plays but the way the men up top are running things. Take this ticket speculating. The managers could stop it in a minute if they wanted to, but half of them are getting rake-offs. They're driving people away from the theater. That boy and his best girl that we used to talk about can't afford to come any more. We're getting the out-of-town buyers—tickets bought for them at inflated prices by the firms they do business with—and the new rich who sprang up during the war. And the kind of audience you get largely determines the kind of plays you get."

"The musicals are better in New York."

"Yes, but the costs are sky-rocketing. They tell me you have to have close on fifty thousand dollars in the kitty to put on a big musical today."

"I wonder what our old friend Hank Savage would say to that."

"Even an *Oh, Boy!* would cost between thirty and thirty-five thousand. In London things are reasonable. And the theaters look so much better here with everyone dressing and most of the men in white ties. It seems as if the audiences are out to enjoy themselves. They don't have that grim I-wonder-if-I'm-going-to-get-my money's-worth attitude of the people who have paid too much for their seats."

"How about Marguerite, is she enjoying London as much as you seem to be doing?"

"Not quite perhaps. She's popped over to Paris. I shall go and join her as soon as the *Sally* cast is settled."

"Since you're so keen on these English plays you've been seeing, you'd better come and lunch with me at the Dramatists Club and meet some of the nibs who write them."

The Dramatists Club had no clubhouse. Its members met once a month in the private dining room of a hotel in Northumberland Avenue, where they lunched and exchanged views. Its president at this time was Sir Arthur Wing Pinero.

Today there was a distinguished gathering. J. M. Barrie was in the seat next to Pinero and on his other side the club's secretary, Ian Hay, who had sprung into fame during the war with his *The First Hundred Thousand*. Knoblock was there. He called a greeting to Guy.

"But the tenth crossing!" he said, and puckered up his face.

The man next to Knoblock, a rather colorless looking little fellow with blondish, graying hair, asked him what he was talking about, and Knoblock turned to tell him the story.

"Who's that?" whispered Guy.

"Jacobs."

"Not W. W.?"

"There's only one Jacobs."

"There certainly is," said Guy reverently. He knew practically all Jacobs by heart. Sam, Ginger, Bob Pretty and the rest of them were his familiar friends. If there had been a deliberate attempt to thrill him, they could not have done better. Louis Parker came in, and with him Clemence Dane, and shortly afterwards Cyril McNiele, who wrote under the name of Sapper. His *Bulldog Drummond*, with Gerald du Maurier starring, had just opened and was a tremendous success. Of those who had big hits running in London only Willie Maugham was missing.

As they were sitting over coffee and cigars, Barrie rose, looking, even when standing, not much taller than his sitting neighbors.

"I know speeches are not in order," he said with his faint Scotch burr, "but I haven't been to one of these meetings for some time and I've got to tell you of the wee little thrill I always get when I come here. It's some years now since we founded this club, Arthur here and poor Haddon Chambers, whom we've just lost, and Harry Esmond and Kipling and Hornung and one or two more. We were all pretty young then and we talked a lot about the things we'd written and the things we were going to write. There was one fellow talked more than all the rest of us put together. A tall, Irish chap with a red beard . . . I've often wondered what became of him."

Guy asked the man seated next to him, if it was true, as Barrie had seemed to imply, that Shaw never came to these lunches and, if so, why.

"There was a lot of unpleasantness during the war," his neighbor told him. "He wrote stuff praising the Germans and it infuriated a good many people, Kipling particularly. The atmosphere got so unpleasant that Shaw finally resigned. Pinero announced it at the next meeting. 'Mr. Shaw has handed in his resignation,' he said. Then paused for a moment, 'Mr. Shaw's resignation,' he added, 'is as nothing compared to ours.' "

· 2 ·

Sally was presented at the Winter Garden in the autumn of 1921 following on the long run *Kissing Time*. The management was again that of Grossmith and Laurillard, and discussions regarding book adjustments, casting and other matters called for daily meetings with George Grossmith, who thus took his place in the Bolton-Wodehouse gallery of theatrical managers.

"Tell me about Grossmith," said Guy one morning.

"What do you want to know about him?"

"He's a strange bird compared with our New York gang."

"George isn't only a manager, he's one of London's top musical comedy actors."

"Yes, I know. He's a brilliant light comedian, but he can't have been so hot in the Donald Brian part in *Kissing Time*."

"Hotter than he was as the Prince in an Austrian operetta I once caught him in. The trouble with George is that if there's a prince in the show you can't keep him away from it with an injunction. Show him a white uniform with gold frogs across the chest and a lot of medals, and he starts making mewing noises."

"A snob perchance?"

"A priceless snob, but the looking-up kind, not the looking-down. The looking-up snob longs to know a duke, the looking-down variety can't afford to know a dustman. George reads himself to sleep with Burke's *Peerage*, but he'll go pub-crawling with the stage doorman."

"I like him."

"Everybody likes him. Women especially."

"Oh, he's a ladies' man?"

"Second to none. I heard a funny story about George the other day. I don't know if it's true or not, but it sounds just like him. He had gone to see the Grand National and, strolling through the paddock, met his friend Lord Latham, who introduced him to a very pretty woman, Lady something—I can't quite remember—Mudge—that's not quite it."

"Peeress?"

"No, wife of a baronet—but that would be enough to endear her to George. They got along together like ham and eggs and, when she said that racing bored her and that she couldn't bear seeing the horses fall at the jumps, he gallantly insisted on remaining with her in the paddock during the running of the race. The friendship ripened on the journey back to London and when they parted she invited George to come and spend the next week end at the old home. She said her husband would be delighted. A touch of gout had kept him away from Aintree but she was sure George would brighten him up.

"George accepted but when he met the gentleman he had misgivings. The Bart had clearly got it in for him. He had heard about the meeting in the paddock and he started right in asking George why the devil he had gone halfway across England to see a race and then chosen to turn his back on it and talk to a woman instead. This had evidently aroused his worst suspicions.

"The dinner was a ghastly affair with the host whipping the carving knife back and forth across the steel until his wife complained that he was setting her teeth on edge. George tried to talk about the house, which was ancient to the point of moldering. Hosts are usually to be drawn out on the subject of the family manse. 'Fascinating old place,' he said.

" 'A lot of people have died in it,' said Bart darkly.

" 'Probably from the damp,' said his wife. 'It's the dampest place I was ever in.'

"This disturbed George. He has a horror of damp. However, he beamed as cheerfully as he could manage. He was glad when the time came for bed.

"But he wasn't glad long. It suddenly came back to him what his hostess had said about the place being damp. The room they had put him in smelled musty, and he was sure the sheets must be wringing. They felt all right to the hand, but you never know with sheets. They fool you into thinking they're dry, and then turn right round and start giving you rheumatism, lumbago and pneumonia."

"I thought it was an established custom before getting into any bed in England to make a test for dampness by putting a hand mirror between the sheets?"

"It is. And don't think old hypochondriac George didn't think of it, but unfortunately the only mirror in the room was a thing six feet by eight, fastened to the wall with brass nails. Then he remembered something. He was pretty sure he had seen a mirror in a carved frame standing on the piano in the drawing room. And what could be simpler than to toddle downstairs and fetch it? With the Grossmiths to think is to act. He set off in his white silk pajamas with the gold frogs across the chest, got the mirror and started back again. As he reached the landing, a door was suddenly thrown open and there was the Bart, looking like Othello.

" 'What the devil are you doing, prowling about the house at this time of night in your pajamas?' he enquired, clenching and unclenching his fists, his eyes burning with a green flame.

" 'I came to get this,' said George, exhibiting the mirror.

"Only it wasn't a mirror. It was a photograph of Lady Mudge."

"Good Lord! What happened then?"

"I don't know," said Plum. "That's where the story ends."

· 3 ·

The chief problem in casting *Sally* was, of course, to find a Sally. There were no Marilyn Millers in England—and only

one in America. It was finally decided to engage Dorothy
Dickson.

Dorothy was an old friend of Guy's and Plum's. Ray Comstock had discovered her dancing with her husband, Carl
Hyson, at the College Inn in Chicago, and had signed them up
as a specialty dance team for *Oh, Boy!*. Their success had been
sensational. Dorothy used to make up with a round spot of
rouge on each cheek like a painted doll, and accentuated this
effect by wearing a little Dutch cap. She was prettier than any
of her rivals in the field of ballroom dancing and, good though
Carl Hyson was, this was the only team—except the Astaires—
in which the female partner was the equal of the male. Vernon
Castle, Maurice, De Marco and the others made it their business to show off the girl they were dancing with, but, had
they wanted to, they could just as easily have shown her up.
Not even the best of them could have done that to Dorothy.

She was ambitious to become something more than a ballroom dancer and took vocal and acting lessons, but the first
two parts she played were in failures—*Girl o' Mine* and *Rock-
a-bye Baby*. She then went to London, rejoining Carl, and
appeared in the Cochran revue, *London, Paris and New York*.
It was not an impressive record, and both Ziegfeld and Kern
were vehemently against entrusting her with such a vitally
important role as Sally, Ziegfeld eclipsing himself in the matter
of violent cables. Guy, however, remained firm and insisted
on her playing the part.

He wanted to get the matter settled so that he could get
over to Paris. He had had a letter from Marguerite in which
she told of an offer from the Opera Comique of an engagement that would assign her the top lyric soprano roles, Louise,
Manon, Mimi and Butterfly. He knew such an opportunity was
her dearest ambition.

"Are you going to say 'yes'?" Plum asked him.

"There's nothing else I can do. I can't help remembering

what she said to me when I wanted to chuck *Sally* and stay in California. 'I don't want you to be looking at me in years to come and saying—for that I gave up my biggest opportunity.' "

"I was afraid it was going to be like that, two ambitious people."

"Oh, well, I can pop back and forth—London, Paris and New York—not a bad life."

"You've got to go to New York for that farce-melodrama, don't you?"

"*The Nightcap*? Yes. I've only a week or two to spend with Marguerite."

Guy raised the question of when they might hope to get together on another show. Plum suggested that they should reunite the old triumvirate, Bolton, Wodehouse and Kern. Guy said it couldn't be a Princess show. Jerry had set his face against writing again for the tiny playhouse.

"If we can't have Jerry, who else is there?"

"Irving."

"Fine, but he wouldn't want me. He writes his own lyrics."

"Do you remember that boy who was rehearsal pianist at the Century?"

"You mean the lad who could make a piano sound like a whole jazz orchestra?"

"That's the one. He said he'd like to show us some of his music."

"Every rehearsal pianist wants to show you his music."

"I know, but I was with some people not long ago and they talked about this chap and someone said he was a genius."

"You're sure it was the same kid?"

"Yes, I'd clean forgotten his name but when they said it I remembered it. I've written it down so I won't forget it again and when I get back I think I'll look him up."

"What was the name?"

"George Gershwin."

"That's right, I recall him now. Pink cheeks, nice smile, a

terrifically strong beard that even the closest shave couldn't conceal."

"If I decide he'll do, will you come over?"

"Yes, but try to get Jerry. After all there's only one Kern."

"True. Still, who knows? Maybe there's only one George Gershwin."

• 4 •

Guy went to Paris. The opera engagement offered to Marguerite was for the autumn. He saw how eager she was to do it and told her to accept. It was for a year with an option for a second one.

"You'll just have to commute," she said.

"I know how you hate to leave the stage for more than a minute but you'll have to when the baby arrives."

"Not necessarily. Tonelli told me he was born in a dressing room at the Scala during a performance of *Traviata.*"

"Don't tell me the lady was playing Violetta?"

"I wouldn't be surprised, dear. Crinolines you know. It's *the* opera for expectant prima donnas."

They went to Italy—Rome, Florence and Venice—returning to Paris where Marguerite was due for rehearsals. *The Nightcap* rehearsals were starting in New York. Guy phoned Plum to say goodbye, Plum again urging him to try and re-establish the Princess team. He sailed from Cherbourg on the "Olympic," the ship that he and Marguerite called their honeymoon boat.

Meanwhile P. G. had retreated to the charming village of Rogate in the Petersfield district and was embarked on that intensive program of novel writing which turned out in rapid succession *Three Men and a Maid, Mostly Sally, Jeeves, Leave It to Psmith, The Heart of a Goof* and *The Small Bachelor,* which last named was *Oh, Lady, Lady* in new guise.

Just to keep his hand in he wrote the lyrics for *The Golden Moth* for which Fred Thompson supplied the book.

The Nightcap opened early and then Guy, who happened to be in Atlantic City, saw the first performance of a show called *Tangerine* which was written by the head of the New York Theatre Guild, Lawrence Langner. Langner had received some help from Philip Bartholomae but it wasn't sufficient. The show fell flat on its face. Carl Carleton, the husband of Edith Day, was the manager. He asked Guy if he thought the piece could be saved. Guy thought it could, and he was right. His revised version ran more than three hundred performances.

Guy barely waited for the opening night, then sailed for Europe. *Sally* was already in rehearsal in London so there was no time to travel via Paris. He wired Marguerite asking her to meet him in London but when he got there he found a letter saying that she was singing *Traviata*. The role sounded significant. She begged him to come over. He phoned and told her he must stick with rehearsals for at least a week or so.

Plum was back in London, living in a house in Onslow Square next door to the one that had been the home of William Makepeace Thackeray. When Guy went to see him, the door was opened by a butler. P. G. explained that this wasn't swank.

"It's business," he said. "This chap is an author's model."

"A what?"

"Come, come, you've heard of artists' models. Audrey Munson, if you remember, was one. Well, he's an author's model. I'm writing some stories about a butler. At least, he's not a butler, he's a valet, but the two species are almost identical. I study this bird and make copious notes. Do you like the name Jeeves?"

"Is that what he's called?"

"No, that's the name of the man in my stories. This one is Robinson. You couldn't sell a butler called Robinson to the public. Not box office. For a long time I was stumped for a name, then I remembered a cricketer in the years before the war called Jeeves. Played for Gloucestershire, I think. Calling a character after a county cricketer is lucky. Sherlock and Holmes were both county cricketers. I believe Doyle had decided on Sherrinford Holmes, when he suddenly thought of Mordecai Sherlock, who used to keep wicket for Yorkshire. Jeeves seemed to me just right for the sort of bloke I wanted."

"What sort of a bloke is this Jeeves of yours?"

"He's omniscient. And, what is more, as Abe Erlanger would say, he knows everything. Robinson's like that. You can't broach a subject he isn't up on. Think of one."

"Spats."

"Too easy."

"Spiders."

"Right." Plum pressed the bell. "Do you know anything about spiders?"

"If you wish to live and thrive, let the spider run alive."

"Damned silly saying. You wouldn't thrive very long with a family of tarantulas running around. Oh, Robinson."

"Sir?"

"Mr. Bolton is writing a play with an entomologist in it and he wants some inside stuff about spiders."

"From what aspect, sir?"

"Their domestic life and all that sort of thing."

"The domestic life of the spider is something that does not bear a close scrutiny, sir."

"Things not too good in the home?"

"No, sir. The spider's is a matriarchal society. The husband, if we may call him such, has but one function . . . if I may put it that way."

"Carry on. Mr. Bolton understands. I've told him all about the bees and the flowers."

"When this function is fulfilled, the lady has him for dinner."

"Nothing formal, I suppose? Just a black tie?"

"I speak in a literal sense, sir."

"You mean she eats him?"

"Precisely, sir. As Shakespeare so well put it, 'Oh, curse of marriage, that we can call these delicate creatures ours, but not their appetites.' "

"Would you say 'delicate' was the—"

"*Mot juste*, sir? Possibly not, sir. One confesses that one is inclined to look askance at the female spider and to view her activities with concern. She deceives the male with a tenderness which in the light of what is to follow one cannot but regard as in dubious taste. She flirts and plays, inviting him to swing with her on a long thread, holding him gently in her arms."

"And all the time she is planning—"

"Precisely, sir."

"Good God! Women! . . . I hope you're listening, Guy."

"Would there be anything further, sir?"

"No, that will be all. Thank you, Robinson."

"Thank *you*, sir."

The door closed.

"There you are," said Plum. "And it would have been just the same if I had asked him about anything else."

"Damn useful," commented Guy. "Saves you a lot of thumbing through the old Encyc. Brit."

"Yes, but I'm a bit sick of book-writing. The sight of you brings the light of battle to my eyes. How about some more Princess shows?"

"No good, I'm afraid. Even Ray has weakened on the Princess. Costs are too high. But he says he'd love to start on a new series at the Longacre."

"Then let's go."

"But Jerry won't write for the Longacre. He says it's too small."

"Heavens, what does the man want—the Hippodrome?"

"The Globe is his bailiwick."

"Dillingham, eh? He'd never understand an intimate show. He'd want to put in a troupe of performing collies."

They left it there for the time being. Guy was busy with a

comedy he had named *Polly Preferred*. He also had another on the stocks that he called *Chickenfeed*. It was the idea on which P. G. had touched when he referred to *Lysistrata*, a strike of wives, wives who were sick of handouts and "What did you do with that five dollars I gave you Saturday?" They struck for the principle of wages for wives.

"Sounds pretty good," said Plum when Guy told him about it. "What's *Polly Preferred?*"

"A chorus kid ambitious to be something runs into an out-of-work publicity man in the Automat. To finance her career he turns her into a company, sells shares in her."

"Yes, I like that. Better idea than *Polly-with-a-Past*—more modern."

Sally opened at the Winter Garden. The only mishap was that Dorothy's toe-slipper came off just as the ballet started. Twice she tried to slip it back on and the audience applauded. Up to that point she had turned in a charming performance. In the dressing room scene that followed she was delightful.

The next morning, after a breakfast of excellent notices, supplemented by a little light refreshment, Guy took off for Paris. Marguerite had reluctantly left the stage, her last performance having taken place ten days previously.

"Even then you were taking chances on being a second Madame Tonelli."

They dined in the seclusion of Marguerite's studio apartment in the Val du Grace. The phone rang. It was from London. Plum reported a complete sell-out. The show had gone like a breeze, the only mishap was that Dot's toe-slipper had come off.

"But, good Lord," said Guy, "is this going to happen every night?"

"Every night, old boy, and at matinees. But don't worry. That pathetic slipping slipper has become one of the high spots of the show."

"She can stop the show with any other kind of dancing."

"She'll stop it in the ballet spot too before she's through. Don't worry."

"It's your birthday this week, isn't it?"

"Yes, this coming Sunday, why?"

"Nothing. I just had an idea."

His idea was right, the baby was born on Sunday. He couldn't call it Pelham so they compromised on Pamela, Pamela Marguerite.

A week or two later Guy had a cable from Sam Harris. It asked him to get together with the Duncan Sisters. He commissioned Guy to write a show for them. Irving Berlin would supply the score. Guy wired back saying he would like to work with Plum. Sam cabled to go ahead only Irving would do his own lyrics.

Guy was delighted. The young lady who had arrived on Plum's birthday seemed to have been a happy omen. He called Plum and told him the news.

"The Duncan Sisters? You can't miss with them. I saw them the other night. They're terrific."

"I'm glad you're so enthusiastic. What about you coming in with me?"

"Good Lord! Do you want me?"

"I sure do."

"Then I'm with you. We can write the show here and then sail."

"But how about Jeeves?"

"Jeeves can wait," said Plum.

Chapter Twelve

T HE Duncan Sisters, in case the present generation needs reminding of it, were two small girls who created the impression of being about twelve years old. Their names were Rosetta and Vivian, though their friends, and their friends were legion, called them Heim and Jake. Their forte was the delivery of numbers like "The Bull-Frog Patrol" in close harmony, and they were—there is no other word—terrific. The revue they were starring in at the Royalty was called *Pins and Needles* and was about London's biggest success, crowded at every performance.

Guy invited them to have supper with him at the Embassy Club. Plum warned him not to, saying that a formal business meeting in the afternoon with pencils and notebooks was the right approach, but Guy would make it the Embassy, a place he adored. Plum said he would not be present. Guy could have the talented artists all to himself.

Guy went to see their show and after a due interval to permit them to change and remove their stage make-up presented himself at their dressing room. He found them ready to leave, but they had not changed their revue costumes, nor had they removed their stage make-up. All they had done was stick huge bows in their hair, one pink, one blue. In the final scene of the revue they had worn short dresses and socks. They were still wearing short dresses and socks. They looked like something left over from a defunct kindergarten, and Guy was conscious of a sinking feeling. The Embassy Club in those days, when the great Luigi presided over it, was the smartest, most exclusive supper place in London, posh to the eyebrows.

Dukes and duchesses jostled countesses and earls, and it was a very exceptional evening when you could throw a brick in it without beaning some member of the royal family. It seemed to Guy that in such surroundings the Sisters Duncan and their socks were likely to make something of a sensation.

Propped up against the wall of the dressing room was a huge floral horseshoe. It was taller than the Duncan Sisters. It was taller than a Duncan Sister mounted on another Duncan Sister's shoulders, and he gazed at it with a wild surmise.

"What's all this?" he asked, and Heim explained that it was a present from their manager, Mr. de Courville, tonight being the two-hundredth performance of the show.

They were now ready to be escorted to the taxi which Guy had asked the stage doorman to have in readiness. Heim spoke to this worthy as they came out, and he ducked back into the theater, emerging a few moments later accompanied by the stage manager and the assistant stage manager. They were cautiously negotiating the horseshoe through the stage door.

"We're not taking that with us?" faltered Guy.

"Of course we're taking it with us. We're not leaving all those lovely flowers here to die."

"But what will we do with it at the Embassy?"

"We'll have it at our table—it'll look cute."

"And another thing," said Jake. "It's lucky. Seems like a good omen to have it there when we sit down to talk about the new show."

Guy tottered on his base. If there was one thing from which his sensitive nature recoiled, it was looking conspicuous, and it was plain that he was scheduled to look even more conspicuous than when giving Marguerite a bite to eat in those Greek reach-me-downs of hers which had so intimidated Plum, the Athenian stole and the serpent armlets. Broodingly he helped the girls into the cab while the driver and the stage manager secured the horseshoe on the trunk stand. He was able to have a brief word with the driver before they started off.

"Ten bob extra," was what he said, and the driver nodded intelligently.

When the cab drew up at its destination, the girls gave a simultaneous cry of dismay.

"It's gone—the horseshoe!"

"My God!" cried Guy, shocked to the core.

The driver was apologetic.

"Sorry, guv'nor, it slipped off and another cab ran over it. Didn't think it was worth while stoppin' to pick it up."

Guy gave the faithful fellow a pound note, and they went into the club.

"It's a bad omen for the new show," said Jake Duncan as they took their seats.

"Yes," agreed her sister. "It's put me clean off it. When you've got a good luck horseshoe and it falls off the taxi, that means something."

"Yessir," echoed Jake, "that sure means something. Maybe we'd best get busy on that Topsy and Eva thing."

Guy was aware of a sinister foreboding. What, he wondered, was the Topsy and Eva thing? He did not like the sound of it.

· 2 ·

Sitting Pretty was the title of the show. They wrote it in Plum's study in Onslow Square. Its central figures were two sisters in an orphan asylum, one of whom was adopted by a wealthy old man whose passion was eugenics. He had already adopted a boy, and it was his aim to marry these two, not knowing that Horace, the boy, was in partnership with an amiable burglar named Uncle Joe who insinuated him into rich houses to prepare the way for him by leaving doors and windows open.

Irving Berlin had written that he had no objection to Plum's contributing a lyric or two if he felt so inclined, and, a comedy song being needed for Uncle Joe, Plum attended to it with a number called "Tulip Time in Sing-Sing."

In a Broadway haunt of pleasure
Where they dine and tread the measure
A young burglar was becoming slowly fried.
When the waiter saw this mobster
Sitting sobbing in his lobster,
He stole up and asked him softly why he cried.
And the yegg said with a quiver
"There's a college up the river
Which I yearn for. That's the reason of my gloom.
For the little birds each Spring sing
Aren't you coming back to Sing-Sing
Now it's April and the tulips are a-bloom?

"When it's Tulip Time in Sing-Sing,
Oh, it's there that I would be:
There are gentle hearts in Sing-Sing
Watching and waiting for me:
Take me back, take me back,
Give me lots of rocks to crack
With my pals of the class of '99:
For I'd rather have neuralgia
Than be tortured by nostalgia
For that dear old-fashioned prison of mine."

Early in the autumn Guy returned with Plum and Ethel to New York.

"Look," said Sam Harris, when they reported at his office, "I'm afraid there's been a hold-up. Irving hasn't been able to work on the score because this *Music Box Revue* has been taking up all his time. I'm going to do *Sitting Pretty* all right, but it will have to be next season. The delay doesn't mean much to you boys, but it does to the Duncan girls, and they've asked me if I will consent to their filling in by doing a thing of their own out on the Coast. I don't have to say yes, because I've got them under contract and I can put them in the Music

Box till we're ready for them, but I don't see any harm in letting them do this thing of theirs if they want to, do you?"

Guy and Plum thought it would be a good idea. If the girls appeared in the *Music Box Revue,* it would take a lot of the freshness out of *Sitting Pretty.*

"What is this thing out on the Coast?" asked Guy.

"Oh, it's some idea of their own that they say they've had for quite awhile. They've written the numbers themselves. It's a sort of half amateur affair. *Topsy and Eva* they're calling it. It's a sort of comic *Uncle Tom's Cabin.*"

Guy's head gave a side jerk as if he had suddenly received a left jab to the jaw. *"Topsy and Eva!"* He recalled the night at the Embassy with a dim foreboding.

"What's the matter?" asked Plum noting his friend's silence.

"I was just thinking. *Uncle Tom's Cabin*—it's never missed yet."

· 3 ·

Some premonition of disaster seemed to be disturbing Irving Berlin when they dined with him two days after seeing Sam.

The dinner took place at Irving's apartment on West Forty-sixth Street. This was a novel duplex penthouse that had taken his fancy. He had had to buy the building in order to get it, but that sort of thing was a trifle to Irving. Like Fabulous Felix, he believed in doing himself well.

There was a broad corridor that descended in a series of steps, each step an eight foot square platform, to the big living room that faced the street. Molded glass panels by Lalique lighted this handsome passage. These were fringed with big potted plants, and standing in front of two of them were tall wooden stands on which stood a pair of brilliant-hued toucans. They added the final touch of magnificence, and it occurred to the authors that Felix must be kicking himself for never having thought of toucans. Only Felix would have had five.

As they came down from the dining room, their host put

179

out his hand to one of the birds, which immediately proceeded to strike like an offended rattlesnake, its terrifying bill missing the hand by the fraction of an inch.

"I'd be a bit more distant with those fowls, if I were you," said Plum. "They're liable to take your finger off."

"Yes," laughed Irving, quite unperturbed. "And it might be the one I play the piano with."

His piano playing was, of course, as exceptional as everything else about him. He could . . . but why are we using the past tense about Irving? If anyone is perpetually present tense, it is the one-man Hit Parade. . . . He can play only in the key of F sharp. But of course if you're a composer, you can't have everything in one key, so Irving's pianos have a transposing keyboard, equipped with a lever that can be set here and there at any key desired, while Irving goes blithely along hitting his black notes. Blithely and magically hit after hit.

After dinner Irving played a couple of tunes he had designed for the Duncan show, then swung round on the piano stool.

"This *Sitting Pretty* book," he said. "I've read it, and I think it's darned good. But . . ."

"But?"

"Well, as I figure it out, it's no use without the Duncans. The high spots come when the sisters, the rich one and the poor one, meet and do numbers together. With the Duncans these'll be smashes. We know what those babies can do with a number when they work it together. But without the Duncans . . ."

"You think we may not get them?"

"I'm wondering. My grapevine tells me this *Topsy and Eva* of theirs is pretty big. It may surprise us all."

"Surely there are other sister acts?"

"You name them."

"The Dollys."

Irving laughed that soft laugh of his.

"What can they do? Kick their legs in unison and carry a

lot of crazy clothes. And those Hungarian accents! No, I can't see the Dollys. I can't see anyone except Jake and Heim."

As they went down in the little push-button elevator, Guy was looking grave.

"I suppose you got that?" he said. "Irving doesn't mean to write that score till he's sure we've got the Duncans. One show more or less means nothing to that bird. He can always make another million or so whenever he feels like it. Lucky devil!"

"Yes, he must have been born in a bed of horseshoes."

"Don't speak of horseshoes, I'm superstitious about them."

"I thought they were lucky."

"Not to me," said Guy.

A day or two later came a letter from George Grossmith saying that the end of the *Sally* run was in sight and that a new show would be needed at the Winter Garden. He proposed that this should be homemade and, indeed, indicated that he was nominating himself as part author. Jerry was to write the score.

"You'd better go and do it with George," said Guy gloomily. "It looks like a long wait on *Sitting Pretty.*"

"Why don't you come too?"

"How can I? I've got *Polly Preferred* going into rehearsal and there's more than a chance that Gilbert will do *The Dark Angel* with Bart Marshall."

So Plum sailed back to London and set to work with George Grossmith on a show called *The Cabaret Girl*, in which Dorothy Dickson was to co-star with Leslie Henson and the author-actor-manager, while Guy went to Paris and to the Val du Grace studio where his infant daughter regarded the stranger with doubtful eyes.

· 4 ·

While Jerry was working with Plum on *The Cabaret Girl* he had read the *Sitting Pretty* book and, waxing enthusiastic, had offered himself as composer if Irving Berlin was dropping out.

Irving was dropping out. *Topsy and Eva* was now in the twenty-seventh week of its Chicago run with no end in sight. Thus when Guy received a letter from Plum saying here was the old firm back together at last, he shot a wire to Ray Comstock and everything was fixed up. He crossed to England and settled down to fit the numbers Plum and Jerry were writing into the *Sitting Pretty* book.

Then one morning the letters that came up with his breakfast tray included one from Marguerite written in her most slapdash style. It seemed that a crisis had arisen, not in Marguerite's affairs but in those of a friend. Marguerite collected crises. She would gladly involve herself in one that was the property of people she hardly knew. Like a boy scout, she believed in doing her daily act of kindness.

A woman of prodigal generosity, she had one pet economy. She hated to waste writing paper. In consequence it was her custom not merely to write on both sides of a piece of thin writing paper but to turn the page sideways and write slap across the writing already there. A great deal of no doubt interesting gossip was thus lost to her friends.

In this letter she had really outdone herself. There was some talk of Robert Milton's wife who was in Paris, and there was some stuff about a child. Whether it was the Miltons' child or the child of a woman travelling with Mrs. Milton was not clear. Guy, remembering somewhat vaguely that the Miltons had a child, inclined to the view that this was it. Anyhow the child was a problem—"I don't mean a problem child," Marguerite wrote in brackets. His name was Ben or possibly Hen—that was Marguerite's handwriting. And his mother was paying a flying visit to Geneva or Genoa where a hick (possibly sick) relative demanded her presence. Meanwhile Ben or Hen—now it looked more like Len—was coming over to spend a week with Guy in England. That part was painfully clear. His mother would collect him at the end of that time on her way back to America. In the meanwhile the little fellow would be entertained by visits to the Tower of London, Madame Tussaud's and the Black Museum at Scotland Yard.

Guy took the letter round to Plum. Bob Milton had staged the Princess musicals for both of them, and it seemed to Guy that they should share this burden that had been thrust upon him, standing shoulder to shoulder like the Boys of the Old Brigade. A partnership, as he pointed out to Plum after Robinson-Jeeves had conducted him to the latter's study, is a partnership.

"How old is this little excrescence?"

"Nine."

"I know that American children are extremely precocious but a child of nine who has his heart set on visiting the Black Museum at Scotland Yard should be given a wide berth. I'll bet that he has six toes on each foot and that his hairline starts one inch above his eyebrows."

"Marguerite says he is extremely well behaved. She goes into details, though unfortunately a good deal of it is impossible to read. I did manage to make out that he does not flip butter pats at the ceiling, a pastime all too prevalent in juvenile American circles."

"That may be as may be, but let me point out to you that people who regard their nine-year-old offspring as a treasure would hardly be shipping it from Paris to London unguarded. The fact that Mrs. Milton is willing to do so is the tip-off."

"Well anyway," said Guy, "the point is I can't put the child up in that mousehole I'm living in at the Mayfair. Here you have lots of space. You also have a butler who might well be a college professor did he not prefer the freer life and higher pay of domestic service. You can turn Ben over to Robinson without a qualm."

"When is the little louse arriving?"

"Tonight on the Golden Arrow. I'm to meet him at Victoria."

The notes of the conversation as given in the Wodehouse diary break off at this point. They are followed by a one line entry: "Went with G. to meet Ben. Biggest mistake of my life."

This cryptic statement is not enlarged on. On the other hand the Bolton entry is extremely detailed, if somewhat incoherent. It was evidently written under the influence of strong emotion.

The basic trouble seems to have lain in the fact that trunks are frequently sent from France to England in bond, thus saving a hold-up in the Dover custom shed. The owner of the trunk can, and usually does, proceed to the spot where these trunks are assembled immediately upon alighting in Victoria Station. Should such a person be travelling with a child it is not unnatural—though perhaps unwise—to tell the little half-wit to take a seat on the platform and look at a picture book of which he, she or it is sick to death after the seven-hour journey from Paris.

"Be a good little honey-cub and sit down there with the bags and the Mommer bear will be back right away."

Why should a poor, unsuspecting American mother imagine that, in orderly England, two kidnappers were on their way ready to pounce on her innocent offspring at this first moment of arrival? Plum and Guy were just a fraction late or they would have seen the Mommer bear and not have found an unaccompanied child goggling vacantly amidst an assortment of hand luggage.

"Sure that's the one?"

"Of course. See his stars and stripes button? Also he looks like Bob Milton, the same sort of puddingy face and red hair."

"How'y'r, Ben?" said Guy, holding out a hand to the youngster.

"I'm okay. How's yourself?"

The complaint, widely circulated, that American children are badly brought up is not necessarily true. This specimen had clearly been taught to be bright and friendly with strangers.

"Come along," said Guy, taking the little fellow's arm. "I bet I know someone who's ready for some ice cream." The chauffeur, who accompanied them, gathered up Ben's surprisingly voluminous hand luggage and they all moved off to the car.

"I hear you want to see Madame Tussaud's?" said Plum chattily.

"Yes, and the Tower of London."

After that the two authors may well be pardoned for believing they were in possession of the rightful Ben. It did not occur to them that all small boys are told when they visit London that they will be taken to Madame Tussaud's and the Tower.

During the journey to Onslow Square the child remained sunk in a gloomy silence. When the car drew up in front of the house, he looked at it disparagingly.

"Rabbit hutch," he said.

The remark wounded Plum, who was rather proud of his little home. He had no notion that his guest was supposing this to be one of London's luxury hotels.

"This is your room," he said, leading the way upstairs. "The bathroom is third door down the passage."

"No bathroom?" rejoined Ben with a haughty stare. "In America hotels that don't have baths with every room is dumps."

"Dinner will be in ten minutes."

"What d'ye mean dinner will be in ten minutes? Mom an' me eat dinner when we like."

Plum went downstairs and joined Guy in the study.

"Correct me in a tendency to dislike this child," he said. "I don't mind a little healthy criticism but this blister treats my home as if it were a Bowery flop-joint."

"He's certainly not what I expected from Marguerite's description."

185

"I don't know why a man like Milton insists on propagating his species unless reasonably assured he can do a bit better than this."

"Wait," said Guy. He seemed agitated. "Do you know what has just occurred to me? I'm pretty sure Milton has only one son."

"One like this is plenty."

"Milton's son, whose name as I recall it is Paul, not Ben, is editor of the *Dance Magazine*."

At this point the door was swung open by the subject under discussion.

"Where's my Mom?" he demanded.

"Your mother is on her way to Geneva—or Genoa."

"You're a liar."

"See here," said Guy, "if you go on like this, there'll be no Tower of London for you."

"Phooey."

"And you must be polite to Uncle Plum. He's being very kind to keep you here for a week."

"A week my foot. We're going back home. My Grannie wants me. My Pop wants me. My Auntie wants me. I guess most everybody wants me."

"You guess wrong," said Plum.

Ben surveyed them malevolently.

"You'd think 'cause they all want me they'll pay you money to get me back. My Mom'll fix you. She'll get the police after you. They'll get you under the lights. They'll beat you up with rubber hoses—that's what they'll do." He turned abruptly and left the room.

"What on earth is the child talking about?"

There was a knock followed by the entrance of Robinson.

"Pardon me, sir, but what are your instructions regarding dinner? Master Breckenridge has informed me that under no circumstances will he eat boiled cod."

" 'Master Breckenridge?' "

"I gather from his observations that that is the young gentle-man's name, sir."

"If it is I shall make it my business to present Mr. Bolton's wife with a typewriter."

Guy leapt to his feet.

"This isn't any question of spelling, of Milton or Wilson. We've got hold of the wrong child!"

"What? Do you think Mr. Bolton is right, Robinson?"

"It seems a tenable theory, sir. It explains certain oddities in Master Breckenridge's behavior."

"Then for heaven's sake let's race this maverick back to the Lost Property Office."

The car was summoned, the bags brought down and Master Breckenridge hustled into his coat.

"Where are we going?" he demanded.

"We're taking you back to your mother."

On the chance that Mrs. Breckenridge might have left Victoria in despair, they asked the youngster if he knew where his mother was planning to stay. He shook his head.

"With your approval, sir," said Robinson, "I will establish telephonic communication with all the leading hotels. The Breckenridges are, I believe, wealthy, and I fancy the lady will have booked rooms at the most expensive."

As they were getting into the car Junior Breckenridge eyed them unpleasantly.

"Are you gorillas taking me for a ride?"

"Don't be crazy."

"Then let me have your guns."

He started to frisk them, rubbing his hands over their pockets. Plum pushed him into the car.

As they arrived at the station, Junior nipped out of the car and rushed to where he saw a policeman standing.

"I bin kidnapped," he said. "I guess it's in the papers. I guess there's a reward—a mighty big reward. You take me to my Mom and you'll get it."

The policeman turned to Plum and Guy.

"What is all this?" he asked. "There's been some talk around here about a missing child. Are you the men who made off with him?"

"Sure. These are the ones," said Junior. "They know my Mom is rich. One of 'em said so. Get 'em under the lights!"

Speaking at once the two writers tried to explain. Guy pulled out Marguerite's letter and held it out waveringly to the policeman.

"I think you'd better come with me over to the Precinct Station."

"Must we? Can't you just take the little fellow and the bags? My man will drive you."

The policeman was unrelenting. He insisted on taking them to the Westminster Police Station. There they found that a police call had been sent out asking for a report on two men seen leaving Victoria Station with a child and some purloined bags. They had, so the blotter read, joined an accomplice at the wheel of a battered car.

The Wodehouse Sunbeam was far from battered. Whoever had supplied the information was, doubtless, a devotee of crime literature. The sergeant in charge took their names. He had clearly never heard of either of them. Something in Guy's accent made him look up.

"You're an American, aren't you?"

"Yes."

"Did you know these people in the States?"

"No."

He eyed Guy keenly. "Sure you didn't follow them over?"

Plum came to the rescue.

"Mr. Bolton is a writer," he said.

"He has no regular business?"

Plum, who might well have been expected to furnish a cutting reply, merely faltered, "No." It was not the stern-faced sergeant that made him go suddenly jittery, it was Junior. The child had become fascinated by a notice on the station bulletin board headed "Wanted for Murder" and depicting two thugs who had figured in a Thames warehouse crime. He was now switching his gaze back and forth from the printed portraits to the faces of the two writers. Plum's nerves, already so many tattered dishrags, could stand no added strain.

"Well," said the sergeant in a tone that suggested capitulation, "it's unfortunate you men got hold of the wrong child. It was a piece of carelessness that caused this little lad's mother a lot of anxiety and distress. I have no doubt your excuse is that the other boy resembled this one. But still—"

"What other boy?" interrupted Junior.

"There was another little boy on the train with you that these gentlemen came to meet."

This sounded better. They were now described as gentlemen.

"That's a lie," said Junior. "There was no kid on that train but me. I went through it and through it looking for someone to play with."

The "gentlemen" period was short-lived. They were now "men" again and men in a most uncomfortable position. Junior Breckenridge was driven off to Claridge's with a policeman guarding him. Plum and Guy were still held answering questions regarding the non-existent Ben, their uncertainty as to his precise name, age or appearance imparting a quality of fishiness to their story.

It was on this intensely delicate situation that Robinson entered. He was looking his most dignified and ambassadorial. The sergeant was visibly impressed.

"Who are you?"

"My name is Eugene Robinson, sir. I am Mr. Wodehouse's major-domo."

"His what?"

"Butler," said Plum.

"Your butler?" repeated the sergeant, looking at Plum with a changed expression. It was clear what was passing in his mind. An employer of butlers, especially such a butler as this, must, like Caesar's wife, be above suspicion.

"What about the child these gentlemen were supposed to meet?"

"That is precisely the point that I have come here to elucidate, sir. In the course of my enquiries regarding Mrs. Breckenridge, I telephoned the Mayfair Hotel where Mr. Bolton resides and was informed that there was a Continental telegram there addressed to him. I took the liberty of having it opened and the contents read to me. It was from Mrs. Bolton and conveyed the information that the child Mr. Bolton was desired to meet would not, after all, be visiting the metropolis, the young gentleman's mother having changed her plans. Might I ask, sir," he added, addressing Plum, "if you plan to return home shortly? When I left the cook was expressing anxiety about the soufflé."

On the way back to Onslow Square Robinson produced the telegram.

"I stopped at the Mayfair and collected this, sir," he said. "However, I feared that if I showed it to the sergeant, it might occasion further confusion."

The telegram read:

LITTLE NAN NOT COMING. HER MOTHER CANCELLING GERMANY VISIT. MRS. NELSON THANKS YOU AND SENDS REGARDS.

There was another wire, a cable. It was from Aarons and Freedley, a newly-established management, asking Guy if he was prepared to write a show for the Astaires with a score by George Gershwin.

Chapter Thirteen

IT was a day or two after this shattering experience that Plum and Guy saw Gertrude Lawrence in a revue called *Rats* at the Vaudeville.

Plum had seen her before in *A to Z* and in the "Midnight Frolic" at the Hotel Metropole, an entertainment that was a close imitation of the one which Flo Ziegfeld had done on the New Amsterdam roof, but in *Rats* she had far greater scope than in either of those vehicles. Her performance affected Guy and Plum rather as his first perusal of Chapman's *Homer* affected the poet Keats. It seemed to them—a view that was to be shared later by the New York public—that she had everything. She could play sophisticated comedy, low comedy, sing every possible type of song, and she looked enchanting. When Guy got back to the Mayfair, he wrote her an enthusiastic note in which he said that if she would come to New York he would guarantee to star her in a revue, a musical comedy or a straight comedy, whichever she preferred.

Getting the Ziegfeld spirit, she replied with a six-page telegram which could have been condensed into the words "Right ho." She was committed to play in a Charlot revue in New York, but after that she would be at his disposal. (The result of this exchange of civilities was *Oh Kay*, the musical comedy which Guy and Plum wrote for her with music by George Gershwin and lyrics by his brother Ira when she was finally free to leave Andre Charlot's management.)

However the immediate problem was the casting of *Sitting Pretty*. Letters passed back and forth with Ray and Jerry who was now back in New York. Frank McIntyre was engaged for the part of Uncle Joe, the sentimental burglar. The sole problem was the two girls who were to take the place of the Duncans. Queenie Smith was decided on for one but who could play the other?

"I've just had a wire from Ray," said Guy, bursting in on Plum at work in his study. "If we cable 'yes' Ray will book Gertrude Bryan."

"Gertrude Bryan? You don't mean that Gertrude Bryan will come back to the stage?"

"I'm just telling you. All he's waiting for is 'yes.' "

"He'll get the loudest 'yes' he's ever heard. Some cocktails, Robinson, and put your best effort into them. This is an occasion."

"Oh yes, indeed, sir. In that brief visit I paid to New York with my late employer I had the privilege of seeing the young lady you refer to in *Little Boy Blue*. You have my warmest congratulations, sir."

There are no doubt by this time a whole generation of voting age who will fail to see the significance of all this enthusiasm. Let them learn now that to have seen Gertrude Bryan in *Little Boy Blue* is to have wandered in a garden of enchantment. Her eyes were like the bluebirds in the spring, and her hair like finches' feathers a-wing. Gertrude Bryan, even more than Marilyn Miller, might well have worn the mantle of Maud Adams, had she not married at the very outset of her career and retired. Alexander Woollcott, who had a shrewd eye for talent, could hardly speak her name without a slight choke in the voice.

"I'll tell you what I think," said Plum. "I vote we board the first liner that's sailing and bend to the task of fitting this reborn star with the material that best suits her."

"Yes, you're right, we mustn't waste a moment."

"Your tone sounds a bit regretful."

"Well, Marguerite and I had planned a little trip in the *roulotte*."

"In the what?"

"Didn't I tell you about it? I suppose you'd call it a caravan, but the front part is a smart little car built by the Minera people. You pull a lever and the *roulotte* is released and away you dash to do the family shopping."

"Where did you acquire this monstrosity?"

"It was made for the King of the Belgians but he passed it up and I bought it for Marguerite. It sleeps four and has a bath, a kitchenette and a bar."

"What, no ballroom?"

"However, I'll forget the *roulotte* until we've got *Sitting Pretty* on. Now where's the *Times*? Let's see what is the first boat going."

"Don't bother. Robinson carries these matters in his head."

Even as he spoke Robinson had entered with the tray containing glasses and shaker.

"If I may be permitted to put two and two together, sir," said Robinson, "I fancy your remark indicates an immediate departure for New York."

"Exactly."

"The 'Mauretania' on Wednesday, sir, the 'Majestic' on Saturday."

"We'll take the 'Mauretania,'" said Plum. "Ask Mrs. Wodehouse if she's prepared to sail on such short notice, then book our passage."

· 2 ·

But, as Robinson might well have said, *surgit semper aliquid amari*. It is sad to have to record that the last effort of the Princess triumvirate, who had worked together so much and so happily, was their least successful, was in fact a flat failure. Jerry turned out a first-class score, the cast was excellent, the staging and mounting all that could be desired, but Irving, the lad who never made a mistake, had put his finger on it when he had insisted that the Duncans were, as Robinson would have said, of the essence. Charming Gertrude Bryan and clever Queenie Smith were not a team. When they met, when they performed together, the electric spark was missing, and the play was so written that these were the vital spots.

Poor *Sitting Pretty*, which had seemed to have so much to offer but which nobody wanted!

"We're like two flower girls," said Plum, waxing sentimental. "Stretching out our small, grubby hands with a pathetic nosegay which the passers-by—blister their insides—curtly ignore as they hurry past."

"For heaven's sake don't talk about flowers," said Guy. "It reminds me of a certain floral horseshoe."

Who knows? Perhaps it is because of that horseshoe—the Horseshoe of Fate it might be called—that *Sitting Pretty* is a name remembered only as that of a film in which Clifton Webb was baby-sitter to an infant Junior Breckenridge.

· 3 ·

There was no time for the licking of wounds. Guy had signed contracts with Aarons and Freedley for two shows, one for the Astaires and one to follow Plum's *Beauty Prize* at the Winter Garden. Since the Astaires were in London, playing in *Stop Flirting,* and Aarons and Gershwin also there busily occupied with the preliminaries of the two shows, an immediate return was indicated. As to Plum there was *Jeeves*.

The new Winter Garden show, which Aarons and Freedley were presenting jointly with Grossmith and Laurillard, had been sketched out by Guy on the voyage to America and a scenario sent back, of which the combined management had approved. It was now at the casting stage, and on arriving in London (he had travelled via Paris) Guy went to report at the Winter Garden, whose bar is the tiny Drury Lane Tavern frequented by Nell Gwynne in her orange-selling days. Plum's *Beauty Prize* was coming to the end of a successful run, and George Grossmith was holding a chorus audition for *Primrose*, which was the name of the new show. He sat together with George Gershwin and Alex Aarons surrounded by press men, yes men, vocal experts and beauty experts, testing applicants as to voice, diction and appearance.

George Grossmith, though one of the boys in private life, was, in his managerial aspect, rather pompous—nay, even stuffy. He had issued a ukase to the effect that all members of the chorus of *The Beauty Prize* should appear and bring a bit of music with them. He had recently lost a girl to Charlie Cochran because her talent had passed unnoticed in the choruses of *Sally* and *The Cabaret Girl*, and he wasn't having that happen again.

As Guy entered the theater, coming in through the Nell Gwynne tavern, George was having difficulty in persuading one of the showgirls to demonstrate her vocal powers. It seemed that here was a young lady who, while willing to accept three pounds a week for decorating the stage of the Winter Garden for a season or two, very definitely had other fish to fry. She was, as a fryer of fish, to make quite a name for herself. Several names in fact, two of them those of peeresses of the realm.

"Must I sing, Mr. Grossmith?"

"Yes, Sylvia, you must. All of you have to sing if you want jobs as showgirls in *Primrose*. The Gershwin score demands it."

"Oh, very well," she replied petulantly, and, going down to what in England are called "the floats," she handed over a piece of music to the pianist in the pit. The piano struck a chord.

> *God save our gracious king,*
> *Long live our noble king,*
> *God save the king.*

George, a strict observer of ritual, rose and stood at attention. His minions rose and stood at attention. Guy, on his way to announce his arrival, stood at attention.

As the anthem came to the normal stopping point, George started to sit down, but there is more, much more of the fine old choral than is generally known. James Carey is credited with a three-stanza version; in another version John Bull, composer, singer and organist at Antwerp cathedral, has expressed the same sentiment in his own way; while James Oswald, a Scot, who was chamber music composer to George III, also got into the act. A printing is extant giving them all. Sylvia Hawkes sang them all. The pianist stopped playing but that didn't stop Sylvia. They wanted her to sing, did they? Well, sing she would. Of course no one dared to call a halt. The national anthem is sacrosanct—especially if you're an actor-manager clinging to the hope of a belated knighthood.

Sylvia Hawkes said afterwards that she expected to be fired then and there. Perhaps she would have been had she not been so pretty. There are, it is true, more pretty girls to the square foot in the U.S.A. than in the British Isles. But, when they're really trying, the parent race can turn out an article of highly exportable value. Witness Ziegfeld's Dolores, also his Kathleen Martin and his June McKay, witness the Jersey Lily, witness Connie Carpenter, Deborah Kerr and, as we say, Sylvia Hawkes.

Sylvia Hawkes was not only pretty, she had a pretty sense of humor. George Gershwin was swept off his feet by her, so was Lord Ashley, heir of the Earl of Shaftesbury, so was Douglas Fairbanks, Sr., so was Lord Stanley of Alderly and so, finally, was the very sure-footed Mr. Clark Gable. All of these, except George Gershwin, laid their fortunes and/or coronets at Sylvia's feet. George might well have done the same had he possessed at the time either fortune or coronet. Starting at the Winter Garden, Drury Lane, even Nell Gwynne didn't cut a much wider swathe than Sylvia Hawkes. But then if you have those looks, combined with those brains, not to mention that charm, you don't have to invent a new mousetrap to have the world beat a path to your door.

Primrose did somewhat less well than the most decorative member of its cast. It managed to hang on for two hundred and fifty-five performances, which was a shade better than its predecessor, *The Beauty Prize,* and definitely better than it deserved.

It was poorly cast—nice enough people but they didn't fit their parts. It had one engaging ditty in which Leslie Henson and Claude Hulbert were overcome with pity when recalling the fate of some of the heroines of history. One quatrain ran:

> *Oh, isn't it terrible what they did to Mary-Queen-of-Scots?*
> *When playing at St. Andrew's she would not replace div-ots,*
> *So, after quite a bothering day,*
> *They locked her up in Fotheringay,*
> *Oh, isn't it terrible what they did to Mary-Queen-of-Scots?*

Though not by Wodehouse, it was written in the Wodehouse style with triple rhymes. It somehow made Guy feel more at home.

Chapter Fourteen

THAT 1924 season in London when the first two of the Gershwin series of shows were written was one of extraordinary gaiety. Was it because the Astaires were there to hobnob with?—the Astaires, George Gershwin and his piano, George Grossmith who knew everybody in London?

Adele had the faculty of making any party from two to fifty-two into a success. Such words as enchanting, delicious, captivating did not seem like tired adjectives from a Hollywood pressbook when applied to her. She could be impish, she could be wise, she could be tender, she could be honest and friendly —are we conveying the impression that we like Adele Astaire? If so, it is all right with us. It is the impression we wish to convey. How nice if she could have gone on and on with brother Fred. How nice if George Gershwin could have gone on and on writing for them. His music suited them to perfection.

One week end Guy encountered Adele at Knole. Knole is one of the top great houses of England. For those who don't know it, or who have not read the books of Victoria Sackville-West, in which its atmosphere is wonderfully evoked, a thumbnail sketch might be in order.

Belonging to Elizabeth's reign, Knole is all of one style as so few great houses are, and is generally conceded to be the finest example of domestic Tudor architecture in England. It is built on a chronological plan, containing three hundred and sixty-five rooms, fifty-two staircases, twelve courtyards, and twenty bathrooms—including one that is haunted. It is packed with art treasures, Vandykes, Reynoldses, Gainsboroughs and Romneys elbowing each other for the spot on the wall with the best light. All in all quite a lot of house.

At the time Adele and Guy were week-ending there the family were living in reduced circumstances. They were huddled into a corner of the cosy edifice where their simple wants were tended by a staff of only twenty-two servants. The gardens, which had been laid out on a scale commensurate with that of the house, had fifteen gardeners hustling round to do the work which had once commanded the services of thirty.

What were Broadway characters doing in such surroundings? Well, Adele had already had several offers to supply her with some such setting of her own, but Guy—?

Guy was there because Lady Sackville had also been, but a few years before, a Broadway character. She had appeared in Guy's first play, *The Rule of Three*, and then again in *Polly-with-a-Past* . . . Anne Meredith, a charming and talented actress.

A wonderful dinner, some satisfactory bridge, a little dancing —there was a fresh supply of American phonograph records, and Adele Astaire to dance with if you could buck the line.

Then came the hour when whiskey and sodas were at the nightcap stage and the company drifted into corners, breaking up into little groups of fours, threes and twos. Lord Sackville made announcement of what the doings would be on the morrow, church or golf, and an expedition, by invitation of the Astors, to visit nearby Hever, home of the Boleyns, where poor Anne had first met Henry. These suggestions were all on a take-it-or-leave-it basis. You could breakfast when you pleased from the row of hot plates in the dining room. You could lunch or not as you pleased so long as you told the butler. The only "must" was the cocktail hour, dinner and a white tie. That was week-ending in England as still surviving in 1924. Not much left of that sort of thing today, alas, save only at dear old Blandings.

Guy was paddling round his bedroom in his pajamas, inspecting the Rowlandsons on its panelled walls, when there was a knock at the door. He opened it to find Adele attired in a heady negligee.

"Come right in," he said heartily. "This is what I call good old-fashioned hospitality. I didn't know Anne made such charming provision for her guests."

"It's a cute idea," said Adele, "but I'm holding out for a wedding ring and I understand the one your girl friends used to rent their apartments with is gone."

"Then to what do I owe the pleasure?"

"I want you to change rooms with me. I've got the haunted bathroom."

"Haunted bathroom? Must be rather a modern ghost?"

"Yes, and the poor thing is very upset or nervous or something."

"How do you know?"

"Well, every fifteen minutes or so you'll hear the johnny flush."

"And there's nobody there?"

"No, but the eerie part of it is that this particular convenience is the difficult kind. You know how it is with English privies—there are the overheads, the buttons, the levers, the foot release and ye olde worlde pull-up. Then with the overheads with dangling handle, of which this specimen is one, for some it's a smart, quick pull, with others a long, steady slow one. This one's a devil—the coax-me variety."

"But yet the ghost?"

"Oh, the ghost has no trouble at all, just a gruesome rattle of the chain followed by an immediate 'whoosh.' Somehow it gives you a creepy feeling when a ghost seems to be more at home in your room than you are. I know I won't sleep a wink."

"We'll change, of course. I'm rather keen on ghosts. A bit of an amateur psychic researcher."

The shiftover was effected. The phenomenon continued at

intervals and was certainly disturbing. Eventually Guy wriggled down under the covers so that hearing was sufficiently impeded for him to get to sleep. He was still in a state of concealment when a soft-footed lady's maid entered, drew the curtains, and then laid him out a pair of demi-tasse shorts, a lace brassière, a pair of stockings and a fetching sports costume.

He wakened during this operation but, being by inclination a slow getter-upper, he decided to remain doggo. As he had supposed would happen, the maid withdrew without disturbing him. He dozed again and this time was awakened by what he presumed to be the ghost taking a bath. He cocked an eye in the direction of the bathroom and was startled to see a feminine form, partly concealed by a towel, flit across the open doorway. He had evidently made some slight noise for the nymph came to the bathroom door rubbing herself with the towel. She was not only very pleasant to look at but she was a lady whose name was one of the most honored in Debrett.

"I thought you wouldn't mind my coming in here, dohling," she said. "George was barricaded in ours and you know what men are in a bathroom. They fall asleep in the tub, I believe."

Guy made some inarticulate noise from under the covers pitched in as high a key as he could manage. The lovely peeress donned her robe and started out. As she passed the bed she gave Guy a hearty smack.

"Get up, you lazy girl," she said. "We're playing golf, re-member?"

She went out into the hall and Guy heard a sharp cry. A moment later Adele appeared.

"For heaven's sake what's happened?" she said. "I just ran into Alex and when she saw me she almost fainted dead away."

Guy put on a scarf and dressing gown and went down to breakfast. Although the custom for ladies was a bedroom tray, there was no rule in the matter. Adele elected to go with him. They found one of Britain's forty marquises lifting the covers of a line of silver hot plates, weighing his choice.

"Did you come into my room this morning and take a bath?" inquired Guy.

"Me? No, but—"

"Funny," said Guy, "I'd have sworn it was you. Of course I wasn't properly awake."

The marquis replaced the lid on the kedgeree.

"Excuse me a minute. I must pop up and have a word with the trouble-and-strife. She was in a bit of a dither about something."

He disappeared.

"Quite the gentleman, what?" laughed Adele, as she helped herself to one of those beautiful Cambridge sausages. "I suppose it's the influence of all these belted earls looking down on you from the walls."

· 2 ·

"So you've been hobnobbing with the upper-crusters, have you?" said Plum, meeting Guy on his return from Knole. "Pleasant enough people, no doubt, but we of the intelligentsia prefer something a bit more brainy. I remember the last time I dined with Johnny Galsworthy—"

"When was that?"

"Two days ago. It was the first time, too. Ethel met Mrs. Galsworthy at a garden party—the house we've taken for the summer is near his—and she invited us to dinner."

"Did he know your books?"

"He'd just bought one."

"How do you know he had 'just' bought it?"

"Because there was a mark in it. It seems it's been his habit when he stops reading to make a pencil note in the margin, so he'll know where he was."

"Which book was it?"

"*Right Ho, Jeeves*. The mark was on the side of page ten."

"Did he say anything matey like, 'I laughed my pants off

at that chapter in which Gussie Fink-Nottle presents the prizes?' "

"I somehow gathered the impression that he found it more tactful not to broach the subject."

"Just you and Ethel?"

"Good Lord, no. There were twelve or possibly fourteen guests. As we took our seats at the dinner table Galsworthy announced that the subject that would be discussed during the meal was the deteriorating effect of educational uniformity on the incidence and development of genius."

"You don't mean that you had to talk about that?"

"Apparently it's a time-honored custom. The woman next me told me that Galsworthy abominates desultory conversation."

"But what happened when the subject became exhausted?"

"It never did. If the conversation lagged, Galsworthy would rap on the table with the end of his knife and present a new aspect of the problem. 'To what extent is genius influenced by the educational standards of parents; with special reference to the cases of Thomas Chatterton and Shakespeare?' "

"What a dinner!"

"I was punch drunk by the time we got to the sweet. I went staggering on and then, how I don't know, I found myself embarked on the plot of a story. I told my companion it was by a young American writer who was recognized as the coming man and who had had even less education than Chatterton. A taxi driver. She clapped her hands and said:

" 'Ah! Another George Meek, Bath Chairman.'

"I told her that it was an exposé of the dishonest psychiatry that was rampant in America. The hero has lost his power to memorize through having been overworked in the censorship service during the war. He ties bits of string round his fingers and then can't remember what they're for. His wife is fed up and takes him to a psychiatrist. She's extremely attractive and the psychiatrist falls for her and she for him. The patient comes one day and finds his wife in the doctor's office and when he lies down on the couch he notices it's quite warm. My neighbor thought that was a very subtle touch.

"Well that warm couch gets him to thinking. He's pretty unhappy although he can't quite remember what he's unhappy about. The unfortunate man keeps asking his wife to tell him what those bits of string round his fingers are to remind him of but she turns mean and won't tell him—or else she tells him wrong. His appointments are a perfect shambles and, in consequence, his business goes completely to pot. He even has a tonsil operation when all he wanted was to remind himself to have his hair cut. Well, just as I was getting to the blowout I realized to my dismay that the whole table was silent. Everybody was listening to me. They'd realized that I was, once more to quote our Joe, pushing the old girl's leg. Worse, I was pushing J. G.'s leg. I paused, appalled, and my girl friend informed the company:

" 'It's by the James Joyce of America . . . taxi driver . . . no education at all.'

"Well, I couldn't stop then. I plunged on telling of how the husband is so unhappy that he decides to hang himself. He tells his wife what he means to do but she does nothing to stop him. She hears him apparently starting to get down to it in the next room, then he suddenly appears with the rope round his neck. He points at it, and says:

" 'Now what the devil was that to remind me of?' "

"Did J. G. join in the shouts of laughter?"

"Shouts of what laughter? Nobody laughed. Somebody said, 'Yes, go on.' "

"I don't believe it."

"It's gospel truth. I had to go stumbling on with some stuff about the husband eventually deciding to leave home and the psychiatrist putting a time bomb in his suitcase. And, being absent-minded, the husband forgets that he's supposed to take the bag with him and shoves it under the couch."

"And the wife and her lover—?"

"Exactly. The female next me called it an O. Henry ending."

"As a matter of fact, you pinched it from Chaliapin. Don't you remember? The bum under the bench, and they put it in the Governor's coat pocket and he stands over them and gloots."

"Good Lord! So I did. That's how one gets stories, I suppose. Unconscious memory."

Chapter Fifteen

Lady Be Good was the new Bolton-Gershwin show for the Astaires, and as soon as the script was ready Guy sailed for New York to help with the staging.

Aarons' and Freedley's idea was to make Lady Be Good the start of a new series of musical comedies like those at the old Princess only on a larger scale, and Guy, while he approved of the scheme, felt a certain melancholy at the thought that he would not be working with Plum. George Gershwin always stipulated that his brother Ira should do his lyrics, and Plum did not blame him, for he had—and has—a great admiration for Ira's work. Any man capable of writing—as Ira did later in Of Thee I Sing—a couplet like

> Let's sing to every citizen and for'gner
> "Prosperity is just around the corner"

got Plum's applause.

The substitution of George for Jerry did not bother Guy. The young man who had played the piano at the rehearsals of The Second Century Show was beginning to look uncommonly like a genius. But it would seem all wrong, working without Plum. There would undoubtedly be a lot of success, but there wouldn't be the same fun. It was with a pang that Guy envisaged the end of the partnership which had begun on that Christmas Eve after the first performance of Very Good Eddie.

The opening of his Grounds for Divorce at the St. James's did nothing to cheer him up. Madge Titheredge, Owen Nares and Lawrence Grossmith were the featured players, and very good they were . . . till on the second night Lawrie collapsed and was taken to hospital, and almost simultaneously Madge Titheredge developed laryngitis and became practically inaudible for three weeks. It surprised Guy that Owen Nares did not fall a victim to some wasting sickness, for once bad luck hits a show, it seldom knows where to stop.

"You're on the right side of the fence," he said to Plum. "Novels don't give you the headaches plays do."

Marguerite's engagement at the Opera Comique had ended but, as she expected to join the Chicago Opera, the change was not greatly for the better. Guy sailed, hoping that after all this he would at least have the consolation of getting a success with *Lady Be Good.*

Success there was. The first scene of Act One showed the Astaires—playing brother and sister—thrown out with their few goods and chattels on the sidewalk. Adele, behaving as she unquestionably would have done in real life, arranged the furniture neatly about a lamp post, hung up a "God Bless Our Home" motto and with the help of a passing workman—destined to become the hero—attached a percolator and fixed the hydrant so that water would be constantly available.

After which, of course, it began to rain, and she and Fred did a number called "Hang On to Me," dancing together under a big umbrella.

Given perfect artists like Fred and Adele, it was just the sort of charming little scene to start a musical comedy off with a bang and, this being so, Alex Aarons, being a manager, could see no virtue in it. Only Guy's proviso that this would have to be done over his dead body had saved it from being thrown into the discard after the dress rehearsal.

He was behind on the opening night when Alex Aarons suddenly appeared, pale and agitated and reproachful.

"I told you!" he cried. "I told you how it would be if we kept that scene in. They're howling and booing!"

"Not so much howling and booing," said Guy, "as cheering their ruddy heads off. You don't often hear cheering like that in a theater. The scene has knocked them cockeyed. But of course you're the boss and what you say goes, so we'll cut it out tomorrow night."

"Over my dead body," said Alex.

Lady Be Good was a smash hit and was equally successful when eventually it arrived in London. There, after a long run, it closed the famous old Empire. The Astaires appeared in one more Gershwin show, *Funny Face*, after which Adele closed her career with a triumphant performance in *The Band Wagon*, by George S. Kaufman, Howard Dietz and Arthur Schwartz. She then married the Duke of Devonshire's second son and retired to Lismore Castle in Ireland, leaving a gap that can never be filled. Fred struggled on without her for a while, but finally threw his hand in and disappeared. There is a rumor that he turned up in Hollywood. It was the best the poor chap could hope for after losing his brilliant sister.

· 2 ·

It was two years before Guy was able to leave America. He had done several shows there, among them the second of the Aarons and Freedley series—*Tiptoes*, written with Fred Thompson, and he came away with a couple of contracts in his pocket. Philip Goodman, an advertising man turned manager, wanted him to do a big musical for Clark and McCullough with score and lyrics by a new team named Kalmer and Ruby. This subsequently became the very successful *The Ramblers*. (In passing, it was to Philip Goodman that Jerry Kern, arriving in his office to discuss a new piece and meeting the manager for the first time, introduced himself with the historic words, "Good morning, Mr. Goodman. I'm Kern. I hear you're a son of a bitch. So am I." Than which nothing could break the ice more effectively.)

The other contract was with Aarons and Freedley for a musical for Gertrude Lawrence, who had written to Guy saying that she was now available. Guy had debated whether to take her to Aarons and Freedley or to Ziegfeld, and it was George Gershwin's connection with Alex and Vinton that tipped the scale in their favor (and eventually put several hundred thousand dollars in their bank accounts). The most attractive aspect of the thing to Guy was that the book was to be written in collaboration with Plum. The old firm was in being again.

Marguerite had returned to Paris and the Opera Comique. She met Guy at Havre with the *roulotte* and Peggy, and they had their long postponed trip through the chateau country. After ten days of perfect weather they rumbled back from Chalons to Paris in a torrential downpour, and then Guy had to go to London to start work with Plum on the Gertie Lawrence show.

"Why don't you come with me?" he said to Marguerite when they were back in the studio.

"How can I? They've given me Thaïs, the one role I've always wanted to sing. Besides," said Marguerite, "you're going to be terribly busy with these two shows to write. You won't want to be bothered with Peggy and me."

Guy agreed that there was certainly no worse company than an author in the throes of composition.

"*L'absence est a l'amour ce qu'est au feu le vent. Il eteint le petit, il allume le grand.*"

"Since I recognize the word *vent*," said Guy, "I conclude that that is something about absence being like the wind. Or does *vent* mean stomach?"

"The wind puts out small flames but fans strong ones."

"It's humiliating, this language thing," said Guy. "There's that daughter of ours—no ball of fire, as you must admit—and I'll bet she grabbed it right off the bat. At three years old!"

"It's your own fault. Why don't you learn the language?"

209

"I've tried, but I don't seem to get anywhere. I decided to start by learning how to count, because, having had some experience with the French, I thought that—next to being able to say '*Ou est le Messieurs?*'—that would come in most useful. And I got along fine till I stubbed my toe on 'seventy.' Apparently *septante* wouldn't do."

"It's *soizante-dix*."

"Exactly. 'Sixty-ten.' A fine way to say 'seventy.' And when you get to 'eighty' it isn't 'seventy-ten,' it's 'four twenty.' And they call the French logical!"

"As a matter of fact, the Belgians do say *septante*. So do the Italians. *Sessanta, settanta, ottanta*. And in Spanish it's *sesenta, setenta, ochenta*."

"It must be great to be educated. My folks set me up with a paper route when I was fourteen. How about this young woman goggling at me over there on the sofa? I suppose she's got the whole thing down cold?"

"Oh, yes, she's wonderful at languages. You understood what Daddy and Mummy were talking about, didn't you, darling?"

Peggy nodded.

"Well, say those figures for **Daddy**."

"*Sechzig, siebzig, achtzig*."

"Before she says it in Russian," said Guy bitterly, "I'll call up and get that reservation on the Golden Arrow."

"*Flèche d'Or*," said Peggy.

· 3 ·

In London Guy found Plum finishing an adaptation of Molnar's *Spiel Im Schloss*—later produced in New York and London as *The Play's the Thing*, and in order to be able to give uninterrupted attention to *Oh, Kay*, the Gertie Lawrence show, they took the train at Paddington and settled in at the Impney Hotel outside what is, next to A. E. Housman's Clun, the quietest place under the sun—Droitwich in Worcestershire, where the brine baths are.

In the long English twilights that last until ten at night—the faint western glow may continue even later—they paced the terrace of the Impney (it's hard to say the name without giving the impression that you have a hare lip) and worked out their plot, pausing occasionally to listen to the nightingales which collect in these parts in gangs. It was probably at Droitwich that the conversation between the romantic man and his deaf friend took place. "Have you ever," sighed the romantic man as they strolled through the lanes one summer night, "heard anything so perfectly wonderful as these nightingales?" "Eh?" said the deaf man. "I said, 'Aren't the nightingales simply marvellous?'" "Huh?" "The nightingales. They're superb, don't you think? The nightingales. The *nightingales*." The deaf man shook his head regretfully. "I'm sorry," he said. "I can't hear a word you're saying. These damned nightingales are kicking up such an infernal noise."

Worcestershire is next door to Shropshire, and they drove there one day in the hope of finding Blandings Castle and catching a glimpse of Lord Emsworth's pig. In this they were unsuccessful, but they found the minute hamlet of Stableford, seven miles outside the town of Bridgnorth, where Plum had lived as a young man.

"Pretty remote sort of spot," said Guy, studying the old home through the window of the car.

"Yes, quite remote," Plum agreed. "I loved it. I've never found a better place for work. At the age of twenty I once wrote fourteen short stories there in ten days. They were never printed, which was a break for the reading public, but I wrote 'em."

"Had you any neighbors in this grim solitude?"

"One family about a mile away. We quarrelled with them two days after we arrived and never spoke to them again. It was milk that caused the rift. At least, they said it was milk when they sold it to us, and we said it was skim milk. Harsh words and dirty looks passed to and fro, and the thing culminated in us cutting them or them cutting us, we never quite made out which. That always happens in rural England. It's pure routine. Directly you have moved in and got your trunks unpacked, you have a hell of a row with the nearest neighbors about milk. Make a note of that."

"I will."

"Father sorts out his things, has a wash and brush-up, and looks in on Mother. 'All set?' he asks. 'All set,' says Mother. 'Fine,' says Father. 'Then let's go and beat the be-jesus out of those swindling crooks down the road who've been selling us that so-called milk.' And off they go, Father with his Roget's *Thesaurus* under his arm in case he runs short of adjectives."

"It sounds a jolly life."

"Oh, it was. Though my mother didn't like it much. She found it a little on the lonely side. My father had seen this house advertised in one of the papers, and he and she went down to take a look at it. As they were driving away, my mother said, 'Well, thank goodness I shall never see that awful place again.' 'Eh?' said my father. 'I was saying that it was a relief to me to think that I should never see that frightful house again.' 'Oh, the house?' said my father. 'You are speaking of the house. I was meaning to tell you about that. I've signed a twenty-years' lease on it.' "

"I'd like to see you springing something like that on Ethel." Plum shivered.

"Don't say such things, even in fun. But, as I was observing, I loved the place. Miles of smiling countryside, and not a Henry W. Savage to be seen as far as the eye could reach. The only thing I didn't like in my formative, or Stableford, period was the social stuff. Owners of big estates round about would keep inviting me for the week end."

"*You?*"

"I don't wonder you're surprised. Even today I'm about as

pronounced an oaf as ever went around with his lower jaw drooping down and a glassy look in his eyes, but you have literally no conception what I was like in my early twenties. Do you remember what Brichou said about the chambermaid in the third act of *The Girl Behind the Gun?*"

" 'She was a nice girl, but she had no conversation.' "

"That was me. I was completely inarticulate. Picture to yourself a Trappist monk with large feet and a tendency to upset tables with priceless china on them, and you will have the young Wodehouse. The solution of the mystery of my mixing with the County is that my brother Armine was very popular. He played the piano like a Gershwin and could converse pleasantly on any subject you cared to bring up, and I suppose what happened was that one of these territorial magnates would run into Mother at a garden party or somewhere and say, 'I do wish you could persuade your son to come to us for the week end.' 'Why, of course,' Mother would reply. 'My sons will be there with their hair in a braid.' The magnate would start like a man seeing a serpent in his path.

" 'Did you say *sons?*'

" 'Yes, I have two—Armine and Pelham.'

" 'Oh? . . . Well, of course, we were rather thinking of Armine, but if Pelham can come as well, we shall be charmed . . . that is to say . . . oh, yes, charmed.'

"And he would totter off and tell his wife that the curse had come upon them and she had better put the best china away till I had blown over. Why are you looking like a stuffed frog?"

"Was I? It was just that I am reminded by the remarks of the last speaker of a little story which may be new to some of you here tonight. I, too, have suffered in country houses. You know I used to be an architect?"

"Yes, you told me."

"Well, when you're in an architect's firm in a fairly junior capacity, you get the dirty jobs shoved off on you, and it was

my lot one day to be sent to a big house in Greenwich to con-
fer with the owner about some alterations he wanted done.
This owner was notorious as the worst-tempered man in Con-
necticut and my employers wished no piece of him, so the cry
went up 'Let Bolton do it,' and I pushed off. I should mention
that in those days I was like you, very gauche and shy. The
least thing embarrassed me."

"What embarrassed you on this occasion?"

"Cats."

"Cats?"

"And dogs. This family I was going to was one of those
animal-loving families and the house was just a frothing mael-
strom of dumb chums. The first thing that happened was that
I started for dinner and looked round for my shirt, which I had
left on the bed, and there was a whacking great cat standing
on it, kneading it with its paws. Well, you know how a fellow
feels about his shirt front, particularly if he has been relying
on its glossiness to start him off with a bang in a strange house.
I scooped the animal up and carried it out on to the balcony—
my room was on the ground floor—and flung it into the void.
And an elderly gentleman, coming round the corner at the
moment, received a direct hit on the back of the neck."

"Your host?"

"My host. The human tiger. I apologized, of course, but
it wasn't very well received. He called me one or two rather
offensive names, and I kept seeing him looking at me in a
nasty sort of way all through dinner, as if he were thinking of
a few more. It was a relief to me when the meal ended and we
all trooped out to the living room for coffee, because I thought
I might make up some of the lost ground over the coffee cups.
The place was stiff with elderly females and I knew that what
registers with these elderly females is the exhibition of those
little politenesses and attentions which were all the go in the
nineties. So my first action was to make a dive for one of the

old geezers who seemed to be trying to find a place to put her cup.

" 'Permit me,' I said, and bounding forward trod on a cat. 'Oh, I beg your pardon,' I said, backing and bringing down my heel on another cat. And tottering to a chair, I sank heavily onto a third cat.

"Well, they all said 'Oh, not at all' and 'Don't mention it,' but I could see that I was now docketed as Bolton, the man who has that curious dislike for animals, and the butler was called in and told in a rather meaning way to remove the cats —before, I suppose, I started setting about them with a hatchet. I was glad when the quiet home evening was over and I was at liberty to go to bed. It seemed to me that at long last my path and that of the animal kingdom would now divide. I, so to speak, was taking the high road while they, as it were, would take the low road. However, remembering that unfortunate episode before dinner, I went down on all fours when I got to my room and looked under beds and things, just to make sure, and it was all right. The eye detected no cats. Relieved, I rose with a gay song on my lips, and I hadn't got much beyond the first couple of bars when a voice behind me suddenly started taking the bass, and turning I perceived on the bed a fine Alsatian dog. And the moment our eyes met I could read the message in his. He had obviously got an entirely wrong angle on the position of affairs and was regarding me purely in the light of an intrusive stranger who had muscled in on his private sleeping quarters. He fixed me with a yellow eye and curled his upper lip slightly, the better to display a long white tooth. Also the twitching nose and the sotto voce imitation of distant thunder."

"It must have been worse than meeting Abe Erlanger the morning after *The Riviera Girl*."

"Much worse. It was difficult to know what avenue to explore. It seemed to me that my best plan would be to steal out and curl up for the night in the living room, so I began to edge for the door, walking with infinite caution like a slackwire artist who isn't any too sure he remembers the correct steps.

"Well, it was a near thing. At the moment when I started, the dog seemed occupied with something that looked like a cushion on the bed. It was licking this object in a thoughtful way and paid no attention to me till I was halfway across No Man's Land. Then it suddenly did a sort of sitting high jump in my direction, and two seconds later I was on top of the wardrobe, with the dog underneath, looking up."

"This, of course, settled your sleeping arrangements for the night?"

"I thought so, but after about half an hour a couple of cats gave tongue in the garden and the next moment the dog had sprung through the window and I heard the thud as he jumped off the balcony."

"You were saved!"

"So it seemed to me, and the relief was stupendous. I climbed down, tottered to the bed and sank down on it. Or, rather, to be accurate, on the dead cat which was lying on the bed. It was this cat which the hound had been licking just before the final breach in our relations, the object, if you remember, which I had supposed to be a cushion.

"Well, you can see the position I was in. Already my reputation in this house was zero, my name mud. After what had occurred in the living room, what would I be able to say if discovered with a dead cat on my person? I had to get rid of it somehow. But how?"

"The old problem of what to do with the body."

"Exactly. The thing that makes life so trying for murderers. Weighing this against that, I came to the conclusion that my best plan was to go out on the balcony and throw the corpse into the garden. There would then be nothing to connect me with it. After all, in a super-catted house like this, cats must

BRING ON THE GIRLS

always be dying like flies all over the place. A gardener would find it in the morning and report to G.H.Q. that the cat strength of the establishment had been reduced by one, and there would be a bit of tut-tutting and perhaps a silent tear or two, and then the thing would be forgotten."

"And no chance this time of hitting your host."

"No. Or at least there wouldn't have been, had it not been his practice during the summer months to sleep in a hammock on the lawn just below my balcony. Scarcely had I released the remains when there came from the darkness the cry of a strong man in his anger.

" 'Who threw that cat?'

"Windows flew up. Heads popped out. I sank to the floor of the balcony and rolled against the wall.

" 'Let me get at the man who hit me in the eye with a cat!' thundered my host.

" 'A cat?' My hostess's voice sounded perplexed. 'Are you sure?'

" 'Sure? What do you mean, sure? Of course I'm sure. I was just dropping off to sleep in my hammock when suddenly a great beastly cat came whizzing through the air and caught me squarely in the eyeball. I insist on the blood of the man who threw that cat.'

" 'Where did it come from?'

" 'Must have come from that balcony there.'

" 'Mr. Bolton's balcony. As I might have guessed!'

"My host bayed like a bloodhound.

" 'So might I have guessed! Bolton, of course. He's been throwing cats all the evening. Somebody come and open the front door. I want my heavy cane, the one with the carved ivory handle. Or a horsewhip will do.' "

Plum was impressed. He had never before realized the fierce, raw excitement of an architect's life. Never a dull moment, it seemed to him. Now drawing blueprints, now sitting on dead cats. One moment making out estimates for sun parlors at clients' country homes, the next, having to look pretty slippy to avoid canes with carved ivory handles. One began to appreciate what Christopher Wren must have had to go through when designing St. Paul's.

"What did you do?" he asked.

"Oh, I left," said Guy. "Nothing to keep me, if you see what I mean."

"Not a thing," said Plum.

· 4 ·

Gertie Lawrence was back in England after playing in the second edition of *The Charlot Revue*. Considering the brilliance of the cast, it had done rather poorly—only a hundred and thirty performances. Both Bea Lillie and Gertie were looking for a follow-up of their 1924 success to establish them as stars of the New York theater.

Guy and Plum felt that it would be advisable to see Gertie and discuss *Oh, Kay* and the part she was to play in it. They telephoned her and arranged a meeting at her flat and drove back to London through those delicious Cotswold villages, Moreton-in-the-Marsh, Stow-on-the-Wold, Lower Slaughter, Weston-Subedge and possibly those hamlets of which Plum had written in his Mulliner stories, Chickenham-infra-Mud, Lower Smattering-on-the-Wissel and Higgleford-cum-Worblebury-beneath-the-Hill! There was time to do some straying. They were not seeing Gertie till teatime.

On the piano in her sitting room there was a photograph of a child dancing. It caught their eyes immediately as they came in.

"Is that you?" enquired Plum.

"Yes, dearies, that's me at the time of my debut in the Brixton Pantomime."

"You took to the stage early?"

"For a good year before that photo was taken I'd been learning the A.B.C. of my trade from dear old Italia Conti."

"What a lot of distinguished pupils she had."

"I'll tell you a little tale about one of them. It was the annual show that was put on for friends and relatives every June. I was just under ten—my birthday's the fourth of July—so you can imagine my surprise when, at the first rehearsal, Madame Conti's assistant handed me a part. Most of the children were 'pixies' or 'villagers' but I was to be a character. I was going to see my name on the program: 'JANE . . . . . Gertrude Lawrence.' The theater has given me a lot of thrills but never one quite as big as that moment when I held my first part in my hand.

" 'JANE' it said on the cover. Jane was one of a party of children who steal out into the garden on Midsummer Night and find the flowers have changed into Little People and are giving a ball, a crafty lead into "The Dance of the Flowers," chief feature of this juvenile turkey. I delayed before turning the slightly battered blue cover, savoring the great moment. I opened it. It wasn't what you would call a hell of a part—it consisted of a single line: 'Oh, look, children! Pansy has turned into a Pierrot and he's dancing with Columbine!'

"I was standing there weighing the problem of how best to characterize Jane when I heard Madame Conti's voice say: 'That's your cue, Gertie.' Good God! I had missed my first cue. Properly flustered, I went charging onto the stage and said: 'Jane pants.'

" 'Jane pants? You don't *say* that, dear. That's the stage direction. You've been running and you're excited.'

" 'Of course, I was upset at being late on cue, I just read it without thinking.'

" 'Well, you *must* think. Never do anything on the stage without thinking. Now make the entrance again and say the line.'

219

" 'Oh, look, children! Pansy has changed into a Pierrot and he's dancing with Concubine.'

"The brats sniggered. Madame Conti explained patiently that the name was 'Columbine,' adding that if I said 'Concubine' on the afternoon of the performance some of the parents might not think this was a very nice school to send their child to.

" 'Whenever you're flustered take a long, deep breath and pause. Always remember a slight pause never hurts.' I paused. I took a long deep breath. And as I did so I heard a childish voice repeat my line, reading it beautifully with wonder and excitement, and just that little catch in the breath that was indicated by 'Jane pants.' 'Don't you think, Madame Conti,' the voice went on, and it had now changed to a budding baritone, 'don't you think it would be *safer* if *I* said the line?'

"I was stunned, speechless, unable to find words in which to protest.

" 'Yes, dear,' I heard Madame Conti say. 'I think perhaps it would be. I'm sure Gertie won't mind. Give Noel the part, will you, dear?'

" 'She doesn't need to,' said Noel grandly. 'I know it.' "

"It wasn't—?" exclaimed Guy.

"Yes, it was, duckie, Noel Coward—the little ham. If I had had a blunt instrument in my hand at the time the English-speaking stage would have lost one of its most brilliant talents."

"He just calmly walked off with your first part?"

"Darned unprofessional, I call it," laughed Plum.

"Yes, but wait, boys. For years I've had a dream. In it I'm playing opposite him and, on opening night, just as we're coming to his favorite line, his most amusing bon mot, I say it myself and then give him the cue. Then, when he's left flat on his bumpty, I whisper, 'Come on, Jane, old girl, let's hear you pant.'

"And let me tell you something—it's coming, Gertie's Revenge." She waved a hand at her desk where stood a photograph of the distinguished author-actor-composer lovingly inscribed. "He's writing a play in which I'm to be with him. He calls it *Private Lives* and it's to be ready by the time I'm finished with your show."

"Well much as I look forward to that opening night, I trust it's a long way off," said Plum.

"So do I," said Gertie. "And now you boys help yourselves to drinks and tell me about this *Oh, Kay*."

The "boys" went back to the Impney. There was one nightingale that Guy had heard when Plum wasn't around and this particular nightingale was, so he insisted, the Caruso of nightingales. The new moon was about due and everyone knows nightingales really try when there's a new moon. It seemed a pretty safe bet that the star singer would be round to show up his rivals and enjoy all these "ahs" and "ohs" from the surrounding nests.

"Why lug Caruso into it? Why not the 'Neapolitan Nightingale.'" They both laughed at the recollection.

Plum was putting the finishing touches to *The Play's the Thing*, while Guy toiled on *The Ramblers*.

"Isn't it rather a ghastly thing writing a show for a couple of comedians like Clark and McCullough?" Plum asked. "Hasn't it got to be just a stream of gags?"

Guy said no. It could better be described as a series of block comedy scenes tied together by a plot. A "block comedy scene" means one written like a revue sketch with a concentration on laughs and a final twist of "blackout" value at the end. He enumerated some of the scenes among them one in a sinister Mexican bedroom where Bobby Clark is stayed in the act of running away by the discovery of a diaphanous nightdress under his pillow, with which he runs about hopefully carolling, "Marquita, Marquita."

They discussed comedians, naming their favorites. Chaplin got the number one spot, then they couldn't quite decide between G. P. Huntley and Bobby Clark. Leslie Henson was well in the running and so was Frank Tinney.

"There's Jack Donahue. He might be the best of all. He's human. Wants comedy to come from character not gags."

"Yes, that's rather a test. Do you remember that chap who went on tour with that turkey we wrote for Al Woods?"

"*See You Later.*"

"*See You Later*—you know for a minute I couldn't remember what it was called."

"Musical version of *The Girl from Rector's*," said Guy coldly. "Score by Gene Schwartz. Lyrics by, and not quite up to the usual standard of, P. G. Wodehouse. Cast . . ."

"Wait a minute," Plum interrupted. "That comedian who played it on the road turned it into a success. You remember his name?"

"I never saw him. I swore I'd never see the show after the opening night and I never did."

"I'm on to something, I think. Help me think of the chap's name. He'd had an early success playing leads for George M. Cohan. That was somewhere around 1907."

"Before my time. I don't remember back of 1908. Even then I was just out of swaddling clothes."

"Well, he disappeared, this bird. Then he turned up in vaudeville with an entirely different style. He'd been brash and tough and now he was soft and apologetic. The sketch he played was quite a success. 'Change Your Act' it was called."

"You are talking about a lad named Victor Moore."

"That's the chap. Victor Moore. Now I'll tell *you* something! He's just the man to play Shorty McGee in *Oh, Kay.*"

"Gosh, you're right! I saw him in that sketch. If he's still alive, there's our Shorty."

This conversation, historic in its consequences, took place on that fondly cherished terrace of the Impney, Droitwich, Worcestershire, on the evening of June 15, 1926. Although he knew nothing about it, it was the beginning of a new career for that sterling comedian, Mr. Victor Moore.

Guy turned toward the west where a rosy glow outlined the ancient oaks that surrounded them. He started to make the ceremonial three bows to a thin silvery crescent that peeped above the topmost branches.

"Turn your money over. It's good luck for your Victor Moore idea."

Plum bowed, turning his money. And at that same moment there was the faint rasping sound of a bird clearing its throat and the Caruso of nightingales let go with a cadenza.

· 5 ·

The comedian's role in *Oh, Kay*, for which they destined Victor Moore, was that of a bootlegger. It was 1926 and the noble experiment had been in operation for seven years. People had learned to cope with it at least to the extent of having their liquor analyzed or, in an emergency, of pouring some into a saucer in a darkened room, setting fire to it, and, if it burned with a reddish flame, changing their bootlegger.

It was the "Hootch Age," and the spirit that made bathtub gin (the human spirit, not the stuff you bought at the druggist's with a doctor's prescription) was the same devil-may-care quality that accounted for flagpole sitters, marathon dancing and the bull market.

It is hard to imagine two worlds more different than the one the authors said goodbye to as they left the Impney and that into which they plunged upon disembarking from the "Aquitania."

It was not only the missing wine card from which they could select, even in that unfashionable retreat, a Chambertin or a Pouilly, as well as the bottle of crusted Taylor '96 that would supply the glass to accompany their after dinner savory. The whole tempo of life was different. People walked faster, laughed louder and became nervously excited—lost their tempers more readily.

The pace had, seemingly, quickened since the *Sitting Pretty* period of two years ago, the last time the two writers had been in New York together. When they dropped in at the Ritz barber shop on the afternoon of their arrival, the barbers of their adjacent chairs both got immediately on to the subject of stocks as if that were the only thing that anybody would want to talk about. The market had taken another upward spurt, it seemed, and each of the lads manipulating the razors had come appreciably nearer to the Easy Street that everyone seemed bent on moving into.

"Have-a you gotta the Alice Charmers?" enquired Plum's barber.

" 'Alice Charmers'? Never met the lady."

The barber laughed.

"Lady! It sure acta like a lady. De mosta sweet stock on de board."

"You watcha your foot with thatta Alice," said the other barber. " 'Like a lady,' you say. Sure, a lady you no canna trust."

The colored boy shining Guy's shoes looked up.

"I got a friend uptown made four hundred dollars last week. Beds it was. He bought beds an' sold 'em again. Four hundred he made."

"Four hundred!" said the barber disparagingly. "Whatsa four hundred?"

"It ain't hay," said the colored boy. "He's gwine back in again an' he's buying a couple for me."

"Coupla beds?"

"No, couple of shares."

"Oh, it's Simmons beds?"

"That's right. Mr. Simmons' beds."

"There's a new bed company started," said the manicurist,

who was sitting at her small table reading the paper. "It'll put Simmons clean out of business."

"Howsa dat, Elsie?" enquired one of the barbers.

"One of my customers was telling me about it. He's in on the ground floor. They got wonderful improvements—buttons you press. One closes the window, another turns on the bath water. They're in the head of the bed. Then there's a radio that you listen to while you go to sleep. It's under your pillow. No one can hear it but you. And if there's someone in bed with you they can listen to a different program under their pillow."

The barber removed the towel from Plum's face.

"What you tink, boss? You tink datta bed business is good thing for to putta de money?"

Plum didn't know.

"I'd like to get the name of the company," said Guy. "I've a theme song for them to play on those radios of theirs."

He started to chant:

> *Bed, bed, beautiful bed,*
> *Pull it all over your head*
> *Wrap up your heels in it*
> *Have all your meals in it*
> *Make a hotel of your bed.*

"What's that?" enquired Plum.

"A relic of my pre-Wodehouse days.

> *Though your wife may desert you*
> *Don't let that fact hurt you*
> *So long as she leaves you the bed.*

"There's a lot more, four verses and four refrains if you'd care to hear them."

"Some other time," said Plum, stepping out of the chair.

"I might have made a lyric writer," said Guy, "if I'd stuck to it."

Plum wasn't listening. The barber was reciting a list of good stock buys based on information gleaned from customers. He wasn't listening to that either.

"This country's gone nuts," he said, as they made their way down the stair.

"Shall we have dinner in the Oak Room or the Oval Room?"

"I never like the Oak Room at night. It's depressing."

"On the other hand in the Oval Room you will have to listen to Vecsey playing 'The Rose of China'—and that is even more depressing."

They were greeted at the door of the Oak Room by the younger of the Ritz's two "Theodores."

"What about a drink, Theodore?"

"Certainly, Mr. Bolton. Two old customers, of course."

When the drinks arrived with a long lemon twist disguising them as "horses' necks," Guy asked Theodore if the essential ingredient was of unquestioned reliability. Theodore reassured him.

"But I heard that two Detroit millionaires woke up dead after drinking some bootleg hootch in this hotel."

Theodore explained that if the story were true (it was) the thing had nothing to do with the hotel.

The gentlemen in question, if they ever existed (he was admitting nothing) had sent a bellboy to a bootlegger they knew of and he had given them a bottle of whiskey made from alcohol that the government had poisoned.

"You don't mean to tell us that the government is running a poisoning department?"

"Oh, yes, Mr. Wodehouse. You've got to be very careful today. They're putting formaldehyde in it."

"Embalming fluid?"

"Yes, sir, and wood alcohol. The enforcement people think it's the best way to stop drinking."

226

"It stopped those two Detroit boys, all right."

"One would think that even Andy Volstead might consider death a somewhat severe punishment for infraction of his famous Act."

Theodore shook his head. Under the Baumes Law a woman had, only last week, been sent to prison for life for selling a pint of gin. Rum-runners were frequently shot down by government officers when crossing the Canadian border. The figure of one hundred and ninety-seven persons killed by prohibition agents had just been published.

They asked Theodore for the names of some reliable speak-easies. He recommended The Hyena Club, The Ha! Ha!, The Jail Club and The Day Breakers.

"We're interested in the subject because we're writing a play in which bootlegging is the main theme," explained Plum.

It was a few minutes later that Bob Benchley strolled in.

"Well, as I live and attempt to breathe," said Bob, "if it isn't Book and Lyrics. How are you, lads, and when does it open?"

They invited him to join them for dinner, and he said he would try to peck a bit, though not having much appetite. He was feeling a little down at the moment, he explained, as he had not yet shaken off the hangover caused by attending a party on the previous night.

"Was it a pleasant party?"

"I can't remember, but I think so. Bob Barbour was our host. Do you know Bob?"

"Yes, quite well." Robert Barbour, the brother of the New Jersey senator, was an old friend.

"Did you ever hear the story about him and his private stock?"

"No."

"Thank God. Now it can be told. He kept it in an old family manse which was next door to the old family plant at Paterson, where I fancy, from the fact that they have so much of it, they print money, and came a day when he decided to move it to his apartment in New York."

"He was taking a risk, wasn't he?"

"A grave risk. The one thing that wakes the fiend that sleeps in the authorities is someone conveying potables across a state line. In some of the more tolerant communities you are given the benefit of a trial, but the general view is that this is a bit sissy."

"We live in stirring times."

"We do, indeed. Well, Bob, knowing this, decided not to risk any minion's hide but to carry through the operation himself. So he loaded the stuff into his station wagon and covered it over with some rugs, a pair of plush portieres and a shepherd's smock that had belonged to his great-great-grandfather."

"Was Bob's great-great-grandfather a shepherd?"

"So the story goes. I believe he herded a beautiful sheep. So, as I say, he rugged, portiered and smocked the alcoholic liquors, and started to wend his way to Gomorrah-on-Hudson. And hardly had he wended a couple of parasangs when he heard that most unpleasant of all noises, the whine of a following motor cycle."

"Golly!"

"You may well say 'Golly.' It was late. The road was empty. There could be no doubt that it was he who was the object of the attention of the hellhound of the Law. He tried turning a corner quickly and doubling back on his tracks, but nothing could shake off the pursuer. Just clear of the town the state trooper rolled up beside him and signalled to him to stop. He stopped, prison bars looming before his eyes.

" 'Mr. Barbour?'

" 'Y-y-y-yes.'

" 'Look, Mr. Barbour,' said the state trooper. 'You're a drinking man, aren't you? Could I interest you in some of our stock? We've got the best line of wet goods in Bergen County.' "

Guy was impressed.

"Is that a true story?"

"You bet it's a true story. I could tell you a dozen more of a similar nature, if you like your stories by the dozen. I'll tell you what you two ought to do, if, as I understand it, you are writing about rum-running on Long Island. You should get this R. Barbour of whom I have been speaking to take you on that floating café of his that he calls a yacht to view the liquor fleet off Montauk. Scores of launches and fishing boats darting back and forth like nesting swallows. It's a heartening sight for those of a convivial kidney. I use the word playfully. Most of us old-timers have only half a kidney left after a seven-year bout with prohibition."

Guy and Plum thought of the Impney and George, the head-waiter, leaning over with the wine card.

"Since it is so warm this evening, sir, perhaps a glass of Chateau Yquem instead of the port? We still have a little of the '92. A very engaging wine, sir."

"Everything ends in 'est' over here," said Guy. "When this country makes a bloomer, it's a beaut."

·6·

They went down to Great Neck. During the short period Marguerite had spent in America, Guy had bought a house there. Immediately behind him lived Ed Wynne, a couple of doors beyond, Joe Santley and his wife, who had played leads in the Princess musicals, and, at the end of the road, Marilyn Miller. Just across Middle Neck Road were quite a lot of old associates —Jack Hazzard, who had been the chief comedian in four Bolton-Wodehouse shows, and his wife, Alice Dovey, who had played opposite to Ernie Truex in *Eddie*. Truex was now their next-door neighbor. Then there was Oscar Shaw, who had also played in four of the team's musicals and had been chosen as Gertie Lawrence's leading man in the forthcoming *Oh, Kay*.

There were other neighbors, Eddie Cantor for one, Ring

Lardner for another, Elsie Ferguson and, most esteemed of all, a young man named Oscar Hammerstein, who was just beginning to make a name for himself in the musical comedy field. The two writers, living *en garçon* with a couple, consisting of mother and son, to look after their wants, found plenty of congenial company for dinners and golf and bridge.

"We have to go to town," said Guy one morning, hanging up after a protracted phone call. "We're to meet the sweetheart of the mayor of New York, and we've got to write in a part for her in the show."

It was rather like that time nine years before when they had gone to Ray's office to meet the two top Follies beauties of the day. Once more there were to be two special girls, one of them Connie Carpenter, who was Gertie Lawrence's understudy in *The Charlot Revue*, and who was to serve in that capacity in *Oh, Kay* and—many years later—in *The King and I*. The other was Betty Compton.

"I hope you're in good voice," said Plum, as they walked to the Aarons and Freedley office. "I take it you'll have to read the thing to them?"

"Good heavens, no," said Guy. "All that reading of scripts to managers has gone out, thank goodness. Even Belasco doesn't expect it nowadays. Talking of Belasco, did I ever tell you about Austin Strong and *The Drums of Oude?* You've heard of Austin Strong?"

"Robert Louis Stevenson's stepson or grand-stepson or something."

"That's the man. He had written this play and he didn't know how to set about selling it, his associations having all been very *Atlantic Monthly*, so he went round asking friends for advice and eventually got in touch with a fellow named Benrimo who was Belasco's road show director and general tuner-upper, and Benrimo said that if he would cut him in fiftyfifty he would show him the places where he had gone wrong and, after the thing was in shape, would introduce him to Belasco. This sounded pretty good to Austin, and he said, 'Fine, go ahead.' You've never met Belasco, have you?"

"Oddly enough, no. All I know of him is that he wears a clergyman's collar."

"He has other eccentricities. He suffers intermittently from an impediment of speech, and when an attack of this comes on, he starts intoning. What troubles him is the letter S. He gets all tangled up with an S and hangs on to it, hissing away like a kettle and then suddenly breaking into this chant like a Druid high priest saying a few words before starting to dig the knife into the human sacrifice. He also has a habit, when you are sitting opposite him at his desk, of resting his elbows on it, bowing his head and playing with his curls, pulling them down over his eyes and peering at you roguishly through the undergrowth."

"He ought to go into vaudeville."

"So a lot of people have thought. Benrimo used to do a wonderful imitation of him. And all the while he sat opposite Austin, showing him where *The Drums of Oude* were off-beat, he would enliven the proceedings with it, and Austin—who didn't know what it was all about, for Benrimo was much too much of an artist to say, 'Look, this is Belasco'—would smile a bit perplexedly and then get on with the work.

"Well, eventually the job was finished and the budding playwright was taken—script under arm—to the famous studio. Belasco sat him down at a refectory table and parked himself on the other side. His stammer was bad that day, so after a few words of fatherly encouragement he started to chant, at the same time going into his curl-twisting act. He pulled his shaggy white locks over his eyes, smiling through them benignly, and Austin gave him a big hand.

" 'That's simply wonderful, Mr. Belasco,' he cried, laughing merrily. 'You've got him to the life.'

" 'What are you s-s-s-s-saying? I don't underssssstand.'

" 'All that s-s-s-stuff. And that business with the hair. It's a sssimply ssssuperb imitation,' said Austin, feeling that he ought to enter into the droll spirit of the thing by doing an imitation of his own. 'It might *be* Benrimo,' he added, wondering a little why his collaborator was looking like that. Benrimo's two eyes, like stars, had started from their spheres, and each particular hair was standing on end like a quill upon the fretful porcupine.

" 'You—' shouted Belasco, turning on his henchman. 'You s-s-s-s-son—'

"Austin clapped his hands.

" 'You ought to go down to the Players where all Benrimo's friends are, Mr. Belasco. You would be a riot there.'

" 'Get out! Both of you!' screamed the Wizard as he reached for a Saracen sword that hung on the wall. He rounded on Austin. 'You s-s-s-s-s-s- . . .' He was still hissing as Austin started for the stairs, closely followed—and halfway down them passed—by Benrimo."

"Did Benrimo lose his job?" asked Plum.

"He did, but he managed to get it back later after prostrating himself before the Master and banging his forehead on the floor a good deal. But Belasco made one condition, that Benrimo was to cut his hair. It put an end to his famous imitation."

"And Austin Strong?"

"There was a happy ending there. He went off to Johnny Golden and wrote *Three Wise Fools* and *Seventh Heaven* for him. *Fools* did three hundred and fourteen performances and *Heaven* seven hundred and four."

The Aarons and Freedley offices were in that same New Amsterdam Theater building which housed both Erlanger and Ziegfeld. There was the usual waiting room with its company of out-of-work actors paying their unsolicited visits; there was the usual guardian of the portal, in the shape of a business-like secretary; the usual posters and photographs telling of past successes, in this particular case, unleavened by failures.

In their inner sanctum Aarons and Freedley faced each other across the top of a large, flat desk. They were the best-dressed managers in New York. They were the best-dressed managers who had ever been in New York. Even in the frenzied hours of the tryout period no one ever saw either of them in need of a shave or a haircut. Save in the matter of titled acquaintances, they could claim social parity with Gilbert Miller.

For the period in which they were operating they were exceedingly well established. Freedley was wealthy both by inheritance and marriage; Aarons' father was one of the powers of the Klaw and Erlanger syndicate. They knew everybody in theater-land who was anybody. The almost equally dapper mayor of New York, Jimmy Walker, was their intimate friend.

When the two authors arrived, there were greetings and an exchange of chit chat with the English Connie Carpenter, then from the street below came the wail of sirens.

The office door opened and Betty Compton came in, followed by the boyish-looking mayor.

Betty Compton wasn't as pretty as Marion Davies but she was well up to Ziegfeld standards and had, in addition, more character in her face than had most of the Follies beauties. When she looked at Jimmy Walker, it was with adoring eyes.

The Mayor, who had, no doubt, primed himself, displayed a flattering degree of knowledge in regard to the past performances of Bolton and Wodehouse.

"With that Lawrence dame, the Gershwin score and you two gentlemen, *Oh, Kay* can't miss," he said. "All it needs is a nice little part for Betty."

He smiled expectantly at the two writers.

"We're going right to work on it," said Guy.

"That word work seems to remind me of something." He

turned to Betty Compton. "How about it, kid, will you ride downtown with me or do you want to stay here and do tricks for the boys?"

"I have no tricks."

"No? What were those things you got me with?"

He turned to Aarons.

"Too bad about that little friend of yours."

"Stella? She was no special friend of mine."

"No, I know that," said Walker. "She had to go and get stuck on a gangster and now he's up for murder and she's held as a material witness."

"And she's expecting, isn't she?" said Betty.

"No, honey, she's not expecting, she's sure. Fine thing having a kid by a fast-finger boy."

"It's terrible," said Freedley, "how many of these girls get mixed up with gangsters. Look at Irene and Larry Fay, and Kiki Roberts and Legs Diamond. Kiki was one of the prettiest kids Ziegfeld ever glorified."

"I've talked to Kiki like a Dutch uncle," said Walker, "but it's no soap. I told her this boyfriend of hers is the clay pigeon of the tommy guns. He's been tattooed with lead so often it's a question whether he belongs in an ambulance or an ammunition wagon. Just because he won't lie down don't mean they won't pin the minus sign on him sooner or later."

"Of course it must be exciting," said Connie Carpenter. "I can see what a thrill it would be going joy-riding in an armored car."

" 'Joy-riding in an armored car,' " repeated Jimmy Walker. "You've hit a phrase there. In a way that's what the whole country's doing."

He and Betty went out, and a few moments later there was a wail of sirens from the street as the big black limousine sped on its way.

As Guy and Plum crossed Times Square, the newstands carried flaming headlines:

CHICAGO KILLINGS
DEAD DISTRICT ATTORNEY IN GANGSTER'S CAR

"Remember Droitwich?" said Guy, as he fished out three cents for his paper. "The terrace of the Impney? The long twilights? The nightingales?"

"Yes, wasn't it dull!" said Plum.

Chapter Sixteen

THE Victor Moore whom Plum had remembered from the touring company of *See You Later* proved to be very much alive. Neither Aarons nor Freedley had ever seen him but they took the word of the authors that he was exactly right to play the bootlegger who had turned the cellar of the hero's summer home into a storehouse for his stock.

But Moore's diffident style, his querulous whine, his fatuous, blundering garrulity, were lost on the two Beau Brummels who were presenting the show. Accustomed to the incisive delivery of a Catlett or an Andy Tombes, they were convinced that the two writers had been crazy in suggesting Moore and were merely stubborn in insisting that he was going to be great in the part. They went so far as to say they would pay ten thousand dollars if Moore would withdraw from rehearsal, and, on the opening night in Philadelphia, they had two comedians watching out front, one of them, Johnny Dooley, having been virtually promised the part.

The staggering triumph of Mr. Moore gave the authors an almost greater satisfaction than the success of the play. So completely did the two managers alter their opinion of him that they employed Moore in five subsequent productions, the final one being *Anything Goes*. Looking back through a past that bristles with mistakes the authors like to recall such occasional triumphs of judgment. The Bolton epitaph: "He wasn't always as much of a damn fool as he was sometimes," will owe something of its validity to Victor Moore.

On the third night of the Philadelphia engagement Guy and

Plum were leaning on the barrier, delighted by the fact that in the whole of the capacious "Shubert Philadelphia" there wasn't a seat for them to sit on.

Shorty McGee, posing as a butler in order to watch over his forty thousand dollars worth of wet goods downstairs, had just gone off to a rousing hand. Gertie Lawrence and Oscar Shaw were in the midst of a romantic passage, and anyone looking at Guy would have realized that here at least was one man who found the scene utterly captivating. Plum, while perhaps equally enchanted, could mask his feelings more readily, nor had he the habit of repeating the words in unison with the actors, a Bolton practice that he, not infrequently supported by members of the audience, had tried vainly to discourage.

A more unfortunate moment for a dog to select in making his appearance on the stage could hardly have been thought of. Long windows stood half open on a moonlit beach; the door to the library was unclosed; there was also a stair. None of these appealed to the canine visitor. He preferred instead to come in through the fireplace, where a log fire was flickering realistically. He paid no attention to the actors but walked straight to the footlights and stared at the audience from under shaggy brows like a Scotch elder rebuking sin from the pulpit.

He then walked over to the proscenium arch, cocked his leg, scuffled with his feet and made his exit—through the fireplace.

Guy was outraged.

"What are you laughing at?" he said. "The love story has gone clean out of the window."

"Out of the fireplace, you mean, don't you?"

The actors had stumbled through the buzzing and the ripples of laughter to the duet.

I remember the bliss
Of that wonderful kiss . . .
Oh, how I'd adore it
If you would encore it.

237

The dog made a second appearance, pausing this time while still in the fireplace, his paws resting on the log as he glanced archly from side to side of the room. He jumped the log and came in wagging his tail. He was a gray, rough-coated animal, something like an oversize Cairn but, if such was his mother's stock, it seemed certain that her pride of race had been tried beyond the breaking point by a lop-eared hound.

Oh, do, do, do what you done, done, done before, baby

sang the lovers.

The storm of laughter drowned the orchestra and, when the wretched animal, as if in response to the repeated admonitions, made his way again to the proscenium arch, there was no continuing with the number.

The pair on the stage were not as badly shaken as was Victor Moore, waiting, on the side opposite the fireplace, to make his re-entrance. He knew the authors had been busy writing in some new stuff for Gertie and Oscar. He knew that Oscar was an accomplished light comedian and he was further aware that, given encouragement, Gertie revelled in "hoke."

But, dash it all, if the so-called "straight" people were going to get laughs like this he would have to pull up his socks. Then, shattering him completely, came a terrific "scene-call" from the audience far in excess of the hand he had received. He could hardly have been expected to guess that a dog had decided that a stage fireplace was an excellent substitute for a kennel.

"I should have left Bugs at his club," said Betty Compton afterward. (Her pet was named after Walker's friend and favorite humorist, Bugs Baer.)

"His club?" queried Plum.

"Oh, yes, there are dogs' clubs in all the big cities. The top one in New York is The Blue Ribbon but poor Buggsie could never get into *that*. You have to have been shown before you're eligible, so of course Buggsie hasn't a hope. Jimmy pulled some strings and got him into The Beefsteak. The food is wonderful but it's full of mutts."

Plum, an old-time dog lover, was interested. Betty explained that there were some single-breed clubs and in those pets of both sexes were catered to. Then should there be any "romances," as Betty termed them, the result would not be too disastrous. There was one for poodles called Colonie Caniche, and another exclusively for police dogs known as The Sentinel. The clubs were, she explained, a great convenience, especially for hotel dwellers.

"A car calls for Buggsie in the morning and he comes home at cocktail time."

"What do the dogs do at these clubs?" asked Guy.

Betty gave him rather a blank look.

"What does anyone do at a club? They eat lunch and play games."

"Of course."

· 2 ·

"They're getting pretty nutty in this land of mine," said Guy a few days later when they were sitting over the Great Neck breakfast table. "I'm reading about the funeral yesterday of the Chicago gangster, Dion O'Bannion. The casket, with handles of solid gold, cost ten thousand dollars and on top of it lay a wreath inscribed 'From Al,' sent by the man who had had him murdered."

"Yes, I've been reading about it, too. There were twenty-six truckloads of flowers. Also three widows in weeds so heavy that they couldn't be identified."

"But life even over here isn't all murders," said Guy. "Turn to the sporting page. 'The Dixmoor Country Club has installed loud speakers round the course so that Sunday morning golfers can listen to the church services and still get their game.'"

"Some game, too, if they play the latest style of golf match which a writer here says is growing in popularity. You're allowed to cheat in any way you like, but if caught cheating you lose the hole."

"The crossword puzzle craze is now at such a pitch, my paper informs me, that a Pittsburgh pastor is handing out crossword slips which, when solved, give the text of his sermon. They're all looney."

"The particular type of looniness that has sprung up in Florida seems to have been given a sharp lesson."

"The hurricane? Yes, pretty ghastly, isn't it?"

"It says that the streets of Miami are littered with yachts—not one of them Hank Savage's, unfortunately—and that a five-masted steel schooner is standing in the garden of one of the new hotels."

"Four hundred dead, fifty thousand homeless. Even Nature goes a bit screwball in America."

"But show business is booming."

"Yes, it's never been better."

"How's *The Ramblers* doing?"

"All the Lyric Theater will hold."

Plum's adaptation of *The Play's the Thing* opened at the Henry Miller on November the third and *Oh, Kay* at the Imperial five days later. They were both instantaneous successes. The old firm was doing all right.

Immediately after the first night of *Oh, Kay*, Guy rushed over to London, where a show he had written, with a score by Rodgers and Hart, was already in rehearsal and due to open at the London Gaiety on December first. It was for Cicely Court-neige, Jack Hulbert and Phyllis Dare and was called *Lido Lady*.

On December fifteenth rehearsals of *Rio Rita* were to begin in New York, so Guy's visit to London was necessarily a brief one. Plum, deciding to remain in America for the winter, had settled down with Ethel in a furnished apartment.

Rio Rita opened the new Ziegfeld Theater on February second. It had a most effective score by Tierney and McCarthy, the team which had written *Kid Boots* for Ziegfeld as well as the record-breaking *Irene*.

Ziegfeld drew Guy aside after the opening and told him that he had signed Marilyn Miller and Jack Donahue for the following season. Would Guy write a show for them and, if so, did he want a partner? He said he did and of course named Plum.

The two set to work immediately and turned out a scenario. The play, tentatively entitled *The Gibson Girl*, was in complete scenario form inside of ten days. They read it to both the stars and both approved. Ziegfeld was in Palm Beach so they decided to go down there and close the deal.

Chapter Seventeen

I T WAS IN 1918 that they had paid their previous visit to the Florida resort—now it was 1927. The real estate boom had come in the interval and, having reached its climax in the previous year, was in a state of recession. It had not yet, however, by any means collapsed.

Plum bought a paper when their train stopped at Fort Pierce and regaled his companion with a joint proclamation by the mayors of the east coast littoral announcing "The Fiesta of the American Tropics"—"Our Season of Mardi Gras when Love, Merrymaking and Wholesome Sport Shall Prevail Throughout Our Domains." They promised unitedly "Parades in which a Glorious Pageantry of Sublime Beauty Shall Depict in Floral Loveliness the Blessings Bestowed upon Us by Friendly Sun, Gracious Rain and Soothing Tropic Winds."

"I wonder," said Guy, "how the sixteen hundred people injured in the great September hurricane feel about those 'Soothing Tropic Winds.'"

Ziegfeld was staying with Leonard Replogle, the financier, and wasn't in when they phoned. They spent the day swimming and playing a round of golf on the new Everglades course. They returned to the hotel expecting to find a message from the manager but there was none. They dressed, dined and went to Bradley's. There the Colonel told them that Ziegfeld was upstairs in the Chemin-de-Fer room. He said he was afraid Flo had had a bad night.

"Lucky that *Rio Rita* of his is such a hit," he said. "He's had nothing but bad luck down here."

A man with a shock of pale straw-colored hair standing nearby turned to them.

"You're talking about Flo?" he said. "Did you ever see anybody like him? He was flat broke before this new show of his went on, with a grocery bill up at Hastings that a greyhound couldn't jump over. But a week after The Ziegfeld opened he came down here in a private car."

"There never was such extravagance," agreed Bradley.

"I knew him out in Chicago when we were both knee-high to a grasshopper," said the light-haired man. "The first thing I remember about him was he'd buy an all-day sucker at six o'clock at night." Everybody laughed.

"Suckers he had even then, had he?" commented a man who had been standing near them listening to the conversation.

As they turned to him he placed a finger on his chest.

"When I say 'suckers' I'm pointing right at the biggest one. Believe me, gentlemen, that loafer still owes me for the costumes of the Follies of 1923. And then he had the nerve to ask for me to dress the Spanish shawl number in *Rio Rita*. Real Spanish shawls he wants and, what you think? I am damn fool enough to get them for him."

"Who was the chap who said he'd known Flo as a kid?" asked Guy as the Colonel escorted them to the stair.

"Jesse Livermore."

"The Wolf of Wall Street!"

"Yes, I don't know why he wastes his time coming in here."

"Shemmy" was an innovation since Guy and Plum had last visited Bradley's. When they were there in 1918, there had been only roulette and "hazzard," or "birdcage" as it is sometimes called. Now Bradley's "shemmy" game had the reputation of being the steepest in the world.

Ziegfeld was seated at the table. He greeted them gaily.

"Hello, boys, what are you doing down here? Bad place, bad game." He addressed the dealer. "Card please."

"I never learned to play 'shemmy,' " said Guy.

"Seems like I never did either," said Ziegfeld, turning over a ten. "You boys got some money on you?"

"Yes." Guy, who was acting as the team's treasurer, pulled out his wallet.

"Give me a thousand."

"That's all we've got."

"That's all I asked for."

Guy handed him a small sheaf of crisp, new hundreds. Ziegfeld tossed them all on the table and pulled the "shoe" toward him.

"That's pretty rich, isn't it?" protested one of the players.

"That's what the bank opens for, gentlemen, a thousand."

As the punters placed their bets, Flo conversed with the two writers standing beside him.

He turned his cards as he spoke. He had eight. The money was raked into the bank. They watched the play for a few minutes, then:

"We've brought down the layout of the Miller show," Guy told him.

"Oh, good. I want it to be the biggest thing I've ever done. Incidentally Erlanger won't come in. He says a hundred thousand is too much to risk on any one show." He turned back to the table.

Ziegfeld continued to win steadily. The croupier announced that there was twenty-four thousand in the bank. A voice said "banco." Ziegfeld looked up and saw Jesse Livermore.

"Hello, Pinkie,"—Livermore, a virtual albino, had that characteristic pink look about the eyes—"don't come round here with that hot streak of yours."

Ziegfeld dealt the cards with the same careless flip.

" 'Shooting for the stick,' eh? That's always been your style."

He turned over a natural.

"The Magoo, Pinkie. Looks like you aren't wearing your horseshoes tonight."

Jesse Livermore laughed and threw in a wad of bills.

"Seems as if you boys have brought me luck," said Ziegfeld.

"You're not going to leave that money in the bank, are you?"

"Why not? I'm doing all right."

"You've run the bank for fourteen coups," said Plum. "You don't think it's going on forever, do you?"

"I'll run it one more."

"Well, I won't watch."

"You stay right where you are. Maybe it's you that's the mascot."

He won again.

"All right, boys, the bank passes. I'm going to go on gambling with this money," he told the table. "I'm going to use it to produce a show by these two gentlemen. What's it called, boys?"

"*The Gibson Girl.*"

"Yes, not bad. Come on, let's go down and have a drink."

The plot of *The Gibson Girl* was designed to show off three colorful American resorts, Saratoga, Bar Harbor and Palm Beach.

Three sisters living on a farm inherit a small legacy and Pat, the one to be played by Marilyn, suggests they employ it in finding a husband. There is not enough for three stylish outfits so her proposal is to take turns. Each of them will have a month in which to disport herself, the two who are "out" serving as secretary-chaperone and lady's maid.

Marilyn, having won first chance and chosen Saratoga, meets a man whom she imagines to be rich but who is a fortune-hunter himself. They fall in love. When their mutually penniless status is revealed, he atones for "wasting her time" by entrapping a rich young man for her. Marilyn's answer is to run away. In the next setting one of her sisters is the glamorous Miss Gibson. She is a lady's maid.

Ziegfeld seemed lukewarm. He raised no objection that could be argued. He listened, nodded and said nothing. A day or two later Guy learned the reason. Flo produced a rough outline for a show which had been sent to him by Bill Maguire. It was "timely," having to do with the recent visit to the United States of Queen Marie of Rumania and her daughter. The Princess was in love with a West Point cadet who, somewhat improbably, had flown the Atlantic with a cadet pal (Donahue). Still more improbably they had landed in Rumania.

Neither Bill nor Ziegfeld was strong on geography, nor were they acquainted with the regulations covering West Point cadets. Guy had, in his architectural youth, spent two years at the Point, and he thought this might give him some advantage in dealing with the cuckoo about to lay its egg (a prophetic phrase he fancied) in the cosy nest that Plum and he were building.

But Maguire had done one thing which, for Ziegfeld, had an irresistible appeal. He had telegraphed his story. As has been pointed out before, Ziggy was the telegraph kid. He handled the forty-two yellow sheets with Bill's name on the last one, with loving care.

So it was that *Rosalie* came into being. Flo told Guy he wanted him to team with Maguire. "I know Bill," he said. "This telegram is about all I'll ever get from him."

"But what about Plum?"

"He can write the lyrics."

"How can he? You're getting Gershwin. He'll only work with Ira."

"I'm having Romberg as well. He knows Rumania. He's been there. Plum knows Europe too. It's a good combination."

"Two book writers, two lyric writers, two composers?"

"Why not?"

"It's all right if you can pay for it."

"If I can't pay for things, I don't pay for them."

This simple axiom summed up the principle on which all Ziegfeld undertakings were based. He had one disciple who adhered to this philosophy as strictly as did he, his pet author, William Anthony Maguire. Bill had his own way of putting it:

"If I haven't got it, they can't get it," was his phrase, and the fact that he so frequently didn't have it because, like Ziegfeld, he'd bought what he couldn't pay for seemingly troubled him as little as it did the manager.

Once when a scene that Bill had written in *Whoopee* was dubbed "old-fashioned," he refuted the criticism hotly.

"Damn it all, Flo and I are ahead of the times. Look at the way we both live on next year's income."

He was constantly just one jump ahead of the sheriff. Once, indeed, the sheriff was one jump ahead of him. Guy was expecting Bill to come and spend a week at a shore cottage he had taken at Westhampton. Together they were going to put the finishing touches to *Rosalie*. Half an hour before the train was due, three men, one of whom wore a large silver star, tramped up the wooden path and displayed a body warrant to the Bolton factotum that called for Bill's arrest and incarceration.

Though clad in a wet bathing suit, Guy flew to his car and drove to Speonk, where he told his collaborator what was awaiting him at Westhampton. Bill and his bag were then driven back to Patchogue so that he could catch a train for New York. All there was of the polishing process took place during the drive.

It was a few days after that that Bill disappeared. He was living at the Warwick but when Guy and Plum, who were working together on a spot where a new number was needed, phoned him, they were told he was no longer there. They called Flo.

"That's where he was last night," said Flo. "I'll see what I can find out. You boys had better come on over to the Ziegfeld."

"I don't know where that damned low-life has got to," were

the words he greeted them with when they entered the office. "His things are still at the Warwick. They're holding them for the rent."

"I hope the revised script of *Rosalie* isn't impounded."

"Holy cats! If that crackpot has got the script, God help us! You know what he did to me once? Sold me a sketch—I bought it outright for fifteen hundred. He put the money in his pocket but forgot to leave the sketch. The *Follies* was already in rehearsal so I combed the town for him. His wife didn't know where he was—but it wasn't often she did. Then *The Passing Show* opened and there was my sketch. The stinker had sold it to Lee Shubert two days before he did to me. And all he'd charged Lee was a thousand!"

The phone rang. It was Bill. Ziegfeld told him to beat it over as fast as he could come and to bring the script.

"He's got it," Ziegfeld told them as he hung up. "The Warwick people wouldn't let him take a thing but he sneaked *Rosalie* out tucked under his waistband. Then what do you think he did? He moved into the Plaza. He says he likes it better there, he's got a nice view of the park."

Bill arrived, cheerful as usual.

"So you're at the Plaza now?"

"Yes, only trouble is it's a bit grand. You have to have a shave before you'd venture into the barber shop."

"What did you do for luggage?"

"Oh, I always keep a bag at the Friars with a couple of old telephone books in it. Then I go buy me what I need and have it paid for at the desk."

The phone rang again. Ziegfeld answered it. "That was the box office," he said, hanging up. "They say there's a sheriff waiting for you downstairs, Bill."

"Jeez! That's what I get for coming here."

"Look," said Flo, "I tell you what. I'll go down and say you've gone. Turn out the lights. I'll tell them there's nobody up here."

It was about seven-thirty. They turned out the lights and sat in the dark discussing the show in whispers. A strange sort of story conference, but then things were apt to be strange around Bill Maguire.

Then the door was opened and Ziegfeld switched on the lights. He held a folded paper in his hands.

"You son-of-a-bitch," he said. "He wasn't after you, he was after me."

Maguire clicked his tongue disapprovingly.

"Why don't you pay your bills, Flo?" he said.

· 2 ·

To compensate Plum for substituting Maguire as Guy's collaborator, Flo engaged him to write *The Three Musketeers*, a musical designed to serve as a twin starring vehicle for Dennis King and Vivienne Segal. The composer was Rudy Friml whom Plum had worked with before on the lyrics of a dead and gone turkey of 1916 called *Kitty Darlin'*.

About the same time he was commissioned by Gilbert Miller to adapt *Her Cardboard Lover* for Jeanne Eagles and Leslie Howard. He had, further, a comedy he had written for an English management called *Good Morning Bill*. All four of these, including *Rosalie*, were produced within the space of four months.

At the same time Guy was engaged with Fred Thompson on a new Astaire show, *Funny Face*, another Philip Goodman musical, *The Five O'Clock Girl*, *Rosalie* and *She's My Baby*. This last was a Dillingham show written in collaboration with Kalmar and Ruby, with a score by Rodgers and Hart, and starring Bea Lillie, Clifton Webb and Irene Dunne.

Guy, finding conflicting demands too much for him, bowed out of *Funny Face* after the play had passed its scenario stage. He suggested Bob Benchley to take his place. Bob took over.

Altogether Plum and Guy had, singly or together, nineteen

opening nights in the three years 1926-7-8. Fourteen of these were new shows, five reproductions in one country of plays first presented in the other.

Looking through the diaries, every day seems to have been given to either writing or rehearsing. The protracted tours of the Princess days had given place to a more or less standard two weeks' tryout. This was a period of intensive effort, of rewriting, of early and late rehearsals, of the continual watching of performances in an effort to gauge audience reactions.

Four shows a year meant two months of this, the hardest and most exacting work of all. The chief intervals of rest were those spent on ocean liners—though even there you would most likely have found the team, rug-wrapped in adjoining deck chairs, busy with pad and pencil.

· 3 ·

Although Plum was deeply preoccupied with his books—*The Small Bachelor, Meet Mr. Mulliner* and *Money for Nothing,* all published in the year, with *A Gentleman of Leisure, Fish Preferred* and *Carry on, Jeeves,* coming along in the next—he still found time to do a little dramatic work. With Ian Hay he wrote *A Damsel in Distress* based on an earlier novel and he accepted a commission from Gilbert Miller to adapt the German play, *By Candlelight.* The fact that Gertie Lawrence was to be the heroine of the last named was too great a temptation to be resisted.

This particular chore took Plum to America in the early summer of '29. He and Guy had not met in exactly a year.

"You're looking a little drawn," said Plum. "I know it can't be 'overdrawn,' ha, ha. So there must be some other reason."

"Just the rat race. I don't quite know why I've been doing it."

"I don't quite know why either of us have. Youth's been knocking at the door for some time now."

"Yes . . . only what do you do when you stop working? Just sit there listening to the hardening of your arteries?"

"It's not as bad as all that. We're still quite young."

"Yes, quite."

"Quite."

"I hate that word 'quite.' "

Plum regarded him speculatively.

"The only symptom of approaching age I detect in you is that you don't talk about *The Little Thing* as much as you used to."

"I'm still as keen about it as ever."

"Are you? Then why the devil don't we put it on ourselves?"

"Become managers?"

"Don't say it in that awed voice. There's no trick to being a manager."

"Are you sure there isn't? All my life—my theatrical life—I've mentally been saying 'sir' to them. They may be 'Ray' and 'Flo' and 'Charlie' to talk to but in my innermost soul they are Mr. Comstock, Mr. Ziegfeld and Mr. Dillingham. I find myself waiting for them to ask me to sit down."

"I never guessed all this."

"You'll find reflections of it in my diary. There are even a couple of 'Mr. Freedley's' crossed out and 'Vinnie' written after them."

The conversation was taking place in the Ritz, where they were both staying. Guy's Great Neck home was rented. In answer to a question he said that Marguerite had been in America but was now in Italy.

"Let's talk over this *Little Thing* thing at lunch."

"Where shall we go?"

"The Algonquin?"

"The Round Table? I'm never comfortable there. I feel like one does when one's trying to think up a funny opening night telegram to the comic, which you know will be pasted on his mirror for the run of the show."

"You seem to be in a very diminished state. What's happened to you?"

"Oh, a bit of this and that—nothing."

"I suspect woman trouble—that old complaint of yours."

"Nonsense. I nailed my flag to the masthead years ago. 'Women are wonderful.' It's still there, a bit tattered and battle-scarred but flying just the same."

They went downstairs to the Japanese Garden where, ironically enough, after their decision not to go to the Algonquin Round Table, Theodore (the big one this time) put them next a table where Alec Woollcott was seated with Bob Benchley, Arthur Richman, and Phil Barry. Plum received a warm welcome and he and Guy were told to move over.

"Don't tell me you two fellows are planning another assault on Broadway," said Phil. "You're a menace."

"Speak to those men respectfully, young fellow," said Bob. "They've written more musical comedies than any other four men in the world. I wrote *one*—that chap Guy landed me with it—and oh, boy, was that something. I always keep saying 'oh, boy!' whenever these two are around," he added. "I like to see those nostalgic smiles steal across their faces."

"What *are* you up to, Plum," said Woollcott, "if it's rude to ask?"

"I'm here to see Gilbert Miller about an adaptation I'm doing for him."

"Gilbert Miller?" echoed Woollcott and, rising, he held up his coffee cup in a toast. "Gentlemen, I give you Gilbert Miller. I give him to you freely. All I ask in exchange is a five-cent cigar and a Coolidge campaign button."

"Come, come now," said Plum. "After all he is our most literate manager. Also, it's the old story—when it's someone you like and admire, their faults are of moment to you. You notice a blemish in your sweetheart that would pass unchallenged in another woman."

"Gilbert may be your sweetheart," said Woollcott. "He isn't mine."

"But you must admit—"

"Yes, yes, yes," interrupted the critic testily. "I admit everything. I admit his impeccable taste in stage decor, his shrewdness in casting, his enterprise, his courage. . . . His stories have both pith and point, and I pay tribute to his admirable restraint when, with far more justification than have others who do, he does not attempt to rewrite his authors' plays. It is on a matter, not of sense, but of sensibility that I arraign him . . . Mr. Arthur Richman has the floor."

"Oh, no you don't!" laughed Arthur. "I'm not telling that story!"

"Are you not the author of the famous line: 'You have to know Gilbert really well in order to dislike him?' "

"That was just a crack—not to be taken seriously."

"Very well if you won't tell the story, I will." He turned to the table:

"The talented gentleman on my right recently received a dinner invitation from the Millers, and, in response to its instructions, presented himself at the door of the Bache-Miller residence, 814 Fifth Avenue, attired in white tie and with dark red carnation in buttonhole.

"Ushered into one of the sumptuous reception rooms where Fragonards and Watteaus rub shoulders, and where berceus encased in lovely Oudry tapestries implore you not to sit on them, our author was set to wondering why he had been invited. It was clearly one of the fancier Miller occasions and he realized that all save himself enjoyed high rating by either social or cash register standards, if not by both.

"In an effort to make him feel more at ease, or possibly because he was tired, Gilbert came and leaned on his shoulder, a rather favorite habit of the most literate of our managers.

" 'Come with me,' he said suddenly and rather abruptly,

253

and, turning, he led the way to the elevator. . . . Oh, yes, there is an elevator, known, because of its being hung with Gobelins, as the *ascenseur*. There are also solid gold fittings on the plumbing fixtures. Kitty maintains they are economical—they never have to be cleaned.

"Little Arthur, following in the wake of big Gilbert, thought to himself hopefully: 'Aha, a business chat . . . Ina Claire . . . that comedy of mine that would have been collecting dust on Gilbert's desk this past twelve months were not Gilbert's desk so constantly dusted.'

"But no, it was not that. Gilbert shot the *ascenseur* upwards and stopped it between floors. He turned to Arthur with that, as always, ominous phrase: 'Arthur, we've known each other a long time, so I think I may speak freely. You have a terrible case of halitosis.'

" 'Oh, no,' protested Arthur, as perspiration beaded his forehead. 'It can't be true. I'm a very healthy man with an excellent digestion and—'

" 'It is true,' broke in Gilbert inexorably. 'Blow at me.'

"Arthur blew.

" 'Blow again.'

"Arthur blew again.

" 'No, it isn't you,' said Gilbert in a matter-of-fact tone and, thereupon, shot the *ascenseur* down again and discharged his tottering guest into the cocktail-drinking assembly. To describe Arthur as shattered is an understatement. His collar had wilted, two damp spots showed on his shirt front, he felt if Gilbert came and leaned on him again he would collapse.

"But Gilbert was leaning on other shoulders. Arthur was free to stand there alone and try to recover his shattered morale. He, naturally, realized the reason for the mistake. Gilbert had not supposed anyone who had his name in the Social Register could possibly have halitosis—well, now he had learned his lesson. Arthur watched as the host ambled off once again to the *ascenseur* with a prominent young upper-cruster in tow.

"When he returned, Arthur could not resist an enquiry.

" 'Yes, he's the one,' said Gilbert, 'but I think I've got him pretty well fixed up with some of Kitty's mouth wash.' "

Woollcott paused.

"If I was a pitiful object," said Arthur, "you should have seen this other poor wretch. Whenever one of the women on either side of him spoke to him, he never turned his head by the fraction of an inch. He spoke straight—out—front."

"An engaging story," said Plum, "but still, reverting from sensibility to sense, isn't it better to know if you've got halitosis? Personally I find it comforting to reflect that if your best friends won't tell you, Gilbert Miller will."

· 4 ·

The idea of turning manager and putting on *The Little Thing* themselves burgeoned as a bud in May. Guy, seemingly dubious when Plum first suggested it, grew daily more enthusiastic. Even when investigation revealed that costs had pyramided so that they must budget for close to a hundred thousand dollars he was not discouraged—what was a hundred thousand dollars? Plenty of smart lads were making that every other day in Wall Street.

The script was hauled out and completely revised. Some of the scenes had the "color" of *Sally*. These were eliminated. Bits of the material that they had designed for *The Gibson Girl* were fitted in. They chose Vincent Youmans as composer. Plum and he set to work on the score.

They took offices in the Brill Building. They interviewed Marilyn, miraculously free. She read the script and liked it.

"Why was this never done before?" she asked. "You say you wrote it some time ago."

"I'd hate to tell you how long."

"It's a shame Jack can't play the comedy part but he's going into something he's written with Fred Thompson."

"*Sons of Guns?* Yes, we know about that. How do you like that new chap they're all talking about who's playing in a thing at the Shubert called *Ups-a-Daisy?*"

"Lester Hope?"

"He's changing his name to 'Bob'—'Bob Hope.' "

"I think he'd be just right."

"We'll get him." It was said with confidence. Not, "We'll get him if Mr. Freedley agrees." No nonsense about the management not being willing to pay the salary—the thing Savage had pulled when they asked for Billy Van.

"You're right," said Guy, "there's no trick to being a manager. "It's like trying the handle of a door that you'd always imagined was locked and bolted, and finding it's been open all the time."

"I suppose we ought to sell some securities and deposit that hundred grand in the bank?"

"Oh, we don't need it yet. My broker says the bull market's good for another six months. Seems a shame to pull the money out when every day you leave it there it keeps getting more."

They hired a company manager, Jim O'Leary, an old-timer who knew the ropes and had costs at his fingertips. They had an excellent secretary, Lillian Hartman, who had worked for Guy years before. Everything seemed set. The only annoyance was what they always referred to as the *ascenseurs*. There never was a building whose elevators were so jammed. People seemed to pour in and out of the Brill Building in waves. Frequently three or four elevators would go by their floor as they were waiting to go to lunch. A little thing but, when you want to go to lunch, you want to go to lunch.

"Let's move before we produce our next show," said Plum.

Guy nodded. "This is an anniversary," he said, "and I suggest that, for good and practical reasons, we go somewhere where they know us."

"What's it an anniversary of?"

"Just thirteen years ago today we walked into Ray Comstock's office. *Go To It* had laid an egg the night before."

"The *Oh, Boy!* contract."

"That's right, the *Oh, Boy!* contract. October the eighth."

"Good old October eighth!"

· 5 ·

It was the following day that the roof started to fall in, but it wasn't till October twenty-fourth that the floor gave way and the two authors began to wonder how far down bottom was. Each hour the seismographs registered a further shock. Auburn Auto, in which they both had holdings, dropped sixty points in one day. After that bit of news came through, things got blurred and there seemed to be a general impression that Judgment Day had set in with unusual severity. Looking over one's shoulder one would not have been surprised to see a brace of those great beasts with an unnecessary number of heads, as described in the Book of Revelation, flexing their muscles before starting in to do their stuff.

Plum and Guy closed the door of their Brill Building office with the knowledge that they would never have need to return. They pressed the "down" button. The elevator that stopped at their floor was miraculously empty.

"That's funny," said Guy.

"Not at all," said Plum. "Everybody is using the windows."

Guy's reception of the witticism was not hearty.

"Where shall we go to lunch?" It was Plum who asked the question.

"Ever try the Automat? The food's darn good. I used to go there when I was writing *Polly Preferred*."

"No," said Plum firmly, "I'm damned if we will. We'll take a leaf out of the Ziegfeld-Maguire book and go to the Ritz."

"What smart fellows those two were: they *spent* their money."

"Yes, I bet they're busy right now popping champagne corks and patting each other on the back."

"Wise guys, eh? I can hear them jeering, 'Now these smart Alecks will be coming round to us for some tips on sheriff dodging.'"

They went to the Ritz and Theodore produced two smashing horses' necks that were not horses' necks. They didn't even mind when Vecsey struck up with "The Rose of China."

"Funny, the failures don't matter any more. If we'd cleaned up with *The Rose of China*, today it would be allee-samee bottomside."

"For heaven's sake, don't start talking pidgin. That'll finish me."

"How do you actually stand?"

"The books balance exactly—the red and the black. They did a thorough job on me."

"They didn't get quite all of mine, thanks to Ethel."

"Well, that's fine."

"What about you taking a bit of it till the tide starts coming in again?"

"No, thanks a lot, but I'm all right. I've got enough for carfare."

Guy took a letter from his pocket and extracted an oblong green slip from it.

"The three sweetest words in the language," said Plum. "'Enclosed find check.' Remember which show that was from?"

"*Very Good Eddie.*"

"Right. Is it a big check?"

"Quite big. I'm sending it back."

"You're doing *what*?"

"Sending it back . . . to Marguerite. She heard about what's happened and sold all the bits and pieces I ever gave her. She even sold her beloved *roulotte*."

"She's a wonderful wife."

"Yes . . . but not mine."

"What on earth do you mean?"

"The divorce was made final that day sixteen months ago . . . the day we lunched with Alec Woollcott and the others at the Ritz. It didn't work, you see. She needed someone who would be on hand to talk to and have a bit of fun with . . . what's the phrase? . . . 'Turn out the pocketful of daily doings.' "

"I'm terribly sorry."

"Oh, I'm all right now. I've found a girl."

"I'm glad to hear that."

"And I've got a job."

"That's odd. *I've* got a job."

"I'm off to Hollywood."

"*I'm* off to Hollywood."

"Well, that's wonderful. I thought this time they really had broken up the old firm. I'm with Paramount."

"*I'm* with Paramount. They're putting me on a picture for W. C. Fields."

Guy drew a deep breath.

"Do you think," he said, "the clientele would object if I sang a few bars? Paramount is putting *me* on that Fields picture, too."

Plum gaped.

"You're kidding."

"It's the truth."

"You mean we'll be working together? But this is terrific!"

"Pretty good, I agree."

"I think this calls for another one, don't you?"

"I certainly do."

"Do you realize," said Plum, "that we've been working together for thirteen years and not a dirty look from start to finish? Most collaborators hate each other's guts after the first couple of shows. It's extraordinary."

"Amazing."

"Twin souls about sums it up, in my opinion."

"In mine, too."

They drank to Hollywood, to Paramount, to W. C. Fields and to the further prosperity of the partnership.

"And now," said Plum, when this ritual was concluded, "tell me about this girl of yours."

"I'd rather wait till you see her."

"When will that be?"

"She'll be meeting me at Pasadena."

"What's her name?"

"No, I'm not even going to tell you that. I'll tell you her nickname, though. And she had it before I met her."

"Yes?"

"The Little Thing," said Guy.

Chapter Eighteen

THE TRAIN TO THE COAST—the famous Chief—was rolling along through the wide open spaces where men are men. It was the second day out from Chicago and Guy and Plum were finishing their lunch in the diner. Ethel was to come on later after they had settled in.

The exodus from the East which had begun with the coming of sound to the motion pictures was at its height. Already on the train the two had met a number of authors, composers, directors and other Broadway fauna with whom they had worked in the days before the big crash. Rudolf Friml was there and Vincent Youmans and Arthur Richman and a dozen more. It was like one of those great race movements of the Middle Ages.

"Well," said Guy, "California here we come. How do you feel?"

"I feel," said Plum, "as I should think Alice must have felt when, after mixing with all those weird creatures in Wonderland, she knelt on the mantelpiece preparatory to climbing through the looking glass."

"I see what you mean—wondering what kind of freaks she was going to meet this time. Still, maybe it won't be so bad. Hollywood can't have many terrors for two men who have survived Erlanger, Savage, little Plymouth, Junior Breckenridge, the Sisters Duncan and Bertie the Seal—not to mention Fabulous Felix and Palmer."

"Palmer?"

"Hank Savage's private poisoner."

"Good Lord, I haven't thought of him for years. I wonder what became of him."

"I hope he perished of his own cooking. I've never forgiven that bird for the supercilious way he sneered at that really excellent plot of ours about the pawnbroker."

"I remember dimly something about a pawnbroker—"

"Good heavens, man, it was a superb plot and we might do worse than spring it on W. C. Fields when we get to Hollywood. You can't have forgotten. Fields was the last of a long line of pawnbrokers and his ancestor had loaned the money to Queen Isabella to finance Columbus . . ."

"I remember! The contract turned up, and Fields found that he owned ten per cent of America."

"It was a darned good idea, and that hash-slinging sea cook crabbed it with a lot of stuff about thematic archaism."

At this moment a man in horn-rimmed spectacles paused at their table.

"Oh, there you are," he said. "I'll come and have a chat in a minute or two. Can't stop now. See you later."

He passed on, and they looked after him, puzzled.

"Now who on earth was that?" said Guy. "He seemed to know us."

"Probably somebody who was in one of our shows. The train's stiff with actors."

They dismissed the man from their thoughts and returned to the subject of Hollywood.

"Have you talked to anyone who's been there?" asked Guy.

"Only Bob Benchley, and you know the sort of information you would get from him. He said I mustn't believe the stories I had heard about ill-treatment of inmates at the studios, for there was very little actual brutality. Most of the big executives, he said, were kindly men, and he had often seen Louis B. Mayer stop outside some nodder's hutch and push a piece of lettuce through the bars."

"What's a nodder?"

"Bob explained that. A sort of yes-man, only lower in the social scale. When there is a story conference and the supervisor throws out some suggestion or idea, the yes-men all say 'yes.' After they have finished saying 'yes,' the nodders nod. Bob said there is also a sub-species known as nodders' assistants, but he didn't want to get too technical."

"What else? Is it true that they're all lunatics out in Hollywood?"

"Bob says no. He says he knows fully half a dozen people there who are practically sane—except of course at the time of the full moon. . . . Good Lord!"

"What's the matter?"

"I've remembered who that chap was who spoke to us."

"Who?"

"Palmer."

"It can't have been."

"It was. Palmer in person. Not a picture."

Guy considered.

"I believe you're right. But we shall soon know. He's coming this way."

It was Palmer—older and with a new and rather horrible briskness about him, but still Palmer. He reached their table and sat down, looking snappy and efficient.

"Well, well," said Guy.

"Well, well," said Plum. "It's a long time since that yacht cruise. How's *Ophelia?*"

Palmer cocked a puzzled eyebrow.

"Ophelia?"

"Your play?"

"Oh, that?" Palmer's face cleared. "I got tired of waiting for the Colonel to do something about it—he kept putting me off and changing the subject to corned beef hash whenever I mentioned it—so I threw up my job as cook on the 'Dorinda' and came out here. Do you know something?"

"What?"

Palmer's voice was grave.

"I don't want to wrong him, but I've sometimes thought that Colonel Savage may have been stringing me along all the time."

"Colonel *Savage?*" cried Guy and Plum, horrified.

"I know the idea sounds bizarre, but it has occasionally crossed my mind that he encouraged me to think that he was going to produce my play simply in order to get a free cook. We shall never know, I suppose. Well, as I was saying, after the seventh—or was it the eighth?—trip to Florida I got tired of waiting and came out here. I had a hard time of it for a year or two, but I won through in the end and am now doing extremely well. I'm a cousin by marriage."

"A . . . what was that?"

"I married the cousin of one of the top executives and from that moment never looked back. Of course, cousins are fairly small fry, but I happen to know that there's a lot of talk going around the front office of giving me brevet rank as a brother-in-law before very long."

"A brother-in-law is good, is it?"

Palmer stared.

"My dear fellow! Practically as high up as a nephew."

The two authors offered suitable congratulations.

"Well, now we're all going to be in Hollywood together," said Guy, "I hope we shall see something of one another."

"We shall. I'm your supervisor."

"Eh?"

"On this W. C. Fields picture. If you've finished your lunch, I'll take you along to meet him. What's the time?"

"Two-thirty."

"Ah, then he may be sober."

They made their way along the train to the Fields drawing room, Guy and Plum a little dubious and inclined to shake their heads. They were not at all sure how they were going to like being supervised by a man who thought that in writing a play—and presumably a talking picture—the scale of values should be at once objective and rational, hence absolute and authentic. And their uneasiness was increased when their over-lord said graciously that he hoped they would come to dinner at his Beverly Hills home on the following Saturday, adding that for the sake of old times he would cook the meal himself.

"I'm as good a cook as I ever was," he said.

Just about, they imagined, and shivered a little.

· 2 ·

In the semi-darkness of the drawing room the first thing the authors heard was a hollow groan and the first thing they saw was a vast something bulging beneath the bed clothes. It stirred as they entered and there rose from the pillow a face rendered impressive by what must have been one of the largest and most incandescent nasal jobs ever issued to a human being since the days of Cyrano de Bergerac.

They were to learn later that the comedian was very sensitive about what he considered the only flaw in an otherwise classic countenance and permitted no facetious allusions to it even from his closest friends.

He switched on the light and regarded the visitors with aversion.

"And to what, my merry buzzards, do I owe this intrusion at daybreak?" he asked coldly.

Palmer explained that Mr. Bolton and Mr. Wodehouse were the two authors to whom had been assigned the task of assembling—under his supervision—the next Fields picture, and the great man softened visibly. He was fond of authors—being, as he often said, an author himself.

"Sit down, my little chickadees," he said, "and pass the aspirin. Are you in possession of aspirin?"

Palmer—who no doubt had foreseen this query—produced a small tin box.

"Thank you, thank you. Don't slam the lid. What I need this morning is kindness and understanding, for I am a little nervous. I was up late last night, seeing the new year in. Yes, I am aware," proceeded Fields, "that the general consensus of informed opinion in these degenerate days—pardon my redundancy—is that the year begins on January the first—but what reason have we for supposing so? One only . . . that the ancient Romans said it did. But what ancient Romans? Probably a bunch of souses who were well into their fifth bottle of Falernian wine. The Phoenicians held that it began on November the twenty-first. The medieval Christians threw celluloid balls at one another on the night of March the fifteenth. The Greeks were broadminded. Some of them thought New Year's Day came on September the twentieth, while others voted for the tenth of June. This was good for the restauranteurs—who could count on two big nights in the year—but confusing for the income tax authorities, who couldn't decide when to send in their demands."

"I never knew that before, Mr. Fields," said Palmer respectfully. There was that about the majestic comedian that made even supervisors respectful.

"Stick around me and you'll learn a lot. Well, you can readily appreciate the result of this confusion of thought, my dream princes. It makes it difficult for a conscientious man to do the right thing. He starts out simply and straightforwardly by booking a reserved table for the last night in December, and feels that that is that. But mark the sequel. As March approaches, doubts begin to assail him. 'Those medieval Christians were shrewd fellows,' he says to himself. 'Who knows whether they may not have had the right idea?'

"The only way he can square his conscience is by going out and investing heavily in squeakers and rattles and paper caps on the night of March the fifteenth. And scarcely has the doctor left his bedside next morning, when he starts to brood on the fact that the Greeks, who were nobody's fools, were

convinced that New Year's Eve was either June the tenth or
September the twentieth. Many a young man in the springtime
of life has developed cirrhosis of the liver simply by overdoing
his researches into New Year's Eve. Last night, being November the twentieth, I was pure Phoenician, and I would
appreciate the loan of that aspirin once more."

He mused in silence for a moment.

"So you're coming out to Dottyville-on-the-Pacific, are you,
boys?" he said, changing the subject. "Poor lads, poor lads!
Well, let me give you a word of advice. Don't try to escape.
They'll chase you across the ice with bloodhounds. And even
if the bloodhounds miss you, the pitiless Californian climate
drives you back. The only thing to do is to stick it out. But
you'll suffer, my unhappy young tenderfeet, you'll suffer. Conditions were appalling enough B. S., but they're far worse
now."

"B. S.?"

"Before Sound—sometimes called the Stereopticon Age,
rich in fossils. Pictures first learned to walk. Now they've
learned to talk. But the thing they've always managed to do is
smell. In this year A. S. confusion is rife. Not a soul at the
studios but is clutching its head and walking around in circles,
saying 'Where am I?' And can you blame them? Think how
they must have felt at M-G-M when they found that Jack
Gilbert could only talk soprano.

"Yes," Fields went on, "confusion is rife. I was out to Pathé
in Culver City last month and found the place in an uproar.
One of their most popular vice-presidents had just been carted
off to the loony-bin, strong men sitting on his head while
others rushed off to fetch strait jackets and ambulances. It
came about thus. As you doubtless know, the Pathé trade-
mark is a handsome white rooster. For years he's been poppin'
up on the screen ahead of their pictures and news reels, flap-
ping his wings and a-gapping open his beak. And when sound
came in, of course the directors held a meeting and it was

duly resolved that from now on he had got to crow right out loud.

"Well, they set to work and brought out all the fancy sound equipment into the front yard. The countryside had been scoured for the biggest, all-firedest rooster the sovereign state of California could provide. It was a beaut—pure white with a great red comb on him—and they had a swell background fixed up behind him and the sound machines all waiting to catch that mighty cock-a-doodle-doo—and—what do you know? —not a yip could they get out of him. He'd strut about, he'd flap his wings, he'd scrabble with his feet, but he wouldn't crow.

"Well, sir, they tried everything. They even went back to the first principle of show business—they brought on the girls. But he wasn't interested, and they began to wonder if it wouldn't be best to send for a psychiatrist. Then one of their top idea men told them that the best way to make a rooster crow was to get another rooster to crow. He remembered that the second vice-president was pretty good at barnyard imitations, though his crow wasn't his best number. His quack was better and his sow-with-a-litter-of-baby-pigs was his topper. But they thought his crow might get by, so they fetched him out of his office.

" 'Crow,' they said.

" 'Crow?' said he.

" 'That's right. Crow.'

" 'Oh, you mean *crow*?' said the vice-president, getting it. 'Like a rooster?'

"And they all said that the more like a rooster he was the better they'd be pleased.

"Well, these vice-presidents don't spare themselves when duty calls. He crowed and crowed and crowed until he had rasped his larynx, but not a sign of audience reaction. The rooster just looked at him and went on scrabbling his feet.

" 'Now let's all be very calm and rational about this,' said the director who had been assigned to shoot the scene. 'I'll tell you what's wrong, Adolf. This bird's no fool. He sees you in those yellow slacks and that hand-painted tie, and he's on to it right away that you're no rooster, so your act don't get over.'

" 'He's right, Adolf,' said the president. 'And here's what you do. You go out in the street round behind the studio wall where the bird can't see you and start crowing out there. That ought to do it.'

"So the vice-president went out on the street and began to crow, and at last the old rooster started to perk up and take notice. He jumped on the perch they had built for him and cleared his throat, and it looked like they were all set to go, when darned if Adolf didn't stop crowing.

" 'What's the matter with the fellow?' said the director, and the president yells over the wall:

" 'Crow, Adolf, crow!'

"But not a yip out of Adolf, and then someone goes outside to see what's wrong, and there's two cops pushing him into the wagon. They're talking to him kinda soft and soothing.

" 'Take it easy,' they're saying. 'Yes, yes, *sure* we understand why you were crowing—you're a rooster, aren't you? So you come with us, pal, and we'll take you back to the hen house.' "

· 3 ·

It was only after they had left the drawing room that Guy remembered that they had not told the comedian their pawnbroker plot. They had not, of course, had much opportunity, and they consoled themselves with the thought that later on there would no doubt be a formal story conference where only business would be talked.

The long journey was coming to an end. They breakfasted next morning as the train was pulling out of San Bernardino. There was a strong scent of orange blossoms in the air, turning Guy's mind to thoughts of marriage. He mentioned this to Plum, as they sat in the diner gazing out at the mountains, at snow-capped Old Baldy and the distant shimmering peak of Mt. Wilson.

"When are you getting married?" Plum asked.

"As soon as possible, now that we are both out here."

"You'll probably settle down in Hollywood and spend the rest of your life there."

Guy shook his head.

"Not if they paid me!"

"Well, they would pay you. Bob Benchley says that's the one redeeming feature of the place—the little man in the cage who hands you out the hundred dollar bills each Thursday."

"I mean, not if they paid me untold gold. Hollywood may turn out all right for a visit, but—"

"—You wouldn't live there if they gave you the place?"

"Exactly. Not even if they made me a brother-in-law, like Palmer. I'm going to get back into the theater again."

"Me, too."

"Vinton Freedley said he liked that story about the fellow who's such a hit with women and the millionaire father who hires him to stop his daughter marrying a titled half-wit."

"You mean *Anything Goes*?"

"Yes. You still like that title?"

"I think it's great."

"Vinton says Cole Porter would write the score."

"Cole does his own lyrics."

"Yes."

"That means I'm out. What pests these lyric-writing composers are! Taking the bread out of a man's mouth."

"You would do the book with me."

"Do you want me to?"

"Of course I do. You had an idea about a crook escaping on the boat from New York dressed as a clergyman."

"Public Enemy Number 13."

"A superstitious crook. Never had any luck when he was Thirteen, so wants to murder one of the top dozen and get promoted to Twelve. We ought to start jotting down some of these ideas before we get all tangled up with Hollywood."

"Write on the back of the menu."

Cups and plates were pushed aside. They paid no further attention to the orange groves, the mountains, the advertisements of the second-hand car dealers, the flaming twenty-four sheets of the picture houses. They were working.

"I see the whole of the action taking place on a transatlantic liner."

"Giving the hero six days to disentangle the girl."

"There'll be another girl—a comic—who's mixed up with the hero. He was out with her on a supper date when the heroine's father gave him the job, and she follows him aboard. You never saw *Girl Crazy*, did you?"

"No, I was in England."

"There was a girl called Ethel Merman in it. It was her first job and she made a terrific hit, singing that 'I've Got Rhythm' thing of Gershwin's. She puts a song over better than anybody and is great on comedy."

"She sounds right for this part."

"Exactly right. We're rolling!"

"Yes, we're rolling."

But they were also rolling into Pasadena. They had to hurry back to their compartment for their things.

Held on the car platform while suitcases, golf bags and typewriters were handed down by the porters, they looked out at the strange new land that was to be their home. Tall eucalyptus . . . blue-flowered jacarandas, feathery pepper trees dotted with red . . . and what looked like a thousand shiny new cars, one of which, they felt, must unquestionably belong to Palmer.

Guy saw all these things without really seeing them. His eyes were on a girl farther down the platform who was searching the faces of the passengers waiting to alight. She turned and saw him . . . smiled and waved.

Journey's End, felt Guy.

Palmer came bustling up.

"I wanted to see you two boys," he said briskly. "I've had an idea for the Bill Fields picture. Just an outline at present, but something for you to be mulling over. Bill's a pawnbroker, the last of a long line of pawnbrokers. His family have been pawnbrokers for centuries. They started originally in Spain and—get this—it was an ancestor of Bill's who loaned Queen Isabella the money to finance Columbus. She signed a regular contract—"

Guy drew a deep breath. His eyes had glazed a little. So had Plum's.

"—giving this ancestor ten per cent of anything Columbus discovered," continued Palmer. "Well, what he discovered—see what I mean—was America. So—this is going to slay you—there's good old Bill with a legal claim to ten per cent of America. Take it from there. Isn't that great?" said Palmer, his horn-rimmed spectacles flashing. "Isn't that terrific? Isn't that the most colossal idea for a comedian's picture anyone ever heard?"

There was a long silence. The two authors struggled for words. Then they found them.

"Yes, Mr. Palmer," said Guy.

"Oh, *yes*, Mr. Palmer," said Plum.

And they knew they were really in Hollywood.

INDEX